WITHDRAWN

F.E.Forbes. delt

THE HUMAN SACRIFICES OF THE EK-GNEE-NOO-AH-TOH.

Lith of Sarony & C? N.Y.

916.6
F739ar

AFRICA

AND

THE AMERICAN FLAG.

BY

COMMANDER ANDREW H. FOOTE,

U. S. NAVY,

LIEUT. COMMANDING U. S. BRIG PERRY ON THE COAST OF AFRICA

A. D. 1850—1851.

NEGRO UNIVERSITIES PRESS
NEW YORK

Originally published in 1854
by D. Appleton & Co.

Reprinted 1969 by
Negro Universities Press
A DIVISION OF GREENWOOD PUBLISHING CORP.
NEW YORK

SBN 8371-1543-4

PRINTED IN UNITED STATES OF AMERICA

TO

COMMODORE JOSEPH SMITH, U. S. N.,

CHIEF OF THE NAVAL BUREAU OF YARDS AND DOCKS,

𝕿𝖍𝖎𝖘 𝖁𝖔𝖑𝖚𝖒𝖊 𝖎𝖘 𝕯𝖊𝖉𝖎𝖈𝖆𝖙𝖊𝖉,

AS A SLIGHT TRIBUTE

OF RESPECT FOR HIS OFFICIAL CHARACTER,

AND AS AN ACKNOWLEDGMENT

OF HIS UNIFORM ATTACHMENT

AS A FRIEND.

CAISep1773

202347

CONTENTS.

8

CHAPTER XXV.

CHAPTER XXVI.

CHAPTER XXVII.

CHAPTER XXVIII.

CHAPTER XXIX.

CHAPTER XXX.

CHAPTER XXXI.

CHAPTER XXXII.

CHAPTER XXXIII.

CHAPTER XXXIV.

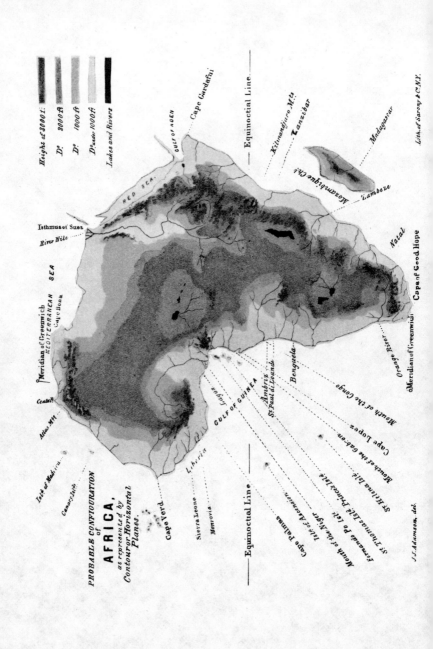

PROBABLE CONFIGURATION
of
AFRICA,
as represented by
Contour or Horizontal
Planes.

Height of 3000 ft.
D.º 2000 ft
D.º 1000 ft
D.º under 1000 ft
Lakes and Rivers

Meridian of Greenwich
MEDITERRANEAN SEA
Cape Bona
Central
Atlas M.ts
Isle of Madeira
Canary Isls
Cape Verd
Sierra Leone
Liberia
Monrovia
GULF OF GUINEA
Lagos
Ambriz
St. Paul d. Loanda
Benguela
Cape Palmas
Isle of Ascension
Mouth of the Niger
Fernando Po I.et
St. Thomas Isle Prince's Isle
Mouth of the Gab-on
Cape Lopez
Mouth of the Congo
Orange River
Meridian of Greenwich
Cape of Good Hope
Natal
Zambeze
Mozambique Ch.l
Madagascar
Zanzibar
Kilimandjaro M.ts
Equinoctial Line
Cape Gardafui
GULF OF ADEN
RED SEA
Isthmus of Suez
River Nile
Equinoctial Line

J. T. Adamson, del.
Lith. of Sarony & C.º N.Y.

AFRICA

AND

THE AMERICAN FLAG.

CHAPTER I.

SUBJECT AND ARRANGEMENT—AREA OF CRUISING-GROUND—
DISTRIBUTION OF SUBJECTS.

ON the 28th of November, 1849, the U. S. brig
"Perry" sailed for the west coast of Africa, to join the
American squadron there stationed.

A treaty with Great Britain, signed at Washington
in the year 1842, stipulates that each nation shall maintain on the coast of Africa, a force of naval vessels "of
suitable numbers and description, to carry in all not
less than eighty guns, to enforce separately and respectively, the laws, rights, and obligations of each of the
two countries, for the suppression of the slave-trade."

Although this stipulation was limited to the term of
five years from the date of the exchange of the ratifi-
cations of the treaty, "and afterwards until one or the

other party shall signify a wish to terminate it;" the United States have continued to maintain a squadron on that coast for the protection of its commerce, and for the suppression of the slave-trade, so far as it might be carried on in American vessels, or by American citizens.

To illustrate the importance of this squadron, the relations which its operations bear to American interests, and to the rights of the American flag; its effects upon the condition of Africa in checking crime, and preparing the way for the introduction of peace, prosperity, and civilization, is the primary object of this work.

A general view of the continent of Africa, comprising the past and present condition of its inhabitants; slavery in Africa and its foreign slave-trade; the piracies upon the coast before it was guarded and protected by naval squadrons; the geological structure of the country; its natural history, languages, and people; and the progress of colonization by the negro race returning to their own land with the light of religion, of sound policy, and of modern arts, will also be introduced as subjects appropriate to the general design.

If a chart of the Atlantic is spread out, and a line drawn from the Cape Verde Islands towards the southeastern coast of Brazil; if we then pass to the Cape of Good Hope and draw another from that point by the island of St. Helena, crossing the former north of the equator, the great tracks of commerce will be traced. Vessels outward bound follow the track towards the South American shore, and the homeward bound are found on the other. Thus vessels often meet in the centre of the Atlantic; and the crossing of these lines off the projecting shores of central Africa renders the coasts of that region of great naval importance.

The wide triangular space of sea between the homeward bound line and the retiring African seaboard around the Gulf of Guinea, constituted the area on which the vigilance of the squadron was to be exercised. Here is the region of crime, suffering, cruelty and death, from the slave-trade; and here has been at different ages, when the police of the sea happened to be little cared for, the scene of the worst piracies which have ever disgraced human nature.

Vessels running out from the African coast fall here and there into these lines traced on the chart, or sometimes cross them. No one can tell what they contain from the graceful hull, well-proportioned masts, neatly trimmed yards, and gallant bearing of the vessel. This deceitful beauty may conceal wrong, violence, and crime—the theft of living men, the foulness and corruption of the steaming slave-deck, and the charnelhouse of wretchedness and despair.

It is difficult in looking over the ship's side to conceive the transparency of the sea. The reflection of the blue sky in these tropic regions colors it like an opaque sapphire, till some fish startles one by suddenly appearing far beneath, seeming to carry daylight down with him into the depths below.   One is then reminded that the vessel is suspended over a transparent abyss. There for ages has sunk the dark-skinned sufferer from "the horrors of the middle passage," carrying that ghastly daylight down with him, to rest until "the sea shall give up its dead," and the slaver and his merchant come from their places to be confronted with their victim.

The relation of the western nations to these shores present themselves under three phases, which claim more or less attention in order to a full understanding of the subject.   These are,

I. Period of Discovery, Piracy and Slaving.

II. Period of Colonizing.

III. Period of Naval Cruising.

CHAPTER II.

THE French of Normandy contested with the Portuguese the honor of first venturing into the Gulf of Guinea. It was, however, nearly a hundred years from the time when the latter first embarked in these discoveries, until, in 1487, they reached the Cape of Good Hope. For about eight centuries the Mohammedan in the interior had been shaping out an influence for himself by proselyting and commerce. The Portuguese discoverer met this influence on the African shores. The Venetians held a sort of partnership with the Mohammedans in the trade of the East: Portugal had then taken scarcely any share in the brilliant and exciting politics of the Levant; her vocation was to the seas of the West, but in that direction she was advancing to an overwhelming triumph over her Eastern competitor.

On the 3d of May, 1487, a boat left one of two small high-sterned vessels, of less tonnage than an ordinary river sloop of the present day, and landed a few weather-beaten men on a low island of rocks, on which they proceeded to erect a cross. The sand which rustled across their footsteps, the sigh of the west wind among the waxberry bushes, and the croakings of the penguins as they waddled off,—these were the voices which hailed the opening of a new era for the world; for Bartholomew Diaz had then passed the southern point of Africa, and was listening to the surf of the Antarctic Sea.

This enterprising navigator had sailed from Lisbon in August, 1486, and seems to have reached Sierra Parda, north of the Orange River, in time to catch the last of the strong southeasterly winds, prevailing during the summer months on the southern coast of Africa, in the region of the Cape. He stood to the southwest, in vessels little calculated for holding a wind, and at length reached the region of the prevailing southwest winds. Then standing to the eastward he passed the Cape of Good Hope, of which he was in search, and bearing away to the northward, after running a distance of four hundred miles, brought up at the island of St. Croix above referred to. Coasting along on his return, the Cape was doubled, and named *Cabo Tormentoso*, or the Cape of Storms. The King of Portugal, on the discoverer's return, gave it the more promising name of *Cabo de buen Speranza*, or Cape of Good Hope.

Africa thus fell into the grasp of Europe. Trade flowed with a full stream into this new channel. Por-

tugal conquered and settled its shores. Missionaries
accompanied the Portuguese discoverers and conquerors
to various parts of Africa, where the Portuguese dominion had been established, and for long periods influenced the condition of the country.

CHAPTER III.

PIRATES—DAVIS, ROBERTS, AND OTHERS—BRITISH CRUISERS—
SLAVE-TRADE SYSTEMATIZED—GUINEAMEN—" HORRORS OF
THE MIDDLE PASSAGE."

THE second period is that of villany. More Africans
seem to have been bought and sold, at all times of the
world's history, than of any other race of mankind.
The early navigators were offered slaves as merchandise. It is not easy to conceive that the few which
they then carried away, could serve any other purpose
than to gratify curiosity, or add to the ostentatious
greatness of kings and noblemen. It was the demands
of the west which rendered this iniquity a trade. Every
thing which could debase a man was thrust upon Africa
from every shore. The old military skill of Europe
raised on almost every accessible point embattled fortresses, which now picturesquely line the Gulf of
Guinea. In the space between Cape Palmas and the
Calabar River, there are to be counted, in the old charts,
forts and factories by hundreds.

The seventeenth and eighteenth centuries were especially the era of woe to the African people. Crime
against them on the part of European nations, had be-

come gross in cruelty and universal in extent. From the Cape of Good Hope to the Mediterranean, in respect to their lands or their persons, the European was seizing, slaying and enslaving. The mischief perpetrated by the white man, was the source of mischief to its author. The west coast became the haunt and nursery of pirates. In fact, the same class of men were the navigators of the pirate and the slaver; and sailors had little hesitation in betraying their own vessels occasionally into the hands of the buccaneer. Slave-trading afforded a pretext which covered all the preparations for robbery. The whole civilized world had begun to share in this guilt and in this retribution.

In 1692, a solitary Scotchman was found at Cape Mesurado, living among the negroes. He had reached the coast in a vessel, of which a man named Herbert had gotten possession in one of the American colonies, and had run off with on a buccaneering cruise; a mutiny and fight resulted in the death of most of the officers and crew. The vessel drifted on shore, and bilged in the heavy surf at Cape Mesurado.

The higher ranks of society in Christendom were then most grossly corrupt, and had a leading share in these crimes. There arrived at Barbadoes in 1694, a vessel from New England, which might then have been called a *clipper*, mounting twenty small guns. A company of merchants of the island bought her, and fitted her

out ostensibly as a slaver, bound to the island of Madagascar; but in reality for the purpose of pirating on
the India merchantmen trading to the Red Sea. They
induced Russell, the governor of the island, to join them
in the adventure, and to give the ship an official character, so far as he was authorized to do so by his colonial commission.

A "sea solicitor" of this order, named Conklyn,
arrived in 1719 at Sierra Leone in a state of great des-
titution, bringing with him twenty-five of the greatest
villains that could be culled from the crews of two or
three piratical vessels on the coast. A mutiny had
taken place in one of these, on account of the chief's
assuming something of the character and habits of a
gentleman, and Conklyn, after a severe contention, had
left with his desperate associates. Had he remained,
he might have become chief in command, as a second
mutiny broke out soon after his departure, in which
the chief was overpowered, placed on board one of the
prize vessels, and never heard of afterwards. The
pirates under a new commander followed Conklyn to
Sierra Leone. They found there this worthy gentleman, rich, and in command of a fine ship with eighty
men.

Davis, the notorious pirate, soon joined him with a
well-armed ship manned with one hundred and fifty
men. Here was collected as fruitful a nest of villany

as the world ever saw. They plundered and captured whatever came in their course. These vessels, with other pirates, soon destroyed more than one hundred trading vessels on the African coast. England entered into a kind of compromise, previously to sending a squadron against them, by offering pardon to all who should present themselves to the governor of any of her colonies before the first of July, 1719. This was equivalent to offering themselves to serve in the war which had commenced against Spain, or exchanging one kind of brigandage for another, by privateering against the Spanish commerce. But from the accounts of their prisoners very few of them could read, and thus the proclamation was almost a dead letter.

In 1720, Roberts, a hero of the same class, anchored in Sierra Leone, and sent a message to Plunket, the commander of the English fort, with a request for some gold dust and ammunition. The commander of the fort replied that he had no gold dust for them, but that he would serve them with a good allowance of shot if they ventured within the range of his guns ; whereupon Roberts opened his fire upon the fort. Plunket soon expended all his ammunition, and abandoned his position. Being made prisoner he was taken before Roberts : the pirate assailed the poor commander with the most outrageous execrations for his audacity in resisting him. To his astonishment Plunket retorted upon him with oaths and execrations yet more tremendous. This was quite to the taste of the scoundrels around them, who, with shouts of laughter, told their captain that he was only second best at that business, and Plunket, in consideration of his victory, was allowed to escape with life.

In 1721, England dispatched two men-of-war to the Gulf of Guinea for the purpose of exterminating the pirates who had there reached a formidable degree of power, and sometimes, as in the instance noted above, assailed the establishments on shore. They found that Roberts was in command of a squadron of three vessels, with about four hundred men under his command, and had been particularly active and successful in outrage. After cruising about the northern coast, and learning that Roberts had plundered many vessels, and that sailors were flocking to him from all quarters, they found him on the evening of the third of February, anchored with his three vessels in the bay north of Cape Lopez.

When entering the bay, light enough remained to let them see that they had caught the miscreants in their lair. Closing in with the land the cruisers quietly ran in and anchored close aboard the outer vessel belonging to the pirates. Having ascertained the character of the visitors, the pirate slipped his cables, and proceeded to make sail, but was boarded and secured just as the

rapid blackness of a tropical night buried every thing
in obscurity. Every sound was watched during the
darkness of the night, with scarcely the hope that the
other two pirates would not take advantage of it to
make their escape; but the short gray dawn showed
them still at their anchors. The cruisers getting under
way and closing in with the pirates produced no movement on their part, and some scheme of cunning or
desperate resistance was prepared for. They had in
fact made a draft from one vessel to man the other
fully for defence. Into this vessel the smaller of the
cruisers, the *Swallow*, threw her broadside, which was
feebly returned. A grape-shot in the head had killed
Roberts. This and the slaughter of the cruiser's fire
prepared the way for the boarders, without much further resistance, to take possession of the pirate. The
third vessel was easily captured.

The cruisers suffered no loss in the fight, but had
been fatally reduced by sickness. The larger vessel,
the *Weymouth*, which left England with a crew of two
hundred and forty men, had previously been reduced
so greatly as scarcely to be able to weigh her anchors;
and, although recruited often from merchant vessels,
landed but one hundred and eighty men in England.
This rendered the charge of their prisoners somewhat
hazardous, and taking them as far as Cape Coast Castle,
they there executed such justice as the place could

afford, or the demerits of their prey deserved. A great number of them ornamented the shore on gibbets—the well-known signs of civilization in that era—as long as the climate and the vultures would permit them to hang.

Consequent on these events such order was established as circumstances would admit, or rather the progress of maritime intercourse and naval power put an end to the system of daring and regulated piracy by which the tropical shores of Africa and the West Indies had been laid waste. This, however, was slight relief for Africa. It was to secure and systematize trade that piracy **had** been suppressed, and the slave-trade became accordingly cruelly and murderously systematic.

The question what nation should be most enriched by the guilty traffic was a subject of diplomacy. England secured the greater share of the criminality and of the profit, by gaining from her other competitors the right by contract to supply the colonies of Spain with negroes.

Men forget what they ought not to forget; and however startling, disgusting, and oppressive to the mind of man the horrors are which characterized that trade, it is well that since they did exist the memory of them should not perish. It is a fearfully dark chapter in the history of the world, but although terrific it has its value. It is more worthy of being remembered than

the historical routine of wars, defeats, or victories; for
it is more illustrative of man's proper history, and of a
strange era in that history.   The evidence taken by the
Committee of the English House of Lords in 1850, has
again thrust the subject into daylight.

The slave-trade is now carried on by comparatively
small and ill-found vessels, watched by the cruisers in-
cessantly. They are therefore induced, at any risk of
loss by death, to crowd and pack their cargoes, so that
a successful voyage may compensate for many captures.
In olden times, there were vessels fitted expressly for
the purpose—large Indiamen or whalers.   It has been
objected to the employment of squadrons to exterminate
that trade, that their interference has increased its enor-
mity.   This, however, is doing honor to the old Guineamen, such as they by no means deserve.   It is, in fact,
an inference in favor of human nature, implying that a
man who has impunity and leisure to do evil, cannot,
in the nature of things, be so dreadfully heartless in
doing it, as those in whose track the avenger follows
to seize and punish.   The fact, however, does not justify this surmise in favor of impunity and leisure.   If
ever there was any thing on earth which, for revolting,
filthy, heartless atrocity, might make the devil wonder
and hell recognize its own likeness, then it was on any
one of the decks of an old slaver.   The sordid cupidity
of the older, as it is meaner, was also more callous

than the hurried ruffianism of the present age. In fact, a slaver now has but one deck; in the last century they had two or three. Any one of the decks of the larger vessels was rather worse, if this could be, than the single deck of the brigs and schooners now employed in the trade. Then, the number of decks rendered the suffocating and pestilential hold a scene of unparalleled wretchedness. Here are some instances of this, collected from evidence taken by the British House of Commons in 1792.

James Morley, gunner of the *Medway*, states : " He has seen them under great difficulty of breathing; the women, particularly, often got upon the beams, where the gratings are often raised with banisters, about four feet above the combings, to give air, but they are generally driven down, because they take the air from the rest. He has known rice held in the mouths of sea-sick slaves until they were almost strangled; he has seen the surgeon's mate force the panniken between their teeth, and throw the medicine over them, so that not half of it went into their mouths—the poor wretches wallowing in their blood, hardly having life, and this with blows of the cat."

Dr. Thomas Trotter, surgeon of the *Brookes*, says : ' He has seen the slaves drawing their breath with all those laborious and anxious efforts for life which are observed in expiring animals, subjected, by experiment,

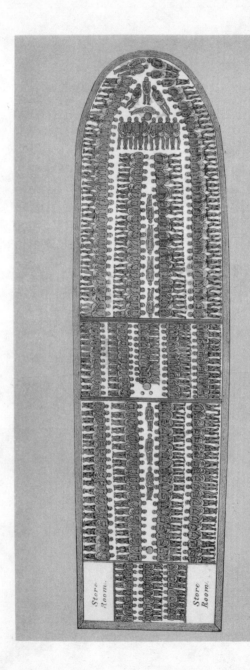

F. E. Forbes, Del.

Lith of Sarony & Co.

THE LOWER DECK OF A GUINEA-MAN. IN THE LAST CENTURY.

Store Room.

Store Room.

to foul air, or in the exhausted receiver of an air-pump; has also seen them when the tarpaulins have inadvertently been thrown over the gratings, attempting to heave them up, crying out 'kickeraboo! kickeraboo!' i. e., *We are dying.* On removing the tarpaulin and gratings, they would fly to the hatchways with all the signs of terror and dread of suffocation; many whom he has seen in a dying state, have recovered by being brought on the deck; others, were irrevocably lost by suffocation, having had no previous signs of indisposition."

In regard to the *Garland's* voyage, 1788, the testimony is: "Some of the diseased were obliged to be kept on deck. The slaves, both when ill and well, were frequently forced to eat against their inclination; were whipped with a cat if they refused. The parts on which their shackles are fastened, are often excoriated by the violent exercise they are forced to take, and of this they made many grievous complaints to him. Fell in with the *Hero*, Wilson, which had lost, he thinks, three hundred and sixty slaves by death; he is certain more than half of her cargo; learnt this from the surgeon; they had died mostly of the smallpox; surgeon also told him, that when removed from one place to another, they left marks of their skin and blood upon the deck, and that it was the most horrid sight he had ever seen."

The annexed sketch represents the lower deck of a

Guineaman, when the trade was under systematic regulations. The slaves were obliged to lie on their backs, and were shackled by their ankles, the left of one being fettered close to the right of the next; so that the whole number in one line formed a single living chain. When one died, the body remained during the night, or during bad weather, secured to the two between whom he was. The height between decks was so little, that a man of ordinary size could hardly sit upright. During good weather, a gang of slaves was taken on the spar-deck, and there remained for a short time. In bad weather, when the hatches were closed, death from suffocation would necessarily occur. It can, therefore, easily be understood, that the athletic strangled the weaker intentionally, in order to procure more space, and that, when striving to get near some aperture affording air to breathe, many would be injured or killed in the struggle.

Such were "the horrors of the middle passage."

CHAPTER IV.*

PHYSICAL GEOGRAPHY—CLIMATE—GEOLOGY—ZOOLOGY—BOTANY.

BEFORE proceeding to the colonizing era, it will be requisite to present an estimate of the value and importance of the African continent in relation to the rest of the world. This requires some preliminary notice of the physical condition of its territories, and the character and distribution of the tribes possessing them. Africa has not yet yielded to science the results which may be expected from it. Courage and hardihood, rather than knowledge and skill, have, from the circumstances of the case, been the characteristics of its successful explorers. We have, therefore, wonderful incidents and loose descriptions, without the accurate observation and statement of circumstances which can render them useful.

---

* The author acknowledges his indebtedness for liberal and valuable contributions on the subject of Physical Geography, Geology, &c., to the Rev. Dr. Adamson, for twenty years a resident at the Cape of Good Hope, and government director and professor in the South African college. He wishes also to express his obligations for frequent suggestions from the same source on scientific subjects, during the preparation of this work.

The vast radiator formed by the sun beating vertically on the plains of tropical Africa, heats and expands the air, and thus constitutes a sort of central trough into which gravitation brings compensating currents, by producing a lateral sliding inwards of the great trade-wind streams. Thus, as a general rule, winds which would normally diverge from the shores are drawn in towards them. They have been gathering moisture in their progress, and when pressed upwards, as they expand under the vertical sun, lose their heat in the upper regions, let go their moisture, and spread over the interior terraces and mountains a sheet of heavily depositing cloud. This constitutes the rainy season, which necessarily, from the causes producing it, accompanies the sun in its apparent oscillations across the equator.

The Gulf of Guinea has in its own bosom a system of hurricanes and squalls, of which little is known but their existence and their danger. A description of them, of rather an old date, specifies as a fact that they begin by the appearance of a small mass of clouds in the zenith, which widens and extends till the canopy covers the horizon. Now if this were true of any given spot, it would indicate that the hurricane always began there. The appearance of a patch of cloud in the zenith could be true of only one place out of all those which the hurricane influenced. If it is meant that *wherever* the phenomenon originated, *there* a mass of cloud gradually formed in the zenith, this would be a most important particular in regard to the proximate cause of the phenomenon, for it would mark a rapid direction upwards of the atmosphere at that spot as the first observable incident of the series. That the movements produced would subsequently become whirling or circumvolant, is a mechanical necessity. But the force of the movement ought not to be strongest at the place where the mischief had its origin.

The squalls, with high towering clouds, which rise like a wall on the horizon, involve the same principles as to the formation of the vapor, and are easily explicable. They are not necessarily connected with circular hurricanes; but the principles of their formation may modify the intensity of the blasts in a circumvolant tornado. Since in the Gulf of Guinea they come from the eastward, it is to be inferred that they are ripples or undulations in an air current. In regard to all of this, it is necessary to speak doubtfully, for there is a great lack of accurate and detailed observation on these points.

Its position and physical characteristics give to this continent great influence over the rest of the earth. Africa, America, and Australia have nearly similar relations to the great oceans interposed respectively between them. Against the eastern sides of these regions are carried from the ocean those strange, furious whirlings in the shallow film of the earth's atmosphere, which constitute hurricanes. It is evident that these oceans are mainly the channels in which the surface winds move, which are drawn from colder regions towards the equator. The shores are the banks of these air streams. The return currents above flow over every thing. They are thus prevalent in the interior, so that the climatic conditions there are different from those on the seaboard. These circumstances in the southern extra-tropical regions are accompanied by corresponding differences in the character of the vegetable world.

These winds are sometimes drawn aside across the coast line — constituting the Mediterranean sirocco, and the African harmattan. Vessels far off at sea, sailing to the northward, are covered or stained on the weather side of their rigging (that next to the African coast), with a fine light-yellow powder. A reddish-brown dust sometimes tinges the sails and rigging. An instance of this occurred on board the "Perry" on her outward bound passage, when five hundred miles from the African coast.

The science of Ehrenberg has been searching amid the microscopic organisms contained in these substances, for tokens of their origin. In the red material he finds forms betraying not an African, but an American source, presumed to be in the great plains of the Amazon and Orinoco. This suggests new views of the meteorology of the world; but the theories founded on it, are not clear of mechanical difficulties.

If we stand on almost any shore of the world as it exists at present, and consider the character of the land surface on the one hand, and of the ocean bottom on the other, we shall see that a very great difference in the nature of the beach line would be produced by a depression of the land towards the ocean, or by an elevation of it from the deep. The sea in its action on the bottom fills up hollows and obliterates precipices; but a land surface is worn into ravines and valleys. Hence a depression, so that the waters overflowed the land, would admit them into its recesses, and river courses, and winding gulleys—forming bays, islands, and secure harbors. Whereas elevation would bring up from the bottom its sand-banks and plains, forming an extent of slightly winding and unsheltered shore. The character of a coast will therefore depend very greatly upon its former history, before it became fixed. We have this contrast in the eastern and western sides of the Adriatic, or in the western and eastern sides of the British islands. These circumstances are to some degree controlled by the effects of partial volcanoes, or of powerful winds and currents. But on the whole, it may generally be inferred that a long unbroken shore indicates that the last change on the land level was one of elevation; while a coast penetrated, broken, and defended by islands has received its conformation from being stopped in the process of subsiding.

The coast of Africa has over almost its whole circuit, that unbroken or slightly indented outline which would arise from upheaval. The only conspicuous exception to this, is in the eastern region, neighboring on the Mozambique Channel, where the Portuguese and the Arab possess the advantage, so rare in Africa, of having at their command convenient and sheltered harbors. There are centres of partial volcanic agency in the islands of the Atlantic, north of the equator, and in the distant spots settled by Europeans outside of Madagascar; but this action has not, as in the Mediterranean or Archipelago, modified the character of the continental shore. It is not known that there exists any active volcano on the continent.

Africa, therefore, if it could be seen on a great model of the world, would offer little, comparatively, that was varied in outline or in aspect. There would be great tawny deserts, with scanty specks of dusky green, or threads of sombre verdure tracing out its scant and temporary streams. There would be forests concealing or embracing the mouths of rivers, with brown mountains here and there penetrating through them, but rarely presenting a lofty wall to the sea. Interior plains would show some glittering lakes, begirt by the jungle which they create. But it is a land nearly devoid of winter, either temporary or permanent. Only one or two specks, near the mouth of the Red Sea, and a short beaded line of the chain of Atlas, would throw abroad the silver splendor of perpetual snow. It is the great want of Africa, that so few mountains have on their heads these supplies for summer streams.

The sea-shore is generally low, except as influenced by Atlas, or the Abyssinian ranges, or the mountains of the southern extremity. There is, not uncommonly, a flat swampy plain, bordering on the sea, where the rivers push out their deltas, or form lagoons by their conflict with the fierce surge upon the shore. Generally at varying distances, there occur falls or rapids in the great rivers, showing that they are descending from interior plains of considerable elevation. The central regions seem, in fact, to form two, or perhaps three great elevated plateaux or terraced plains, having waters collected in their depressions, and joined by necks; such as are the prairies of Illinois, between the St. Lawrence and the Mississippi, or the llanos of South America between its great rivers. The southern one of these African plains approaches close to the Atlantic near the Orange River. Starting there at the height of three thousand feet, it proceeds round the sources of the river, and spreads centrally along by the lately visited, but long known lakes north of the tropic. The equinoctial portion of it is probably drained by the Zambeze and the Zaire, flowing in opposite directions. It appears to be continuous as a neck westward of Kilmandjaro, the probable source of the Nile; till it spreads out into the vast space extending from Cape Verde to Suez, including in it the Niger and the Nile, the great desert, and the collections of waters forming Lake Tzad, and such others as there may be towards Fitre.

The mountains inclosing these spaces form a nearly continuous wall along the eastern side of Africa. The snows of Atlas form small streams, trickling down north and south; and, in the latter case, struggling almost in vain with the tropical heats, in short courses, towards the Desert of Sahara.

There are found separate groups of mountains, forming for the continent a broken margin on the west. There may also be an important one situated centrally between Lake Tzad and the Congo; but there appears no probability of a transverse chain, stretching continuously across this region, as has hitherto had a place on maps, under the title of the "Mountains of the Moon."

No geological changes, except those due to the elevation of the oldest formations, appear to have taken place extensively in this continent. The shores of the Gulf of Guinea, and of the eastern regions, abound with gold, suggesting that their interior is not covered by modern rocks. The two extremities at Egypt and Cape of Good Hope, have been depressed to receive secondary and tertiary deposits. There may be other such instances; but the continent seems, during a time, even geologically long, to have formed a great compact mass of land, bearing the same relations as now to the rest of the world.

The valleys and precipices of South Africa have been shaped by the mighty currents which circulate round the promontory of the Cape; and the flat summit of Table Mountain, at the height of three thousand six hundred feet, is a rocky reef, worn and fretted into strange projections by the surge, which the southeasters brought against it, when it was at the level of the sea.

The present state of organized life in Africa tells the same tale. It indicates a land never connected with polar regions, nor subjected to great variations of temperature. Our continent, America, is a land of extremes of temperature. Corresponding to that condition, it is a land characterized by plants, the leaves of which ripen and fall, so that vegetation has a pause, waiting for the breath of spring. All the plants of southern Africa are evergreens. The large browsing animals, such as the elephant and rhinoceros, which cannot stoop to gather grass, find continuous subsistence in the continuous foliage of shrubs. America abounds with stags

or deer—animals having deciduous horns or antlers.
Southern Africa has none, but is rich in species of
antelopes, which have true or permanent horns, and
which nowhere sustain great variations of heat and cold.
Its fossil plants correspond apparently in character to
those which the country now bears.

Its fossil zoology offers very peculiar and interesting
provinces of ancient life. These have been in positions
not greatly unconformable to those of similar phenom-
ena even now. Great inland fresh-water seas have
abounded with new and strange types of organization,
in character and office analogous to the amphibious
forms occurring with profusion in similar localities of
the present interior. These, and representatives of the
secondary formations, rest chiefly on the old Silurian
and Devonian series, the upheaving of which seems to
have given the continent its place and outline. Coal is
found at Natal, near the Mozambique Channel, but not
hitherto known to be of value.

Africa still offers, and will long continue to offer,
the most promising field of botanical discovery. Much
novelty certainly remains to be elicited there, but it is
very dilatory in finding its way abroad. Natal is the
region most likely to be sedulously explored for some
time. Vegetable ivory has been brought thence, and
elastic, hard, useful timber abounds. Much lumber of
good and varied character is taken to Europe from the

western regions of the continent; but so greatly has scientific inquiry been repelled by the deadly climate, that even the species affording it are unknown, or doubtfully guessed at.

The vegetation of the south is brilliant, but not greatly useful. It affords the type of that which covers the mountains, receding towards the northeast, until they reach perpetual snow near the equator. That which is of a more tropical character, stretches round their bases and through their valleys, with its profusion of palms, creepers, and dye-woods. These hereafter will form the commercial wealth of the country, affording oil, india-rubber, dye-stuffs, and other useful productions.

The wild animals of Africa belong to plains and to loose thickets, rather than to timbered forests. There is a gradation in the height of the head, among the larger quadrupeds, which indicates the sort of country and of vegetation suitable to them.

The musket, with its "villanous saltpetre," in the hands of barbarians is everywhere expelling from the earth its bulkier creatures, so that the elephant is disappearing, and ivory will become scarce. Fear tames the wildest nature; even the lion is timid when he has to face the musket. The dull ox has learned a lesson with regard to him; for when the kingly brute prowls round an unyoked wagon resting at night, and his growl or smell makes the oxen shake and struggle with terror, they are quieted by the discharge of firearms.

When Europeans first visited the shores of Africa, they were astonished at the tameness and abundance of unchecked animal life. The shallow bays and river lagoons were full of gigantic creatures; seals were found in great numbers, but of all animals these seem the most readily extirpated. The multitudes which covered the reefs of South Africa are nearly gone, and they seem to be no longer met with on the northern shores of the continent. The manatee, or sea-cow, and the hippopotamus, frequented the mouths of rivers, and were killed and eaten by the natives. They had never tamed and used the elephant: that this might have been done is inferred from the use of these animals by the Carthaginians. But as the Carthaginian territory was not African in the strict sense of the term, it may be doubted whether their species was that of Central Africa. This latter species is a larger, less intelligent looking, and probably a more stubborn creature than the Asiatic. The roundness of their foreheads and the size of their ears give them a duller and more brutal look; the magnitude of their tusks, and the occurrence of these formidable weapons in the female as well as in the male, are accommodated to the necessity of conflict with the lion, and indicate a wilder nature.

Lions of several species, abundance of panthers, cats, genets, and hyenas of many forms, mainly constitute the carnivorous province, having, as is suitable to the climate, a high proportion of the hyena form, or devourers of the dead. A foot of a pongo, or large ape, "as large as that of a man, and covered with hair an inch long," astonished one of the earliest navigators. This animal, which indicates a zoological relationship to the Malayan islands, is known to afford the nearest approach to the human form. The monkey structure on the east coast of Africa tends to pass into the nocturnal or Lemurine forms of Madagascar, where the occurrence of an insulated Malayan language confirms the relationship indicated above.

The plains with bushy verdure nourish the ostrich and many species of bustards over the whole continent. Among the creatures which range far are the lammergeyer, or bearded eagle of the Alps, and the brown owl of Europe, extending to the extremity of the south. Among the parrots and the smaller birds, congregating species abound, forming a sort of arboreal villages, or joint-stock lodging-houses. Sometimes hundreds of such dwellings are under one thatch, the entrances being below. The weaving birds suspend their bottle-shaped habitations at the extremities of limber branches, where they wave in the wind. This affords security from monkeys and snakes; but they retain the instinct of forming them so when there is no danger from either the one or the other.

Reptiles abound in Africa. The Pythons (or Boas) are formidable. Of the species of serpents probably between one-fourth and one-fifth are poisonous; but every thing relating to them in the central regions requires to be ascertained. The Natal crocodile is smaller than the Egyptian, but is greatly dreaded.

The following instance of its ferocity occurred to the Rev. J. A. Butler, missionary, in crossing the Umkomazi River, in February, 1853. "When about two-thirds of the way across, his horse suddenly kicked and plunged as if to disengage himself from the rider, and the next moment a crocodile seized Mr. Butler's thigh with his horrible jaws. The river at this place is about one hundred and fifty yards wide, if measured at right angles to the current; but from the place we entered to the place we go out, the distance is three times as great. The water at high tide, and when the river is not swollen, is from four to eight or ten feet deep. On each side the banks are skirted with high grass and reeds. Mr. Butler, when he felt the sharp teeth of the crocodile, clung to the mane of his horse with a death hold. Instantly he was dragged from the saddle, and both he and the horse were floundering in the water, often dragged entirely under, and rapidly going down the stream. At first the crocodile drew them again to the middle of the river, but at last the horse gained shallow water, and approached the shore. As soon as he was within reach natives ran to his assistance, and beat off the crocodile with spears and clubs. Mr. Butler was pierced with five deep gashes, and had lost much blood."

CHAPTER V.

AFRICAN NATIONS—DISTRIBUTION OF RACES—ARTS—MANNERS
AND CHARACTER—SUPERSTITIONS—TREATMENT OF THE DEAD
—REGARD FOR THE SPIRITS OF THE DEPARTED—WITCH-
CRAFT—ORDEAL—MILITARY FORCE—AMAZONS—CANNIBAL-
ISM.

WHENCE came the African races, and how did they
get where they are? These are questions not easily
answered, and are such as might have been put with
the same hesitation, and in view of the same puzzling
circumstances, three thousand years ago. On the mon-
uments of Thebes, in Upper Egypt, of the times of
Thothmes III., three varieties of the African form of
man are distinctly portrayed. There is the ruling race
of Egypt, red-skinned and massy-browed. There are
captives not unlike them, but of a paler color, with
their hair tinged blue; and there is the negro, bearing
his tribute of skins, living animals, and ivory; with the
white eyeball, reclining forehead, woolly hair, and
other normal characteristics of his type.

Provided that these representations are correct, and
that the colors have not changed, the Egyptian has

been greatly modified as to his tint of skin; whether we consider them as represented by the Copts, or the Fellahs of that country at present, the former bearing clearer traces of the more ancient form. The population of Africa, as it is at present, seems to be chiefly derivable from the other two races. There are, however, circumstances difficult to reconcile, in the present state of c knowledge, with any hypothesis as to the dispersion of man.

Southern and equatorial Africa includes tribes speaking dialects of two widely-spread tongues. One of them, the Zingian, or the Zambezan, is properly distinguished by the excess to which it carries repetition of certain signs of thought, giving to inflections a character different from what they exhibit in any other language. This tongue, however, bears, in other respects, a strong relationship to the many, but, perhaps, not mutually dissimilar dialects, of northern Africa. It may be considered as the form of speech belonging to the true or most normally developed African race.

The other of these two tongues offers also circumstances of peculiar interest. We may consider it, first, as it is found in use by the Hottentot or Bushman race, of South Africa. It has even among them regular and well-constructed forms of inflection, and as distinguishing it from the negro dialects, it has the sexual form of gender, or that which arises from the poetical or personify-

ing view of all objects—considering them as endowed
with life, and dividing them into males and females.
In this respect it is analogous to the Galla, the Abyssinian, and the Coptic. Nay, at this distant extremity
of Africa, not only is the form of gender thus the same
with that of the people who raised the wonderful mon-
uments of Egypt, but that monumental tongue has its
signs of gender, or the terminations indicating that
relation, identical with those of the Hottentot race.

We have, therefore, the evidence of a race of men,
striking through the other darker ones, on perhaps
nearly a central line, from one end of the continent to
the other. The poor despised Bushman, forming for
himself, with sticks and grass, a lair among the low-
spreading branches of a protea, or nestling at sunset in
a shallow hole, amid the warm sand of the desert, with
wife and little ones like a covey of birds, sheltered by
some ragged sheepskins from the dew of the clear sky,
has an ancestral and mental relationship to the builder
of the pyramids and the colossal temples of Egypt, and
to the artists who adorned them. He looks on nature
with a like eye, and stereotypes in his language the
same conclusions derived from it. He has in his words
vivified external things, as they did, according to that
form which, in our more logical tongues, we name poetical metaphor. The *sun*—"Soorees"—is to him a
female, the productive mother of all organic life; and

rivers, as Kuis-eep, Gar-eep, are endowed with masculine activity and strength.

To this scattered family of man, which ought properly to be called the *Ethiopic* race, as distinguished from the negro, may probably be ascribed the fierce invasions from the centre, eastward and westward, under the names of Galla Giagas, and other appellations, which occasionally convulsed both sides of Africa; and, perhaps, by intermixture of races, gave occasion to much of the diversity found among native tribes, in disposition, manners, and language. The localities occupied by it have become insulated through the intrusion of the negro. Its southern division, or the Hottentot tribes, were being pressed off into an angle, and apparently in the process of extinction or absorption by the Zambezan Kaffirs from the north and east, when Europeans met and rolled them away into a small corner of desert.

Egypt was evidently the artery through which population poured into the broad expanse of Africa. That the progenitors of the negro race first entered there, and that another race followed subsequently, is one mode of disposing of the question, which, however, only removes its difficulties a little farther back.

This supposition is unnecessary. Any number of human families living together, comprises varieties of constitution, affording a source from which, by the force of external circumstances, the extreme variations may be educed. If we examine critically the representations of the oldest inhabitants of Egypt, we shall see in the form of man which they exhibit, a combination of characteristics, or a provision for breaking into varieties corresponding to the conditions of external nature in the interior regions.

The dissatisfied, the turbulent, the defeated and the criminal would in these earliest times be thrown off from a settled community in Egypt, to penetrate into the southern and western regions. They would generally die there. Many ages of such attempts might pass before those individuals reached the marshes of the great central plateau, whose constitutions suited that position. Many of them, moreover, would die childless. Early death to the adult, and certain death to the immature, would sweep families off, as the streams bounding from southern Atlas intrude on the desert, and perish there. The many immigrants to whom all external things were adverse would be constantly weeded out; so it would be for generation after generation, until the few remained, whom heat, exposure, toil, marsh vapor, and fever left as an assorted and acclimated root of new nations.

Such seems to have been the process in Africa by which a declension of our nature took place from Egypt in two directions; one through the central plains down to the marshes of the Gaboon or the Congo river, where the aberrant peculiarities of the negro seem most developed; and the other along the mountains, by the Nile and the Zambeze, until the Ethiopian sank into the Hottentot.

The sea does not deal kindly with Africa, for it wastes or guards the shores with an almost unconquerable surf. Tides are small, and rivers not safely penetrable. The ocean offered to the negro nothing but a little food, procured with some trouble and much danger. Hence ocean commerce was unknown to them. Only in the smallest and most wretched canoes did they venture forth to catch a few fish. If strangers sought for regions of prosperity, riches, or powerful government, their views were directed to the interior. Benin, in 1484, confessed its subordination to a great internal sovereign, who only gave responses from behind a curtain, or permitted one of his feet to be visible to his dependents, as a mark of gracious favor. It was European commerce in gold and slaves, received for the coveted goods and arms they bought, which ultimately gave these monarchs an interest in the seashore.

Cruelty and oppression were everywhere, as they still are. It is not easy for us to conceive how a living man can be moulded to the unhesitating submission in which a negro subject lives, so that it should be to him a satisfaction to live and die, or suffer or rejoice, just as his sovereign wills. It can be accounted for only from the prevalence and the desolating fury of wars, which rendered perfect uniformity of will and movement indispensable for existence. It is not so easy to offer any probable reason for the eagerness to share in cruelty which glows in a negro's bosom. Its appalling character consisted rather in the amount of bloodshed which gratified the negro, than in the studious prolongation of pain. He offers in this respect a contrast to the cold, demoniac vengeance of the North American Indian. Superstition probably excused or justified to him some of his worst practices. Human sacrifices have been common everywhere. There was no scruple at cruelty when it was convenient. The mouths of the victims were gagged by knives run through their cheeks; and captives among the southern tribes were beaten with clubs in order to prevent resistance, or "to take away their strength," as the natives expressed it, that they might be more easily hurried to the "hill of death," or authorized place of execution.

The negro arts are respectable, and would have been more so had not disturbance and waste come with the slave-trade. They weave coarse narrow cloths, and dye them. They work in wood and metals. The gold chains obtained at Wydah, of native manufacture, are well wrought. Nothing can be more correctly formed for its purpose than the small barbed lancet-looking point of a Bushman's arrow. Those who shave their heads or beards have a neat, small razor, double-edged, or shaped like a shovel. Arts improve from the coast towards the northeast.

Their normal form of a house is round, with a conical roof. The pastoral people of the south have it of a beehive form, covered with mats; the material is rods and flags. If the whole negro nations, however, were swept away, there would not remain a monument on the face of their continent to tell that such a race of men had occupied it.

One curious relation to external nature seems to have prevailed throughout all Africa, consisting in a special reverence, among different tribes, for certain selected objects. From one of these objects the tribe frequently derives its national appellation: if it is a living thing, they avoid killing it or using it as food. Serpents, particularly the gigantic pythons or boas, are everywhere reverenced. Some traces of adoration offered to the sun have been met with on the west coast; but, generally speaking, the superstitions of Africa are far less intellectual. These and many of their other practices have a common characteristic in the disappearance of all trace of their origin among the tribes observing them. To all inquiries they have the answer ready, that their fathers did so. There is in this, however, no great assurance of real antiquity, for tradition extends but a short way back.

A reliance on grisgris, or amulets, worn about the person, belongs to Africa, perhaps from very ancient ages. Egypt was probably its source : a kind of literary character has been given to it by the Mohammedans. Throughout inland central Africa, sentences written on scraps of paper or parchment have a marketable value. An impostor or devotee may gain authority and profit in this way. As we pass southward we find this superstition sinking lower and lower in debasement : men there really cover or load themselves with all kinds of trumpery, and have a real and hearty confidence in bones, buttons, scraps, or almost any conceivable thing, as a security against any conceivable evil. The Kroomen, even, with their purser's names, of *Jack Crowbar*, *Head Man*, and *Flying-Jib*, *Bottle of Beer*, *Pea Soup*, *Poor Fellow*, *Prince Will*, and others, taken on board the " Perry," in Monrovia, were found now and then with their sharks', tigers' and panthers' teeth, and small shells, on their ankles and wrists ; although most of these people, from contact with the Liberians, have seen the folly of this practice, and dispensed with their charms.

The Africans also have stationary *fetishes*, consisting in sacred places and sacred things. They have practices to inspire terror, or gain reverence in respect to

which it is somewhat difficult to decide whether the
actors in them are impostors or sincere. Idols in the
forms of men, rude and frightful enough, are among
these fetishes, but it cannot be said that idolatry of this
kind prevails extensively in the country.

In two respects they look towards the invisible: they
dread a superhuman power, and they fear and worship
it as being a measureless source of evil. It is scarcely
correct to call this Devil-worship, for this is a title of
contrast, presuming that there has been a choice of the
evil in preference to the good. The fact in their case
seems to be, that good in will, or good in action, are
ideas foreign to their minds. Selfishness cannot be
more intense, nor more exclusive of all kindness and
generosity or charitable affection, than it is generally
found among these barbarians. The inconceivableness
of such motives to action has often been found a strong
obstacle to the influence of the Christian missionary.
They can worship nothing good, because they have no
expectation of good from any thing powerful. They
have mysterious words or mutterings, equivalent to
what we term incantations, which is the meaning of
the Portuguese word from which originated the term
fetish.

The other reference of their intellect to invisible
things consists in acknowledging the continued existence of the dead, and paying reverence to the spirits of

their forefathers. This leads to great cruelty. Men of rank at their death are presumed to require attendance, and be gratified with companionship. This event, therefore, produces the murder of wives and slaves, to afford them suitable escort and service in the other world. From the strange mixture of the material and spiritual common to men in that barbarian condition, the bodies or the blood of the slain appear to be the essentials of these requirements. Thus, also, the utmost horror is felt at decapitation, or at the severing of limbs from the body after death. It is revenge, as much as desire to perpetuate the remembrance of victory, which makes them eager for the skulls and jaw-bones of their enemies, so that in a royal metropolis, walls, and floors, and thrones, and walking-sticks, are everywhere lowering with the hollow eyes of the dead. These sad, bare and whitened emblems of mortality and revenge present a curious and startling spectacle, cresting and festooning the red clay walls of Kumassi, the Ashantee capital.

Such belief leads to strange vagaries in practice. They sympathize with the departed, as subject still to common wants and ruled by common affections. A negro man of Tahou would show his regard for the desires of the dead by sitting patiently to hold a spread umbrella over the head of a corpse. The dead man's mouth, too, was stuffed with rice and fowl, and in cold

weather a fire was kept burning in the hut for the benefit of their deceased friend. They consulted his love of
ornament, also, for the top of his head and his brow
were stained red, his nose and cheeks yellow, and
the lower jaw white; and fantastic figures of different
colors were daubed over his black body.

Dingaan, the Zulu chief, was exceedingly fond of
ornament. He used to boast that the Zulus were the
only people who understood dress. Sometimes he came
forward painted with all kinds of stripes and crosses, in
a very bizarre style. The people took all this gravely,
saying that "he was king and could do what he
pleased," and they were content with his taste. It is
this unreflecting character which astounds us in savages. They never made it a question whether the
garniture of the king or of the corpse had any thing
unsuitable.

All along the coasts, from the equator to the north of
the Gulf of Guinea. they did not eat without throwing
a portion on the ground for those who had died. Sometimes they dug a small hole for these purposes, or they
had one in the hut, and into it they poured what they
thought would be acceptable. They conceived that
they had sensible evidence of the inclinations of the
dead. In lifting up or carrying a corpse on their
shoulders, men may not attend to the exact direction
of their own muscular movements or those of their as-

sociates. There are necessarily shocks, jolts and struggles, from the movements of their associates. People will, in some cases, pull different ways when hustled together. All these unconscious movements, not unlike the "table turnings" of the present era, were taken as expressive of the will of the dead man, as to how and whither he was to be carried.

Their belief, as we have seen, influenced their life : it was earnest and heartfelt. When the king of Wydah, in 1694, heard that Smith, the chief of the English factory, was dangerously ill with fever, he sent his fetishman to aid in the recovery. The priest went to the sick man, and solemnly announced that he came to save him. He then marched to the white man's burial-ground with a provision of brandy, oil, and rice, and made a loud oration to those that slept there. "O you dead white people, you wish to have Smith among you ; but our king likes him, and it is not his will to let him go to be among you." Passing on to the grave of Wyburn, the founder of the factory, he addressed him, "You, captain of all the whites who are here! Smith's sickness is a piece of your work. You want his company, for he is a good man ; but our king does not want to lose him, and you can't have him yet." Then digging a hole over the grave, he poured into it the articles which he had brought, and told him that if he needed these things, he gave them with good-will, but he must not expect to get Smith.   The factor died, notwithstanding.   The ideas here are not very dissimilar to those of the old Greeks.

It is remarkable, however, that in tracing this negro race along the continent towards the south, we find these notions and practices to fade away, and at last disappear.   Southeast of the desert, along the Orange River, there is scarcely a trace of them.

The dread of witchcraft prevails universally.   In general, the occurrence of disease is ascribed to this source.   In the north they fear a supernatural influence; in the south this is traced to no superhuman origin, but is conceived to be a power which any one may possess and exercise.   Among these tribes, the man presumed to be guilty of this crime is a public enemy (as were the witches occasionally found among our own venerated pious, and public-spirited puritan forefathers—a blemish in their character due to the general ignorance of the age), to be removed if possible, as a lion, tiger, or pestilence would be annihilated.   Even the force of civilized law, when introduced among them, has not saved a man under this stigma from being secretly murdered by the terrified people.   It has yielded only to the enlightening influence of Christian missionaries.

These delusions are often rendered the support of tyranny by the chiefs, for the property of the accused is confiscated. Scenes sad and horrible are exhibited as the consequence of a chief's illness. In order to force a discovery of the means employed, and to get the witchcraft counteracted, some native, who is generally rich enough to be worth plundering, is seized and tortured, until, as an old author expresses it, "he dies, or the chief recovers." They extend the horror of the infliction, by calling in the aid of vermin life, destined in nature to devour corruption, by scattering handfuls of ants over the scorched skin and quivering flesh of their victim.

Generally among the Guinea negroes, the ordeal employed to detect this crime, is to compel the accused to drink a decoction of sassy-wood. This may be rendered harmless or destructive, according to the object of the fetishman. It is oftener his purpose to destroy than to save, and great cruelty has in almost all cases been found to accompany the trial.

Plunder is the reward of the soldier. In the central regions this was increased by the sale of captives. Captives of both sexes were the chief's property. Thus the warriors looked to the acquisition of wives from the chief, as the recompense of successful wars. They announced this as their aim in their preparatory songs. The chief was, therefore, to them the source of every thing. Their whole thought responded to his movements, and sympathized with his greatness and success.

Women in Africa are everywhere slaves, or the

slaves of slaves. The burdens of agricultural labor fall on them. When a chief is announced as having hundreds or thousands of wives, it signifies really that he has so many female slaves. There does not appear to be any tribe in Africa, in which it is not the rule of society, that a man may have as many such wives as he can procure. The number is of course, except in the case of the supreme chief, but few. The female retinue of a sovereign partakes everywhere of the reverence due to its head. The chief and his household are a kind of divinity to the people. His name is the seal of their oath. The possibility of his dying must never be expressed, nor the name of death uttered in his presence. Names of things appearing to interfere with the sacredness of his, must be changed. His women must not be met or looked at.

In war, as long as success depends alone on individual prowess, the strong and athletic only can be successful soldiers. Where the weapons, rather than the person are the source of power, docility and endurance are qualities more valuable than strength. In these the weaker sex, in savage life, surpasses the other; hence women have appeared in the world as soldiers. It was probably the introduction of the arrow, killing at a distance, as superior in effect and safety to the rude clubs and spears of earlier conflict, which originated the Amazons of old history. The same fact is resulting in Africa from the introduction of the musket. Females thus armed were found, commonly as royal guards, in the beginning of the last century. The practice still continues in the central regions.

In Dahomey a considerable proportion of the national troops consists of armed and disciplined females. They are known as being royal women, strictly and watchfully kept from any communication with men, and seem to have been trained, through discipline and the force of co-operation, to the accomplishment of enterprises, from which the tumultuous warriors of a native army would shrink. A late English author (Duncan) says, " I have seen them, all well armed, and generally fine, strong, healthy women, and doubtless capable of enduring great fatigue. They seem to use the long Danish musket with as much ease as one of our grenadiers does his firelock, but not of course with the same quickness, as they are not trained to any particular exercise; but on receiving the word, make an attack like a pack of hounds, with great swiftness. Of course they would be useless against disciplined troops, if at all approaching to the same numbers. Still their appearance is more martial than the generality of the men, and if undertaking a campaign, I should prefer the female to the male soldiers of this country."

The same author thus describes a field review of these Amazons, which he witnessed : "I was conducted to a large space of broken ground, where fourteen days had been occupied in erecting three immense prickly piles of green bush. These three clumps or piles, of a sort of strong brier or thorn, armed with the most dangerous prickles, were placed in line, occupying about four hundred yards, leaving only a narrow passage between them, sufficient merely to distinguish each clump appointed to each regiment. These piles were about seventy feet wide and eight feet high. Upon examining them, I could not persuade myself that any human being without boots or shoes would, under any circumstances, attempt to pass over so dangerous a collection of the most efficiently armed plants I had ever seen."

The Amazons wear a blue striped cotton surtout, manufactured by the natives, and a pair of trowsers falling just below the knee. The cartridge-box is girded around the loins.

The drums and trumpets soon announced the approach of three or four thousand Amazons. "The Apadomey soldiers (female) made their appearance at about two hundred yards from, or in front of, the first pile, where they halted with shouldered arms. In a few seconds the word for attack was given, and a rush was made towards the pile with a speed beyond conception, and in less than one minute the whole body had passed over this immense pile, and had taken the supposed town. Each of the other piles was passed with the same rapidity, at intervals of twenty minutes." " When a person is killed in battle, the skin is taken from the head, and kept as a trophy of valor. I counted seven hundred scalps pass in this manner. The captains of each corps (female), in passing, again presented themselves before his majesty, and received the king's approval of their conduct." These heroines, however, say that they are no longer women, but men.

The people of Ashantee and Dahomey are considerably in advance of those on the coast. They cultivate the soil extensively, manufacture cotton cloth, and build comparatively good houses. They have musical instruments, which, if rude, are loud enough. Their drums and horns add to the stateliness of their ceremonies. Of such exhibitions they are very fond, and consider it a national honor if they can render them impressive to strangers. The Dahomeans are about one hundred miles in the interior, west of the Niger.

Necessity has occasionally driven some of the southern tribes to adopt the practice of cannibalism. There it has ever excited horror and disgust. Those who have practised it are distinguished by an appellation setting them apart from other men. Among some of the central tribes it has prevailed rather, however, in all appearance, from superstitious motives, or as an exhibition of triumphant revenge, than in the revolting form which it assumes among some of the Polynesian islanders.

CHAPTER VI.

TRADE—METALS—MINES—VEGETABLE PRODUCTIONS—GUMS—
OIL—COTTON—DYE-STUFFS.

THE trade of Africa for an almost indefinite time must consist of the materials for manufactures.

The fact that old formations reposing on granite, or distorted by it, form a large proportion of its geological surface, indicates that useful metals will probably be found in abundance. In comparing it with California and Australia as to the probability of finding deposits of the more valuable metals, two circumstances of great importance must be kept in view. These countries were possessed by natives who had no domesticated animals, and therefore were not called upon to exercise over the soil the same inquisitive inspection for herbage and water as were required from the races among the mountains and deserts of Africa, so that the chances of finding any thing were not the same.

The other circumstance is, that metals were comparatively little known to the aborigines of California, and not at all to those of New Holland, so that discoveries of the kind would neither be sought for, nor reckoned of much value when they occurred. On the other hand, metals of all kinds have during indefinite eras been regarded as of high importance, and have been used in various ways by the African nations. Copper, and some alloys of it, seem to be used for ornaments throughout the whole south. These are smelted from the ores by the natives. They also manufacture their own iron. Their desires, therefore, and their necessities, and their arts, render it probable that no deposits of metals exist, except such as require scientific skill to discover, and mechanical resources to procure.

Gold is not in this predicament. Wherever it occurs in abundance, it has been collected by elemental waste from disintegrated rocks, and is mixed with gravel and alluvial matters in those portions where men of nomadic habits, and familiar with metal ornaments, would most readily meet and appropriate it. Some, probably a great proportion, of the gold of ancient Egypt, was got by a laborious process of grinding, on which their wretched captives were employed. This would not have been the case if the metal had been found plentifully throughout the extensive regions with which they were acquainted.

An addition to the metallic riches of the world from Africa, is therefore to be looked for in the discovery of deep-seated mines, if there are any, and in better modes of working those which exist, particularly the alluvial deposits of gold along the northern shores of the Gulf of Guinea and the shores of the Mozambique Channel. The present export of gold from all Africa, probably amounts to about two millions of dollars per annum.

The vegetable articles of export are of great value. Cotton may be produced in unlimited abundance. The African dye-stuffs are already recognized as extensive and valuable articles of commerce. Indigo is used extensively by the natives. When we recollect that the vast trade of Bengal in this article has been created within the memory of men still living, and that India possesses no natural advantages beyond those of Africa, we may infer what a profusion of wealth might be poured rapidly over Africa by peace and good government.

Gums, of various kinds, constitute a branch of trade which may be considered as only commencing. The extensive employment of india-rubber, and the knowledge of gutta-percha, are only a few years old. Africa gives promise of a large supply of such articles. Its caoutchouc has already been introduced into the arts.*

---

* The Rev. J. Leighton Wilson, who was a missionary of the American Board of Commissioners for Foreign Missions, at Cape Palmas and at the Gaboon River for more than twenty years, first called attention to a vine, or creeper, as affording india-rubber. It is now collected from this plant in the Gaboon district; and two or three cargoes have already been shipped to this country, with a prospect of its becoming a lucrative article of trade. We may look to intelligent missionaries, like Mr. Wilson, for securing such benefits to traffic and art, as well

It may be long before the natural sources of supply found in its marshy forests can be exhausted. Be that as it may; when men are induced, as perhaps they soon will be, to substitute regular cultivation for the wild and more irregular modes of procuring articles which are becoming every day of more essential importance, Africa may take a great share in the means adopted to supply them.

Palm-oil has become pre-eminently an object of attention. The modes of procuring it are very rude and wasteful. The palm-nuts are generally left for a day or two, heaped together in a hole dug in the ground. They are then trodden by the women, till they form a greasy pulp; out of this the oil is rudely strained through their fingers, or water is run into the hole to float the oil, and it is skimmed off with their hands into a calabash. In Benin they employ the better mode of boiling it off. The oil occurs in a kind of pulp surrounding the seed, as is the case with the eatable part of the common date; it is evident, therefore, that more suitable modes of producing it may be put in practice.

What may be done in the production of sugar and coffee, no man can tell. James Macqueen, who has, during great part of his life, devoted his attention to

---

as to science and literature. We are glad to learn that he contemplates an extended work on Africa, which will no doubt be highly acceptable to the public.

the condition and interests of Africa, gave evidence before a committee of the British House of Peers, in 1850,
to the following effect: "There is scarcely any tropical
production known in the world, which does not come to
perfection in Africa. There are many productions
which are peculiarly her own. The dye-stuffs and dye-
woods are superior to any which are known in any other
quarter of the world, inasmuch as they resist both acids
and light, things which we know no other dye-stuffs,
from any other parts of the world, can resist. Then
there is the article of sugar, that can be produced in
every part of Africa to an unlimited extent. There is
cotton also, above all things—cotton of a quality so
fine; it is finer cotton than any description of cotton
we know of in the world. Common cotton in Africa I have seen, and had in my possession, which was
equal to the finest quality of American cotton.

"Egyptian cotton is not so good as the cotton away
to the south; but the cotton produced in the southern
parts of Africa is peculiarly fine. Africa is a most ex-
traordinary country. In the eastern horn of Africa,
which you think to be a desolate wilderness, there is the
finest country, and the finest climate I know. I know
of none in South America equal to the climate of the
country in the northeastern horn of Africa. It is a very
elevated country; and on the upper regions you have all
the fruits, and flowers, and grain of Europe growing; and

in the valleys you have the finest fruits of the torrid
zone. The whole country is covered with myrrh and
frankincense; it is covered with flocks and herds; it
produces abundance of the finest grain. Near Brasa,
for instance, on the river Webbe, you can purchase as
much fine wheat for a dollar as will serve a man for a
year. All kinds of European grain flourish there. In
Enarea and Kaffa, the whole country is covered with
coffee; it is the original country of the coffee. You can
purchase an ass's load (200 lbs.) of coffee in the berry
for about a dollar. The greater portion of the coffee
that we receive from Mocha, is actually African coffee,
produced in that part."

CHAPTER VII.

THE Portuguese commercial discoverers having succeeded those of France, and founded trading establishments on the coast of Africa, were driven from the seashore by the rivalry and power of the Dutch and the English, about the year 1604. They retired into the interior, and commingled with the negroes. From their intermarriages arose a race of mulattoes, who have long exercised considerable influence. As early as 1667, this influence had become detrimental to commerce and discovery. They closed against others the entrances to the great region of more elevated lands, and carried on trade, without rivals, from Benin to Senegambia, over two thousand miles. They had generally little chapels near their houses, and spared no pains to make proselytes.

How much might these men have done for the good

of Africa and the progress of the world! Following their lines of commerce, and cresting the high lands, which feed, with rains and rivulets, the Gambia and the Niger, as well as the streams by which they dwell, they might have saved two centuries of doubt and hazardous attempts, and much sacrifice of good and talented men. They might earlier have let in Christian civilization to repel the Moslem and redeem the negro. Portuguese influence is gone, and has left the world little reason to regret its extinction. On the rising and almost impervious forest-lands which are at the distance of from twenty to fifty miles back from the coast, these Portuguese mulattoes are still found, watching for their monopoly, with the same jealous exclusiveness as of old. These forests thus inhabited, form, at present, a serious obstacle to the extension of the influence of Liberia. An enterprising people, however, occupying the great tracts of cleared lands along the coast, which constitute the actual territories of the republic, will, with the progress of the settlements, and the increase of their power, soon be enabled, notwithstanding the short navigable distance of the rivers, to open communication with the far interior.

The Portuguese founded cities and missions. A more extensive authority was gained by them over great and populous regions, both on the eastern and western shores, than has been attained by any other people. The title of "Lord of Guinea" was fairly claimed for the King of Portugal, by the establishment of this sovereign's supremacy over various native kingdoms. But Portugal wanted the light and strength of a nation —a righteous and intelligent policy.

The establishments on the east coast now scarcely keep their ground, ever shrinking before the barbarian and the Arab. St. Paul de Loando, on the southwest coast, is shrivelled down from its former greatness. Both regions have rich capabilities; both might have extended a useful influence, until they met and embraced in the centre, uniting these vast regions with the great movements of human progress; but they clui to the slave-trade, and its curse has clung to them.

They misunderstood human nature, and overlooked its high destiny. Of the Spaniards and Portuguese concerned in slaving, Captain Dunlop, of the British Navy, long attached to the English squadron on the African coast, says: "They speak of the African as a brute, who is only fit to be made a slave of, and say that it is quite chimerical and absurd in us to attempt to put down the trade, or to defend men who were only born to be slaves."

Other nations only founded slave factories. Every thing peculiar to this influence was bad. Compared with the ounces of gold and tusks of ivory which drew the cupidity of early navigators, there arose everywhere a traffic, far more rapid, but it was that of cruelty, bringing with it vice. Brandy and arms, drunkenness and war, followed as the remuneration of rapine and slaving. The gross vices of Europe added to the mischief. Legitimate trade, which might have flourished for centuries, withered; and the rank which the white man held among the natives, made him a source of wide corruption. Little good could come out of the state of society in Europe during the last century, for little good was in it. This state of things has improved.

The three nations whose interference seems likely to have a conspicuous effect upon the interests of Africa in the future, are *France*, *England*, and the *United States*.

France will have all the Mediterranean shore, and the caravan trade across the deserts. But this will diminish in activity and value, as the trade of the other shores extends, and as the way across from them to the interior becomes easier. No great influence can, therefore, be in this way exercised over the prosperity of the African people.

England holds the south; but the natives around the Cape of Good Hope are greatly isolated from the interior by deserts and climates hostile to European life. Democracy has a footing there, inasmuch as Dutch colonists have retired from under English jurisdiction, and formed a government for themselves, which has been acknowledged by England. After suffering, and trial,

and privation shall have taught independence of thought
and patriotism, a respectable confederacy of states may
be formed in these regions.

Every effort that is just and suitable, is made to extend English influence along the shores of negro lands.
The expenditure in endeavoring to extirpate the slave-
trade is very great; and great devotedness and heroism
have been seen in attempts to explore the interior.
Both objects are drawing towards completion; but the
permanently beneficial influence of England rests on the
establishment of Sierra Leone and the extended coasting
trade, arising from the semi-monthly line of English
steamers which touch there.

England has established twenty-four treaties with
native kings, chiefs, or powers, for the suppression of the
slave-trade; seventeen of these are with chiefs whose
territories have fallen under the influence of the Republic of Liberia and Cape Palmas. The influence of these
governments has now replaced that of England, by
sweeping the slave-trade from their territory of about
six hundred miles. The great proportion of recaptured
slaves, chiefly men and boys, who have been thrown
into the population of Sierra Leone, has loaded it heavily. Of these, altogether not less than sixty thousand
have, at different times, been introduced; yet, with the
original colonists—the Novascotians, Canadians and
the Maroons from Jamaica—the whole do not now ex

tend beyond forty-five thousand; still, Sierra Leone has long been a focus of good emanations. It embraces a territory small compared with Liberia. The government is repressive of native energy, on account of the constant superintendence of white men, and the subordination of the colony to a distant and negligent government.

One momentous effect of its influence, however, has come permanently forward, tending to carry rapid improvement widely over the western regions of Africa. These recaptured slaves, and their descendants, many of them, are returning to their native lands, elevated in character by the instruction they have received. Three thousand of them are now settled among their brethren of the Yoruba tribe, near the mouth of the Niger, and there, superintended by two or three missionaries, are sending abroad, by their influence and example, the light of Divine truth.

Sierra Leone and the naval squadrons have rendered great service to Liberia. It is perfectly obvious that the colony could not have existed if left to itself under the old system of pirating and slave-trading. Those who did not spare European forts, would have had no scruple at plundering and extinguishing such opponents of their traffic. It must in justice be admitted, that a fair surrender of what might, in reality, be considered as conquered territory, has been made by England to

Liberia. The instances of such transactions show a greatly advanced state of morality in the public dealings of nations, and in this, even, the African has begun to partake.

Sierra Leone was founded on the 9th of May, 1787, by a party of four hundred negroes, discharged from the army and navy. They were joined by twelve hundred from Nova Scotia in 1792.

In 1849, the country around the river Sherboro, intervening between Sierra Leone and Monrovia, had been carrying on a war for about seven years, and at length commenced plundering the canoes of the Sierra Leone people. The acting governor soon brought them to terms. This vexed the slavers at the Gallinas, who had long been an annoyance to the Liberian authorities. It was the slavers' policy to keep up the excitement and strife, that they might in the mean time drive a brisk trade unmolested.

The English cruisers at length blockaded the Gallinas. They ascertained that, notwithstanding the blockade, abundance of goods were received by the enemy. The mystery was at length solved by discovering that the slave-traders, through small creeks and lagoons, had received what they wanted from Sierra Leone. The case was referred to the governor to have this prevented, and by the governor it was referred to the lawyers. They shook their wigs solemnly over the complaint, and decided that nothing within the compass of the law suited the case, and therefore nobody could interfere.

Captain Dunlop, in command of the cruisers, a good naval diplomatist, ready in the cause of justice and humanity to make precedents where none could be found, informed the Sherboro chiefs, that a treaty existed between them and his government for the suppression of the slave-trade; and suggested to them the virtue and the profit of seizing the goods brought from Sierra Leone. The chiefs had the smallest possible objections which honest men could have, to appropriate the slavers' goods to themselves. On the principle of employing a thief in office for the moral benefit of his companions, this matter was easily settled. The goods were seized in their transit. It was also stipulated with these chiefs, that they should stop all trade and intercourse between their own people and the slave barracoons. Having now no chance of sending off slaves, and no means of getting any thing from Sierra Leone or elsewhere, the slavers, established at the Gallinas—regarded for the present as no man's land— were obliged to come to terms.

Captain Dunlop landed to receive their surrender. But to spare his own men in the sickliest season of the year, he applied to a chief for one hundred and fifty hands; these he obtained, and soon after three hundred

more joined him, and remained for the five or six
weeks, while the affair was being settled. These men
behaved as well as disciplined troops, or rather better,
for although among an enemy's property, there was no
drunkenness or plunder.

An idea of the extent of the slave-establishment may
be had from the fact that sixty foreigners were made
prisoners. They hailed from everywhere, and were sent
to Sierra Leone to find passage to Brazil, Cuba and
other places.

The chiefs who had been in partnership with them,
found themselves none the worse for this summary
breaking up of the firm. They cleared off their national
debt. In the way of trade they had come under obligations to this establishment to the extent of seven
thousand slaves, and they found themselves at liberty
honestly to "repudiate," or rather their obligation was
discharged, as slaves were no longer a lawful tender.
The chiefs, however, were required to set at liberty all
slaves collected but not delivered. These amounted to
about a thousand. A preparation was here made for
the extension of Liberia, and afterwards, as will be
seen, that government came into possession of this territory, and thus secured a still greater extent of coast
from the intrusion of the slaver.

English influence is extending by means of factories
and agents all along the coast, from Cape Palmas to

the Gaboon (about twelve hundred miles), for commercial purposes and for the suppression of the slave-trade. These establishments are supported by the government. Commissioners proceed from them to enter into negotiations on the subject of the slave-trade with the powerful chiefs of the interior, and curious results sometimes occur from the prestige thus gained.

One of the great Ashantee chiefs came over to the English, during the war in which Sir Charles McCarthy was killed, and retained his independence on the borders of the two powers. Governor McLean, at Cape Coast Castle, learnt that this chief had offered human sacrifices as one of his " customs." A summons, in a legal form, was dispatched to him by a native soldier, citing him to appear for trial for this offence. Agreeably to the summons, he marched to the court in great state, surrounded by his chiefs and attendants. He was tried, convicted, and heavily fined. He was then dismissed, with an order to remit the money. This he immediately did, although there was no force, except moral supremacy, to constrain him to obey. There has been no slaving at Cape Coast Castle since the trade was abolished forty years ago.

There are only forty British officers and soldiers in all the line of forts, with one hundred of the West India regiment, and about fifty native militia-men. The annual expense of the establishments is about twenty thousand dollars; although, as the government has lately purchased, for fifty thousand dollars, the Danish forts, the expense will be materially increased.

The interior is improving. Captain Winniet visited Ashantee in October, 1849. He found on the route large thriving additional villages, as far as English protection extended. He was received at Kumassi with the usual display of African music, musketry, and marching. He was led for a mile and a half through a lane at heads and shoulders, clustered thick on both sides. There were here and there diverging branches of a like character, as thick with heads and shoulders; and at the end of each, a chief sitting in his chair of state. To and by each chief, a hand was waved as a salutation, until the monarch himself was reached. He rose, came forward, and, with heavy lumps of gold dangling at his wrists, exhibited his agility in dancing. When this act of state ceremony had been properly *done up*, he offered his hand to shake, and thus completed the etiquette of a reception at court. The houses, with piazzas projecting to shelter them from the sun—public-rooms in front, and dwelling-rooms behind, nicely plastered and colored—were greatly admired.

The pleading about the slave-trade was the main business and the main difficulty; but the nature of such negotiations appears, in its most impressive aspect, in the case of Dahomey.

This chief professes great devotedness to England. In consequence of some difficulty, he gave notice to European foreigners, " that he was not much accustomed to cut off white heads, but if any interfered with an agent of the English government, he would cut off their heads as readily as those of his black people." By murderous incursions against his neighbors, he seized about nine thousand victims annually. He sold about three thousand of these directly on his own account, gave the rest chiefly away to his troops, who sold them : a duty of five dollars being paid on each slave exported, afforded him altogether a revenue of about three hundred thousand dollars.

This was a serious matter to argue against. He stated the case strongly : " The form of my government cannot be suddenly changed, without causing such a revolution as would deprive me of my throne, and precipitate the kingdom into anarchy. . . . I am very desirous to acquire the friendship of England. I and my army are ready, at all times, to fight the queen's enemies, and do any thing the English government may ask of me, except to give up the slave-trade. No other trade is known to my people. Palm-oil, it is true, is engaging the attention of some of them, but it is a slow method of making money, and brings only a very small amount of duties into my coffers. The planting of cotton and coffee has been suggested, but that is slower still. The trees have to grow, and I shall probably be in my grave before I reap any benefit from them; and what am I to do in the mean time? Who will pay my troops in the mean time? Who will buy arms and clothes for them? Who will buy dresses for my wives? Who will give me supplies of cowries, rum, gunpowder and cloth, for my annual 'customs?' I hold my power by the observance of the time-honored customs of my forefathers. I should forfeit it, and entail on myself a life full of shame, and a death full of misery, by neglecting them. The slave-trade has been the ruling principle of my people. It is the source of their glory and wealth. Their songs celebrate their victories, and the mother lulls the child to sleep with notes of triumph over an enemy reduced to slavery. Can I, by signing such a treaty, change the sentiments of a whole people? It cannot be!"

The case was a puzzling one for this intelligent, open-hearted, and ambitious barbarian. He had trained an army of savage heroes, and as savage heroines, thirsting for distinction and for plunder. This army cowers at his feet as long as he satiates its appetite for excitement, rapine and blood. But woe to him if it turn in disappointed fury upon him! Such is military despotism; perilous to restrain, and perilous to let loose. Blessed is that people which is clear of it!

There is this strange incident in the affair. that the

English power, which sent an ambassador to plead the
case with him in this peaceful mode, was at the same
time covering the sea with cruisers, and lining the shore
with factories, and combining every native influence to
extinguish the sole source from which flowed the security and splendor of his rule. He knew this, and could
offer no moral objection to it, although complaining of
the extent to which it reduced his authority, and crip-
pled his resources.

The urgency to which the King of Dahomey was
subjected, ended, in 1852, in his yielding. England
had proposed to pay him some annual sum for a time,
as a partial compensation for the loss of his revenue: it
may therefore be presumed that he is a stipendiary of
the British government; and as the practices given up
by him can scarcely, in any circumstances, be suddenly
revived, his interest will retain him faithful to the en-
gagement. It is a strange, bold, and perilous undertaking, that he should direct his disciplined army, his
hero and his heroine battalions, to the arts of peace!
But to these he and they must henceforward look as
the source of their wealth, security, and greatness.

Queen Victoria, it is said, has lately sent the King of
Dahomey two thousand ornamental caps for the Amazon soldiers.

CHAPTER VIII.

DAHOMEY——SLAVISH SUBJECTION OF THE PEOPLE——DEPENDENCE
OF THE KING ON THE SLAVE-TRADE——EXHIBITION OF HU-
MAN SKULLS——ANNUAL HUMAN SACRIFICES——LAGOS——THE
CHANGES OF THREE CENTURIES.

DALZIEL, in slave-trading times, shocked the world
with details in reference to Dahomey. Duncan and
Forbes have again presented the picture in the same
hues of·darkness and of blood. Ghezo is a good king as
things go, and rather particularly good for an African,
for whom the world has done nothing, and who, therefore, cannot be expected to do much for the world. He
has a threatening example before him. His elder
brother is a prisoner, with as much to eat and more to
drink than is good for him—caged up by a crowd of
guards, who prevent him from doing any thing else.
He was deposed, and reduced to this state, because his
rule did not suit his subjects.

Ghezo, therefore, has the office of seeing men roll on
the earth before him, and scrape up dust over themselves; of being deafened by vociferations of his dignity
and virtue and glory and honor, by court poets and par-

asites, on state occasions ; the office of keeping satisfied, with pay and plunder, the ferocious spirit of a bloodthirsty people ; the office of looking out for some victim tribe, whom, by craft and violence, they may ruin ; and the office of procuring, catching and buying some scores of human victims, whom he and his savages murder, at different set seasons, in public.

A good share of this used to be effected by means of the slave-trade. But that is gone, or nearly so, and with it may go much of the atrocity of Dahomean public life. Things are yet, however, and may long remain, in a transition state. He and his people will not suddenly lose their taste for the excitement of human suffering; and it would be a danger for which, it is probable, he has not the moral courage, or a result for which he has no real wish, to bring old national ceremonies to a sudden pause. But there are circumstances likely to act with effect in producing the change, which is a matter destined to occur at some time or other, and to be obtained when it occurs only in one mode ; and the sooner the process is begun, the sooner it will end.

As to what it is that higher principles must banish from the world, Commander Forbes, of the British Navy, in 1850, the latest visitor of that country who has given an account of it, tells us what he saw. He says: " There is something fearful in the state of sub-

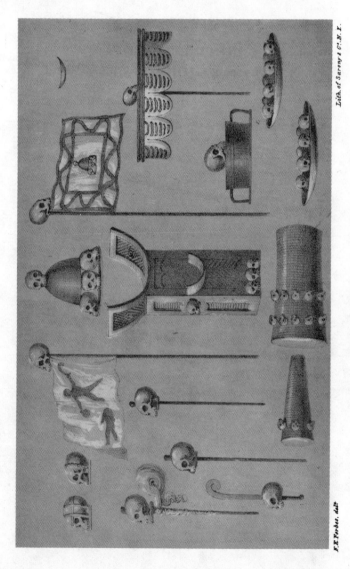

F.E.Forbes, delt

Lith. of Sarony & Co. N.Y.

SKULL ORNAMENTS & BANNERS OF DAHOMEY.

jection in which, in outward show, the kings of Dahomey hold their highest officers; yet, when the system is examined, these prostrations are merely keeping
up of ancient customs. Although no man's head in
Dahomey can be considered warranted for twenty-four
hours, still the great chief himself would find his
tottering if one of these customs was omitted."

They were preparing for the ceremony of watering
the graves of the royal ancestors with blood; during
which the king also presents some victims as a royal
gift to his people. This merely means that they are
knocked down in public, and their heads cut off, amidst
trumpeting, and clamor, and jesting.

"With much ceremony," we read, "two large cala-
bashes, containing the skulls of kings," conquered by
the Dahomeans, "ornamented with copper, brass, coral,
&c., were brought in and placed on the ground. Some
formed the heads of walking-sticks, distaffs; while
those of chiefs and war-men ornamented drums, um-
brellas, surmounted standards, and decorated doorways.
They were on all sides in thousands."

"There was much to disgust the white man in the
number of human skulls and jaw-bones displayed; but
can the reader imagine twelve unfortunate human beings lashed hands and feet, and tied in small canoes
and baskets, dressed in clean white dresses, with a high
red cap, carried on the heads of fellow-men? These,

and an alligator and a cat, were the gift of the monarch
to the people—prisoners of war."…. "When carried
round the court, they bore the gaze of their enemies
without shrinking. At the foot of the throne they
halted, while the *Mayo* presented each with a head
(bunch) of cowries, extolling the munificence of the
monarch, who had sent it to them to purchase a last
meal, for to-morrow they must die."

Again: "But of the fourteen now brought on the
platform, we the unworthy instruments of the Divine
will, succeeded in saving the lives of three. Lashed as
we have described before, these sturdy men met the
gaze of their persecutors, with a firmness perfectly astonishing. Not a sigh was breathed. In all my life
I never saw such coolness before, so near death…. The
victims were held high above the heads of their bearers,
and the naked ruffians thus acknowledged the munificence of their prince…… Having called their names,
the nearest one was divested of his clothes; the foot of
the basket placed on the parapet, when the king gave
its upper part an impetus, and the victim fell at once
into the pit beneath. A fall upwards of twelve feet
may have stunned him, and before sense could return,
his head was cut off, and the body thrown to the mob;
who, now armed with clubs and branches, brutally muti-
lated it and dragged it to a distant pit." Forbes and
his companion had retired to their seats away from the

F. E. Forbes, del.

THE PLATFORM OF THE AH-TOH.

Lith. of Sarony & Co. N.Y.

sight. Two sons of Da Souza, the notorious slaver, remained to look on.

The circumstance most likely to have effect in restrain-
ing these barbarities, is the value which slaves will now
bear as the means of cultivating the ground, and raising exportable produce, to which alone the monarch
and people must look, in the diminished state of the
slave-trade, to furnish means for their expenses. Victims and slaves will also be more difficult to be procured by warfare, inasmuch as civilized people have
more general access to the country, and will introduce
a better policy, and more powerful defensive means
among the people. Christianity also is adventuring
there, and carrying its peaceful influence and nobler
motives with it.

Lagos plundered recaptured slaves returning to their
homes. The authorities deserved no favor. A better
man—perhaps a more legitimate claimant for the royal
dignity—was found, and after a severe fight, in which
the British cruisers warmly participated, he was seated
on the throne. A severe blow was given to the slave-
trade. Affairs seemed to be going on smoothly until
early in the autumn of 1853, when a revolution broke
out, amidst which the king died, and the country, as far
as is known, remains in confusion.

The present is an interesting period in the history of
the world. Changes are rapid and irrevocable. Cir-

cumstances illustrative of the condition of our race as
it has been, are disappearing rapidly.   The future
must trust to our philosophic observation, and faithful
testimony, for its knowledge of savage life.   The help-
lessness, and artlessness, and miserable shifts of barbarism are becoming things of the past.   There is perhaps no region of the earth which is now altogether
beyond the reach of civilized arts.   Shells, and flints,
and bows, and clubs, and bone-headed spears are everywhere giving way to more useful or more formidable
implements.   Improvements in dress and tools and
furniture will soon be universal.   The history of man
as he has been, requires therefore to be written now,
while the evidence illustrative of it has not altogether
vanished.

The changes of the last three centuries have, to only
a slight degree, influenced the African races.   An
inaccessible interior, and a coast bristling with slave-
factories, and bloody with slaving cruelties, probably
account for this.   The slight progress made shows the
obduracy of the degradation to be removed, and the
difficulty of the first steps needed for its removal.
Wherever the slave-trade or its effects penetrated, there
of course peace vanished, and prosperity became impossible.   This evil affected not only the coast, but
spread warfare to rob the country of its inhabitants, far
into the interior regions.   There were tribes, however,

uninfluenced by it, and some of these have gained extensive, although but temporary authority. Yet nowhere has there been any real civilization. It is singular that these people should have rested in this unalloyed barbarism for thousands of years, and that there should have been no native-born advancement, as in Mexico, or Peru, or China; and no flowing in upon its darkness of any glimmering of light from the brilliant progress and high illumination of the outside world. It has been considered worthy of note, that a few years ago one of the Veys had contrived a cumbrous alphabet to express the sounds of his language; but it is surely, to an incomparable degree, more a matter of surprise, that centuries passed away in communication with Europeans, without such an attempt having been made by any individual, of so many millions, during so many generations of men.

The older state of negro society, therefore, still continues. With the exception of civilized vices, civilized arms, and some amount of civilized luxuries, life on the African coast, or at no great distance from it, remains now much the same as the first discoverers found it.

As it was two hundred years ago, the food of the people consists of rice, maize and millet; or the Asiatic, the American and the African native grains. A few others, of comparatively little importance, might be added to these. Many fruits, as bananas, figs and pumpkins, compose part of their subsistence.

Flesh of all kinds was used abundantly before European arms began to render game scarce. Fish along the coast, and beside the rivers and interior lakes, are used, except by some tribes, who regard them as unclean. The Bushmen south of Elephants' Bay, reject no kind of reptile. The snake's poison arms their weapon, and its body is eaten. As the poisons used act rapidly, and do not affect the flesh of the animal, it is devoured without scruple and without danger. Throughout all the deserts, as in ancient times, the locust, or large winged grasshopper, is used as an article of food, not nutritive certainly, but capable of sustaining life. The wings and legs are pulled off, and the bodies are scorched, in holes heated as ovens, and having the hot sand hauled over them.

In Dahomey, according to Duncan, there is some improvement in agriculture, traced to the return from the Brazils of a few who had been trained as slaves in that empire. This influence, and that of ideas imported from civilized society, seem to be more prevalent in Dahomey than elsewhere. The present sovereign has mitigated the laws, diminished the transit duties, and acted with such judicious kindness towards tribes who submitted without resistance, that his neighbors, tired of war and confusion, have willingly, in some instances, preferred to come under his jurisdiction.

These circumstances, together with the treaty formed by England with the King of Dahomey, in 1852, for the suppression of the slave-trade, indicate that a new destiny is opening for the African races. It may be but rarely that a man of so much intelligence gains power; and the successor of the present king may suffer matters to decline; but still great sources of evil are removed, and the people are acquiring a taste for better practices. Human sacrifices have, to a great extent, been abolished; and the wants of cultivation will of themselves render human life of higher value. The two great states of Ashantee and Dahomey, now both open to missionary influence, are likely to run an emulative race in the career of improvement.

CHAPTER IX.

STATE OF THE COAST PRIOR TO THE FOUNDATION OF LIBERIA—
NATIVE TRIBES—CUSTOMS AND POLICY—POWER OF THE FOL-
GIAS—KROOMEN, ETC.—CONFLICTS.

THE lands chosen as the site of the American colony
excited attention in olden times. "Africa would be
preferable to Europe," said the French navigator
Villault in 1667, "if it were all like Cape Mount."
He launches out with delight on the beauty of the prospects, and the richness of the country. He says, "There
you find oranges, almonds, melons, pumpkins, *cherries*
and plums," and the abundance of animals was so great
that the flesh was sold "for almost nothing." Of the
Rio Junco he remarks, "The banks are adorned with
trees and flowers; and the plains with oranges, citrons
and palms in beautiful clumps. At Rio Cesters he
found a people rigidly honest, who had carefully preserved the effects of a deceased trader, until a vessel
arrived to receive them.

Another Frenchman, Desmarchais, in the succeeding
century was invited by "King Peter" to form an establishment on the large island at Cape Mesurado, but

he preferred the Cape itself, on account of the advantages of its position.

The country adjoining Mesurado, although subsequently harassed and wasted by the slave-trade, had in early times a national history and policy, containing incidents which illustrate the character of savage man as displayed in such social arrangements as his dull apprehension can contrive. This will be apparent from circumstances in its history during the sixteenth century.

The country was held chiefly by divisions of a great community, known by the common name of Monoo. The Gallas and the Veys were intruders, but nearly related. The Mandi, or head of the Monoo, retained reverence and dignity, but had lost dominion.

The subordinate tribes ranged themselves in rank, according to the power they possessed, which varied with temporary circumstances. Thus the Monoo lorded it over the Folgias; the Folgias over the Quojas, and the Quojas over the Bulams and Kondos.

Their fortresses were square inclosures, surrounded by stout palisades, driven close together, having four structures somewhat in the form of bastions, through which, and under their defence, were the entrances to the place. Two streets in the interior, crossing each other in the centre, connected these entrances. They had a kind of embrasures or port-holes in these wooden walls, out of which they threw assagays or spears and arrows.

Along the eastern bank of the Junco, stretched the lands of the Kharoo Monoos, the *Kroomen* so well known to our cruisers of the present day. The Folgias weakened in warfare had recourse to the sorceries of a celebrated performer in that line, whose policy in the case savored very greatly of earthly wisdom. He recommended religious strife as the best mode of weakening the enemy. They therefore contrived to excite some "old school and new school" controversy with regard to the sacredness of a pond held in reverence by the Kroos.

It was a matter of Kroo orthodoxy, that into this pond the great ancestor and author of their race had descended from heaven, and there first made his appearance as a man. Hence it was the faith of their established church to make offerings to the pond in favor of the fish that dwelt there.

Now it was also an old and ever-to-be-respected law among them, that no fish should be boiled with the scales on. Amid their career of victory, the audacious and criminal fact was one day discovered, that into the sacred pond, the just object of reverence to an enlightened and religious people, there had been thrown a quantity of fish boiled in a mode which indicated contempt for every thing praiseworthy and national, inasmuch as not a scale had been scraped off previously to their being boiled.

The nation got into a ferment about the fish-scales. From arguments they went to clubs and spears. Parties accusing and parties accused defended their lives, in "just and necessary wars," while the Folgias looked on until both were weak enough to be conquered. The victors, however, were generous. Their chief married the sister of Flonikerri, the leader of the Kroos, and left him in sovereignty over his people. Flonikerri showed his loyalty by resisting an attack on the Folgias by the Quabo of the southeast.

In the mean time the great sovereign Mendino, king of the Monoos, had died; and as negro chiefs are or ought to be immortal, and as no king can die except by sorcery, his brother Manomassa was accused as having contrived his death. He drank the sassy-wood, and survived, without satisfying the people. As the sorcerers proposed to hold a kind of court of inquiry upon the case, Manomassa, indignant at the charge, surrendered himself to the care of the "spirits of the dead," and went away among the Gala.

There his character gained him the office of chief. But annoyed at their subsequent caprice, he threw himself upon the generosity of the Folgias, who employed Flonikerri to reinstate him in his dominion over the Gala. Flonikerri had in fact become a kind of generalissimo of the united tribes.   He was afterwards employed in subduing the Veys of Cape Mount; and after various battles, reduced them to offer proof of their submission.   This consisted in each swallowing some drops of blood from a great number of chickens, which were afterwards boiled; they ate the flesh, reserving the legs, which were delivered to the conqueror, to be preserved as a memorial of their fealty.

Flonikerri fell in battle, resisting a revolt of the Galas.   Being hard pressed, he drew a circle round him on the ground, vowing that within it he would resist or die.   Kneeling there he expired under showers of arrows.

His brother and successor, Killimanzo, extended the authority of the tribe by subduing the Quilligas along the Gallinas river.   The son of the latter, Flanseer, extended their conquests to Sierra Leone, crushed some rebellions, and left a respectable domain under the sway of his son Flamburi.   Then it was that the energy, skill and vices of Europeans came powerfully into action among the contentions of the natives, until they rendered war a means of revenue, by making men an article of merchandise for exportation.

The same language prevailed among all their tribes. The most cultivated dialect was that of the Folgias, who prided themselves greatly on the propriety and the elegance of their speech, and on the figurative illustrations which they threw into it. They retained their supremacy over the Quojas, notwithstanding the extended dominion of the latter. This was indicated by the investiture of the chief of the Quojas with the title of Donda, by the king, or Donda, of the Folgias. The ceremony bore the character of abasement almost universal among the negro race. The Quoja aspirant, having approached the Folgia chief in solemn state, threw himself on the ground, remaining prostrate until the Folgian had thrown some dust over him. He was then asked the name he chose to bear. His attendants repeated it aloud. The king of the Folgians pronounced it, adding the title of Donda; and the whole multitude seized and shouted it with loud acclamations. He was invested with a bow and quiver. Mutual presents concluded the ceremony.

State and dignity, of such a character as could be found among savages, were strictly enforced in these old times. Ambassadors did not enter a territory until they had received permission, and until an officer had been sent to conduct them. There were receptions, and reviews, and stately marchings, trumpetings, drummings, and singing of songs, and acclamations, and flatteries.

The attendants of the ambassador prostrated themselves. He was only required to kneel, but, having bent his head in reverence, he wheeled round to the people, and drew the string of his bow to its full bent, indicating that he became the king's soldier and defender. Then came his oration, which was repeated, sentence by sentence, in the mouth of the king's interpreter. The Quojas claimed the credit of best understanding the proper ceremonies of civil life. How great is the difference between this population, and the few miserable slave-hunters, who subsequently ravaged, rather than possessed, these shores!

CHAPTER X.

THE views of men in founding colonies, have varied
in different ages of the world. Although, however,
some special inducement may have been pre-eminent at
different times, yet a multiplicity of motives have generally combined in leading to such undertakings. Hannibal found the municipal cities, or Roman colonies of
Italy, the obstacles to his conquest of the republic. It
was with provident anticipation of such an effect that
they were founded. Lima in Peru, and other places
in Brazil and elsewhere, had their origin in similar
aims. Differences in political views have led to the
foundation of many colonies; and, superadded to these,
religious considerations have had their influence in the
settlement of some of the early North American colonies.

In the small republics of Greece, the seditious, or the criminal—sometimes whole classes of men, whose residence was unsuitable to the general interests—were cast adrift to go where they chose, probably making a general jail delivery for the time being.

Modern efforts of the kind are, upon the whole, more systematic. A colony sent for settlement or for subsistence, is purely so. A military colony is purely military, or, more generally, is nothing else than a garrison. A colony of criminals is restricted to the criminals. In this case a new element characterizes the modern system, for the object is not merely to remove the criminal, but to reform him. England has done much in this way. It is a great result, that in Australia there are now powerful communities, rich with the highest elements of civilization; constituted to a great extent of those who otherwise, as the children of criminals, would have been born to wretchedness and depravity, to cells and stripes and brandings and gibbets, as their inheritance.

But such experiments are not capable of indefinite repetition; space is wanting for them in the world. Nations are now called by the imperious force of circumstances, or more properly speaking, by the decree of Providence, to the nobler task of preventing rather than punishing; of raising society from the pollution of vice rather than curing or expelling it. This higher effort, which is natural to the spirit of Christianity, should have accompanied it everywhere. A nation is responsible for its inhabitants, and ought to master whatever tends to crime among them. Those whom it sends abroad should be its citizens, not its reprobates. It owes to the world, that the average amount of virtue in it accompany its transferred communities, so that the world does not suffer by the transferrence. This must be the case when a race unsuitably placed is, on account of that unsuitableness only, transported to a location more suitable.

A case which is exceptional in regard to common instances, will be when the higher and better motives to colonization take precedence of all others. Such an instance is that of returning the negro race to their own land. It is exceptional in this respect, that the transfer of that race to its more suitable locality is mainly an effort of philanthropic benevolence. Its motives, however, excel in degree, not in kind. The same inducements which at all times influenced colonizing measures, have had their place, with more or less force, in these schemes. In deriving support for them it has been necessary to appeal to every motive, and seek assistance by every inducement.

The increase of national prosperity, the promotion of national commerce, the relief of national difficulties, the preservation of national quiet, have all been urged

on the different orders of men appealed to. It has
been shown how all these circumstances would influence
individual interests, while the higher Christian and
philanthropic aims to be fulfilled by these efforts have
not been overlooked. All this is perfectly right; and
if right in us, it is also right in others. It would have
been satisfactory if in the two parties, America and
England, in respect to their measures towards African
establishments, there had been more nobleness in their
discussions, less national jealousies in all parties, less of
sneering censure of national ambition, selfishness or
grasping policy, while both parties were in fact making
appeals to the very same principles in human nature,
which foster national ambition, or selfishness, or grasping policy.

Although African colonization originated with, and
has been sustained wholly by individuals, in the United
States, England has regarded it in the same light with
which this country has looked upon her acquisition of
foreign territory.

There is, however, a high superiority in these schemes
of African colonization, although it be but in degree.
The best and holiest principles were put prominently
forward, and men of corresponding character called
forth to direct them. They sought sympathy and aid
from the English African Association, and from the
Bible. and Missionary Societies of this land.   They

were truly efforts of Christianity, throwing its solid intelligence and earnest affections into action for the conquest of a continent, by returning the Africans to their home, and making this conquest a work of faith and labor of love.

The slavery imported and grafted on this country by foreign political supremacy, when the country was helpless, has been subjected to a trial never undergone by such an institution in any other part of the world. An enemy held dominion where slavery existed, and while the masters were called upon to fight for their own political independence, there was opportunity for the slave to revolt or escape if such had been his wish. Those who are not acquainted with the ties uniting the slave to his master's household, and the interest he feels in his master's welfare, would expect that when a hostile army was present to rescue and to defend them, the whole slave population would rise with eager fury to avenge their subjection, or with eager hope to escape from it. But the historical truth is, that very few indeed of the colored men of the United States, whether slaves or free, joined the English or Tory party in the Revolutionary War. Thus the character impressed on the institution frustrated the recorded expectation of those who forced this evil upon a reluctant people—that the position and the influence of the negro in society would forever check republican spirit and keep the country in dependence.

The small number of colored persons who did join the English produced no slight difficulty. That small number ought perhaps to have been easily amalgamated somehow or other with the vast amount of the English population. That this did not happen, and did not seem possible, is perfectly evident. Either color, or character, or position, or something else, which it is for the English people to explain, prevented this. Many of them were found in the lanes and dens of vice in London, without the prospect of their ever amalgamating with the Londoners, and therefore only combining incumbrance, nuisance, and danger by their presence there.

This condition of things, as is well known, excited the attention and sympathy of Granville Sharpe, and led to the foundation of the colony of Sierra Leone, as a refuge for them.

Great Britain found herself hampered on a subsequent occasion with the charge of a few hundreds of the Maroons, or independent free negroes of Jamaica. It was known that it would not answer to intermingle them with the slave population of that island. The public good was found imperiously to require that they should be removed elsewhere. They afterwards constituted the most trustworthy portion of the population of Sierra Leone.

Similar difficulties have pressed with a manifold

weight on society in this country.   Jefferson, with other
distinguished statesmen, endeavored to remedy them.
Marshall, Clay, Randolph, and others shared in his
anxieties.   A suitable location was sought after for the
settlement of the free negroes in the lands of the West.
The Portuguese government was afterwards sounded
for the acquisition of some place in South America.
But these schemes were comparatively valueless, for
they wanted the main requisite,—that Africa itself
should share in the undertaking.

When Christian benevolence looked abroad upon the
face of the world to examine its condition and its wants,
Africa was seen, dark, gloomy, and vast and hopeless,
with Egyptian darkness upon it,—" darkness that
might be felt,"—while Europe guarded and fought for
it as a human cattle-fold, to be plundered with an extent and atrocity of rapine such as the world elsewhere
had never beheld.   Africa, therefore, became the object
of deep interest to the Christian philanthropy of this
country, and all things concurred to bring out some
great enterprise for its benefit and that of the African
race in America.

In 1773 slavery was not only common in New England, but the slave-trade was extensively carried on in
Rhode Island and other northern states.   Dr. Hopkins
became convinced of the injustice of the traffic, and in
conjunction with Dr. Stiles, afterwards President of

Yale College, made an appeal to the public in behalf of some colored men whom he was preparing for an African mission. These men were nearly qualified for proceeding to Africa when the Revolutionary War frustrated the scheme, which, in its character, was rather missionary than colonial.

Paul Cuffy, a colored man born in New Bedford, Massachusetts, who had risen to the possession of considerable wealth, and commanded a vessel of his own, induced about forty colored people to embark in his vessel for Sierra Leone, where they had every facility for a settlement afforded them.

Dr. Thornton, of Washington, in 1783, suggested the practical course of establishing a colony in Africa, and obtained in some of the New England States the consent of a number of colored persons to accompany him to that coast. This project failed for want of funds. No better success attended an application of Mr. Jefferson, as secretary of state, directed to the Sierra Leone company.

The State of Virginia, in legislative session, 1800–1805, and 1816, discussed the subject of colonization, and contributed greatly to prepare the public mind for subsequent action on the subject.

The Rev. Dr. Finley, of New Jersey, matured a plan for the purpose, and proceeded to Washington, where, after consultation with a few friends, a meeting was called on the 25th of December, 1816. Henry Clay presided; Andrew Jackson, William H. Crawford, Dr. Finley, and others, were elected vice-presidents. The American Colonization Society was formed with the resolution to be free, and christian, and national.

There was peace in the world. Society was awakening to a remorseful consideration of the iniquities which had been practised on the African race in their own land, and of the condition of its population in this. The gradual emancipation of slaves, as favored by Jefferson and others in the early days of the republic, was discussed. But the objects sought in the formation of the Colonization Society, were the removal and benefit of the free colored population, together with such slaves as might have freedom extended to them with the view of settlement in Africa. And thus the work of forming an African nation in Africa, with republican feelings, impressions and privileges, and with Christian truth and Christian civilization, was commenced.

CHAPTER XI.

FOUNDATION OF THE AMERICAN COLONY—EARLY AGENTS—
MILLS, BURGESS, BACON, AND OTHERS—U. S. SLOOP-OF-WAR
"CYANE"—ARRIVAL AT THE ISLAND OF SHERBORO—DISPO-
SAL OF RECAPTURED SLAVES BY THE U. S. GOVERNMENT—
FEVER—SLAVES CAPTURED—U. S. SCHOONER "SHARK"—
SHERBORO PARTIALLY ABANDONED—U. S. SCHOONER "ALLI-
GATOR"—SELECTION AND SETTLEMENT OF CAPE MESURADO
—CAPTAIN STOCKTON—DR. AYRES—KING PETER—ARGU-
MENTS WITH THE NATIVES—CONFLICTS—DR. AYRES MADE
PRISONER—KING BOATSWAIN—COMPLETION OF THE PUR-
CHASE.

IN November, 1819, the Colonization Society appointed the Rev. Messrs. Samuel J. Mills and Ebenezer
Burgess as its agents; with directions to proceed, by
the way of England, to the west coast of Africa, for the
purpose of making inquiries and explorations as to a
suitable location for a settlement. They arrived in
Sierra Leone in the month of March following, and visited all the ports from thence to the island of Sherboro.

At Sherboro, about sixty miles S. S. E. from Sierra
Leone, the agents found a small colony of colored people, settled by John Kizel, a South Carolina slave, who
had joined the English in the Revolutionary War, and

at its close was taken to Nova Scotia, from whence he sailed, with a number of his countrymen, to the coast of Africa. Here he became prosperous in trade, built a church, and was preaching to his countrymen. By Kizel and his people the agents were kindly received. He expressed the opinion, that the greater part of the people of color in the United States would ultimately return to Africa. "Africa," said Kizel, "is the land of black men, and to Africa they must and will come."

After the agents had fulfilled their duties, they sailed for the United States. Mr. Mills died on the passage. In a public discourse, by the Rev. Dr. Leonard Bacon, of New Haven, Mr. Mills is thus alluded to: "He wandered on his errands of mercy from city to city; pleading now with the patriot, for a country growing up to an immensity of power; and now with the Christian, for a world lying in wickedness. He explored in person the devastations of the West, and in person he stirred up to enterprise and to effort the churches of the East. He lived for India and Hawaii, and died in the service of Africa." Mr. Burgess gave so satisfactory a report of his mission, that the society was encouraged to proceed in its enterprise.

The political friends of colonization, being desirous of affording aid to the incipient efforts of the society, accomplished their object through Wm. H. Crawford, one of the vice-presidents, who proposed to the government, that recaptured slaves should be sent in charge of an agent to the colonies in Africa. He called the attention of the government to a number of slaves who had been received in the state of Georgia, subsequently to the law of Congress, in 1807, prohibiting the slave-trade. These slaves were to have been sold in payment of expenses incurred in consequence of their seizure and detention by the state authorities. The Colonization Society proposed to take them in charge, and restore them to Africa, provided the government would furnish an agent for the purpose.

Agreeably to the views of the Colonization Society, and to guard against an occurrence of a character similar to that in Georgia, Congress passed an act, on the 3d of March, 1819, by which the President of the United States was authorized to restore to their own country, any Africans captured from American or foreign vessels attempting to introduce them into the United States in violation of law; and to provide, by the establishment of a suitable agency on the African coast, for their reception, subsistence and comfort, until they could return to their relatives, or derive support from their own exertions. Thus the government became indirectly connected with the society.

It was determined to make the site of the government agency on the coast of Africa, that of the colonial

agency also; and to incorporate into the settlement all
the blacks delivered by our men-of-war to the government agent, as soon as the requisite arrangements
should be completed.

The Rev. Samuel Bacon received the appointment of
both government and colonial agent, having associated
with him John P. Bankson and Dr. Samuel A. Crozer,
the society's agents; and with eighty emigrants, sailed
on the 6th of February, 1820, for the coast of Africa.
The U. S. sloop-of-war Cyane, also bound to the coast,
under orders from the government, accompanied the
emigrant vessel, but parted company after being a few
days at sea. The vessels met at Sierra Leone, whence
they proceeded to the island of Sherboro.

The confidence of the new agents in Kizel was
greatly impaired by finding that he had given impressions of the place where he resided, which were much
too favorable. The fever made its appearance among
the people, who were loud in their complaints of every
thing, and their conduct was any thing but commendable. Many were detected in petty thefts, falsehoods
and mischiefs of a disgraceful nature. About twenty
or twenty-five of the emigrants died. The remainder
survived the acclimating fever, and in a few weeks regained their health. Mr. Bacon himself fell a victim to
it; but to the last his confidence in the ultimate success
of African colonization was unabated. He remarked

that he had seen ninety-five native Africans landed together in America, who, the first year, were as sickly as these. And regarding himself, he said: " I came here to die; and any thing better than death, is better than I expected." Lieutenant Townsend, one of the officers of the Cyane, also died of the fever. After this disastrous attempt at forming a settlement, Sherboro was partially abandoned, and several of the emigrants were removed to Sierra Leone.

Had timid counsels prevailed, the cause of colonization would have been no longer prosecuted. But the society determined to persevere, trusting that experience and the choice of a more salubrious situation would guard against a repetition of these disasters.

The U. S. sloops-of-war Cyane and John Adams in cruising off the coast captured five slavers, which were sent to the United States for adjudication.

In the year following Messrs. Winn and Bacon (brother of the deceased agent) on the part of the government, and Messrs. Andrews and Wiltberger by the society, were appointed agents, and proceeded to Sierra Leone, with forty effective emigrants to recruit the party sent out the preceding year. In a personal interview with Mr. Wiltberger, and from some notes communicated by him, the author has derived much interesting and reliable information relating to the colony

during his agency, extending to the purchase and settlement of Liberia.

The island of Sherboro was wholly abandoned, and
the remaining emigrants removed to Sierra Leone.

In 1822, Dr. Ayres was appointed colonial physician
and agent, and proceeded in the U. S. schooner Shark
to Sierra Leone. Soon afterwards the U. S. schooner
Alligator arrived with orders from the government to
co-operate with the agents of the society at Sierra Leone. Captain Stockton, her commander, with Dr.
Ayres and seven of the emigrants, proceeded on a
cruise of exploration down the coast, and on the 12th
of December anchored off Cape Mesurado, in lat. 6° 19′
N., and long. 10° 48′ W.

"That is the spot we ought to have," said Captain
Stockton, pointing to the high bluff of the cape; "that
should be the site of our colony. No finer spot on the
coast." "And we must have it," added Dr. Ayres.

They landed without arms, to prove their peaceful
intentions, and sent an express to King Peter for negotiations. The natives collected in large bodies, until the
captain and agent were surrounded without the means
of defence, except a demijohn of whiskey and some
tobacco, which convinced the natives that no hostility
was then intended.

King Peter at length appeared, and a long palaver
took place, when the agent informed him that their

object was to purchase the cape and islands at the mouth of the river. He strongly objected to parting with the cape, saying, " If any white man settle there, King Peter would die, and his woman cry a plenty." The agents represented to him the great advantages in trade, which the proposed settlement would afford to his people. After receiving a vague promise from the king that he would let them have the land, the palaver broke up.

On the 14th instant the palaver was renewed at the residence of the king, whither, as a measure of the last resort, Captain Stockton and the agent had determined to proceed. The first word the king said was, " What you want that land for ?" This was again explained to him. One of the men present accused them of taking away the King of Bassa's son and killing him; another of being those who had quarrelled with the Sherboro people. A mulatto fellow also presented himself to Captain Stockton, and charged him with the capture of a slave-vessel in which he had served as a seaman. The prospects now looked very gloomy, as here were two men in the midst of a. nation exasperated against them. But by mixing a little flattery with threatening, Captain Stockton regained his advantage in the discussion. He explained his connection with the circumstances, and complained of their constant vacillation of purpose in reference to the lands. The old king was at length pacified, and promised to call some more kings, and have a meeting the following day for the purpose of ceding the lands.

Several palavers of a more amicable nature were afterwards held, and the kings at last consented to cede a tract of land, receiving as a compensation goods to the value of about three hundred dollars. The deed bears on it the marks for signatures of King Peter, King George, King Zoda, King Long Peter, King Governor, King Jimmy, and the signatures of Captain Robert F. Stockton and Eli Ayres, M. D.

The tract ceded included Cape Mesurado and the lands forming nearly a peninsula between the Mesurado and Junk rivers—about thirty-six miles along the sea-shore, with an average breadth of about two miles.

Captain Stockton then left the coast with the Alligator, placing Lieutenant Hunter in command of a schooner, who, with Dr. Ayres and the men, proceeded to Sierra Leone, and brought from thence all the working men to Cape Mesurado. They disembarked on the smaller of the two islands amidst the menaces of the natives.

It was ascertained on their arrival that King Peter had been denounced by many of the kings for having sold the land to a people who would interfere with the slave-trade, and were hostile to their old customs. The king was threatened with the loss of his head ; and it was decreed that the new people should be expelled from the country. Dr. Ayres at length succeeded in checking the opposition of the kings, and restored apparent tranquillity.

The island on which the colonists first established themselves, was named Perseverance. It was destitute of wood and water, affording no shelter except the decayed thatch of a few small huts. Thus exposed in an insalubrious situation, several of the people were attacked with intermittent fever. By an arrangement with King George, who claimed authority over a part of the northern district of the peninsula of Mesurado, the colonists, on their recovery, were permitted to cross the river, where they cleared the land, and erected a number of comparatively comfortable buildings; when, in the temporary absence of Dr. Ayres, a circumstance occurred which threatened the extinction of the colony.

A small slaver, prize to an English cruiser, bound to Sierra Leone, ran into the port for water. During the night she parted her cable, and drifted on shore, near King George's Town, not far from Perseverance Island. Under a prescriptive right, when a vessel was wrecked, the natives claimed her, and accordingly proceeded to take possession. The English prize-officer resisted, and after one or two shots the assailants hastily retreated. The officer learning that another attack was meditated, sent to the colony for aid. One of the colonists—temporarily in charge during the absence of the agents to bring the women and children from Sierra Leone—regardless of the admonition to avoid " entangling alliances," and approving " the doctrine of intervention," promptly afforded assistance. The second attack was made, but the colonists and prize-crew, with the help of one or two rounds of grape and cannister from a brass field-piece on the island, which was brought to bear on the assailants, soon scattered them, with the loss of two killed and several wounded. On the following day, they renewed their assualt with a greater force, and were again repulsed, but an English sailor and one colonist were killed.

This interference on the part of the colonists, in behalf of the slave-prize, greatly exasperated the natives; not merely from the loss of their men and the vessel, but from the apprehension that their most valued privileges were about being invaded; and especially that the slave-trade, on which they depended for their gains and supplies, would be destroyed. The natives, therefore, determined forthwith to extirpate the colony while in its feeble and defenceless state.

In the mean time, Dr. Ayres, having returned, found the colonists confined to the island; and as the stores had become nearly exhausted, and the rainy season was about setting in—superadded to the vindictive feelings of the natives towards the people—the agents proposed to re-embark for Sierra Leone, and abandon the new settlement. Mr. Wiltberger strenuously opposed the agents' proposal, and, after ascertaining that the colonists were disposed to remain at Mesurado, Dr. Ayres cheerfully assented.

The kings then adopted the deceitful policy of pretending to be conciliated, and inveigled Dr. Ayres into their power. He became their prisoner, and in that condition appeared to consent to take back the portion of goods which had been received towards the payment of the land, but evaded their peremptory order for the immediate removal of the people, by showing its impossibility, on account of the want of a vessel for the purpose. They finally gave permission that they might remain, until he should have made arrangements to leave the country. In this dilemma, Bă Caiă, a friendly king, at the suggestion of Dr. Ayres, appealed to King Boatswain,* whose power the maritime tribes well un-

---

* Boatswain was a native of Shebar. In his youth, he served in some menial capacity on board of an English merchant vessel, where he acquired the name which he still retains. His personal qualifications were of the most commanding description. To a stature approaching seven feet in height, perfectly erect, muscular and finely proportioned ; a countenance noble, intelligent and full of animation, he united great comprehension and activity of mind ; and, what was still more imposing, a savage loftiness, and even grandeur of sentiment—forming altogether an assemblage of qualities obviously disproportioned to the actual sphere of his ambition. He was prodigal of every thing except the means of increasing the terror of his name. " I give you a bul-

derstood, and with whom he was in alliance. King
Boatswain came down to the coast, and by a direct ex-
ertion of his authority, convoked the hostile kings.   He
also sent for the agents and principal settlers to appear
before him, and explain the nature of their claims, and
present their grievances. The respective allegations of
the parties were heard. King Boatswain decided in
favor of the colonists. He said that the bargain had
been fair on both sides, and that he saw no grounds for
rescinding the contract. Turning then to King Peter,
he laconically remarked: "Having sold your country,
and accepted payment, you must take the consequences. . . . Let the Americans have their lands immediately. Whoever is not satisfied with my decision, let
him tell me so." Then turning to the agents: "I
promise you protection. If these people give you further disturbance, send for me; and I swear, if they
oblige me to come again to quiet them, I will do it by
taking their heads from their shoulders, as I did old
King George's, on my last visit to the coast to settle
disputes."

In this decision both parties acquiesced, whatever

---

lock," said he to an agent of the society, "not to be considered as
Boatswain's present, but for your breakfast." To his friend Bă Caiă, he
once sent: "King Boatswain is your friend; he therefore advises you
to lose not a moment in providing yourself plenty of powder and ball;
or, in three days (the least possible time to make the journey), let me
see my fugitive woman again."

their opinion might have been as to its equity. The settlers immediately resumed their labors on the grounds near the Cape.

The Dey tribe (King Peter's) saw that a dangerous enemy had been introduced among them. King Peter, with whom we must have sympathy, was impeached, and brought to trial on a charge of having betrayed the interests of his people, and sold part of the country to strangers. The accusation was proven; and, for a time, there was reason to believe that he would be executed for treason.

Soon after King Boatswain had returned to his country, the colony was again threatened. The agent called another council of kings; and after some opposition to his claim for the disputed territory, the whole assembly —amounting to seventeen kings, and thirty-four half-kings—assented to the settlement; and on the 28th of April, 1822, formal possession was taken of Cape Mesurado.

Dr. Ayres and Mr. Wiltberger now returned to the United States, the former to urge the wants of the colony, and the latter from ill health. Before they left, Elijah Johnson, of New York, one of the colonists, who had on various occasions distinguished himself, was appointed to superintend the colony during their absence.

CHAPTER XII.

THE acting agent of the colony judiciously managed
its affairs until the arrival of Mr. Ashmun and his wife,
with thirty-seven emigrants, part of whom were recaptured slaves, who had been delivered over to the
Colonization Society by the Marshal of Georgia, under
the Act of Congress already noticed. Mr. Ashmun
held the appointments of government and society's
agent. He took a comprehensive view of the colony.
The entire population did not exceed one hundred and
thirty, of whom thirty only were capable of bearing
arms. The settlement had no adequate means of defence. He found no documents defining the limits of
the purchased territory—explaining the state of the

negotiations with the natives, or throwing light on the duties of the agency.

It was now perceived that means, as well as an organized system of defence were to be originated, while the materials and artificers for such purposes were wanting. One brass field-piece, five indifferent iron guns and a number of muskets, ill-supplied with ammunition, comprised all the means for defence. These were brought from the island and mounted, and such fortifications as the ability and resources of the agent could construct were erected. Public stores and more comfortable houses were also raised. The settlement, except on the side towards the river, was closely environed with the heavy forest. This gave an enemy an important advantage. The land around was, consequently, cleared up with all possible dispatch.

Mr. Ashmun experienced an attack of fever. On the following day his wife was seized, and soon afterwards died: she thus closed a life of exemplary faith and devotedness.

It has been observed, that the dread of provoking King Boatswain's resentment, led the hostile kings to assume a show of friendship; but the disguise could not conceal their intentions. The chiefs attributed the departure of the agents to a want of spirit, and dread of their power. The arrival of Mr. Ashmun had delayed the execution of their purpose, of a general attack on the colony; but when the vessel sailed, early in October, which had brought out the agent and emigrants, a council of kings determined upon instant hostilities.   King George had abandoned his town early in September, leaving the Cape in possession of the colonists.   This had been regarded by the natives as the first step of colonial encroachments; if left alone for a few years, they would master the whole country. The natives refused, throughout the consultation, to receive any pacific proposals from the colony.

On the 7th of November, Mr. Ashmun, although still suffering from the effects of fever, examined and strengthened the defences.   Picket guards were posted during the night, and every preparation made for a vigorous defence.   On the 11th the attack was commenced by a force of eight hundred warriors.   The picket, contrary to orders, had left their station in advance of the weakest point of defence; the native force, already in motion, followed close in the rear of the picket, and as soon as the latter had joined the detachment of ten men stationed at the gun, the enemy, presenting a front, opened their fire, and rushed forward to seize the post; several fell, and off went the others, leaving the gun undischarged.   This threw the small reserve in the centre into confusion, and had the enemy followed up their advantage, victory was certain; but such was their avidity for plunder, that they fell upon the booty in the outskirts of the town. This disordered the main body. Mr. Ashmun, who was too ill to move at any distance, was thus enabled, by the assistance of one of the colonists, Rev. Lot Carey, to rally the broken forces of the settlers. The brass field-piece was now brought to bear, and being well served, did good execution. A few men, commanded by Elijah Johnson, passed round on the enemy's flank, which increased their consternation, and soon after the front of the enemy began to recoil. The colonists now regained the post which had at first been seized, and instantly brought the long-nine to bear upon the mass of the enemy; eight hundred men were in a solid body, and every shot literally spent itself among them. A savage yell was raised by the enemy, and the colonists were victors.

In this assault the colonists (who numbered thirty-five) had fifteen killed and wounded. It is impossible to estimate the loss of the natives, which must have been very great. An earnest but ineffectual effort was made by the agent to form with the kings a treaty of peace.

Notwithstanding this disastrous result, the natives determined upon another attack. They collected auxiliaries from all the neighboring tribes who could be induced to join them. The colonists, on the other hand, under Ashmun, the agent, were busily engaged in fortifying themselves for the decisive battle, upon which the fate of the settlement was suspended.   On the 2d of December the enemy attacked simultaneously the three sides of the fortifications.   The colonists received them with that bravery and determination which the danger of total destruction in case of defeat was calculated to inspire.   The main body of the enemy being exposed to a galling fire from the battery, both in front and flank, and the assault on the opposite side of the town having been repulsed, a general retreat immediately followed, and the colonists were again victorious.

Mr. Ashmun received three musket-balls through his clothes ; three of the men stationed at one of the guns were dangerously wounded ; and not three rounds of ammunition remained after the action.   Had a third attack been made, the colony must have been conquered ; or had the first attack occurred before the arrival of Mr. Ashmun, it would have been extirpated.   But its foundations were now secured by a firm and lasting peace.

The British colonial schooner Prince Regent, with a prize crew in charge of Midshipman Gordon, R. N., opportunely arrived, with Major Laing, the African traveller, on board, by whose influence the kings, being tired of the war, signed a truce, agreeing to submit all their differences with the colony to the Governor of Sierra Leone.   Midshipman Gordon and his crew volunteered to assist the colonists, and see that the truce was preserved inviolate. The Prince Regent furnished a liberal supply of ammunition. Four weeks after sailing, Midshipman Gordon and eight of his men had fallen victims to the malaria of this climate, so inimical to the constitution of white men.

At this period, 1823, the colonists were in a sad condition: their provisions were nearly consumed, trade exhausted, lands untilled, houses but partially covered; the rainy season was approaching, and the people, in many instances, had become indolent and improvident. Captain Spence, of the Cyane, arrived at the Cape, and proceeded to adopt efficient measures for the benefit of the colony. He fitted out the schooner Augusta, under the command of Lieutenant Dashiell, with orders to cruise near the settlement and render it aid. Dr. Dix, the surgeon of the Cyane, died of the fever. Upon her leaving the coast, Richard Seaton, the captain's clerk, volunteered to remain as an assistant to Mr. Ashmun. In the course of two or three months he fell a victim to the fever, and his death was soon followed by that of Lieutenant Dashiell, of the Augusta. On the homeward-bound passage of the Cyane forty of the crew died from the effects of the African climate, superadded to those of the climate of the West Indies, where she had been cruising previously to proceeding to the African coast.

The slave-trade had received no effectual check. King Boatswain, although one of the best friends of the colony, partook in no degree of the views for which it had been established, and at this time committed an act of great atrocity, in making an attack at night upon an inoffensive tribe, murdering all the adults and infants, and seizing upon the boys and girls, in order to fulfil his engagements with a French slaver.

In the month of May, Dr. Ayres brought a reinforcement of sixty emigrants. He announced his appointment as the government and colonial agent. Mr. Ashmun was at the same time informed that a bill drawn by him to defray expenses for the necessities of the colony had been dishonored, and that the board of directors of the society had withdrawn from him all authority except as sub-agent. Very soon after this, Dr. Ayres was obliged on account of ill health again to leave for the United States. Had Mr. Ashmun acted under the impressions of indignation naturally flowing from such treatment, the colony would have been utterly extinguished. But he was of nobler spirit than to yield to any such motive, and therefore resolved to remain in this helpless and disorganized community, sending home at the same time to the board a proposal that he should receive from them less than one-third the sum which a man of ordinary diligence might in his position gain by traffic. This proposal he had made from the most honorable sense of duty, in order in fact that the people for whom he had done and suffered so much should not utterly perish. And yet he had the mortification to learn afterwards that the directors, influenced by slanderous reports to the detriment of his character, had refused to sanction this proposal.

At this period a number even of the principal colonists became disaffected, in consequence of the regulations of the board, requiring that any emigrant who received rations from the public store, should contribute two days' labor in a week on the public works. About twelve of the colonists not only refused work and threw off all restraint, but exerted their influence to induce others to follow their example. Soon after this occurrence Mr. Ashmun published the following notice :

"There are in the colony more than a dozen healthy persons who will receive no more provisions out of the public store until they earn them." On the 19th of December he directed the rations of the offending party to be stopped. This led to a riotous assembly at the agent's house, which endeavored by denunciations to drive him from his purpose ; but finding him inflexible, they then proceeded to the public store, where the commissary was issuing rations to the colonists, and each one seized a portion of the provisions and hastened to their homes.

The same day Mr. Ashmun directed a circular to the people, in which he strongly appealed to their patriotism and conscience. This measure induced the disaffected to return to their duty. The leader of the sedition acknowledged his error, and by his subsequent good conduct fully redeemed his character.

A faithful history of the colony would furnish, at intervals, a dark shady as well as a sunny side. The friends of the cause are prone to exaggerate its success, while its enemies regard the colored race, judging them in their condition when in contact with the whites, to be incapable of developing the mind and character, which, under their own independent government, is now manifested.

Early in February, 1824, a vessel arrived, after a short passage, with one hundred and five emigrants in good condition.

Mr. Ashmun had heard nothing from the board for some time after the departure of Dr. Ayres; and finding his health beginning to fail, and that his services had been received with calumny instead of approbation, he applied to be relieved from the service of the board. After making this application, he appointed Elijah Johnson to act as agent during his absence, and proceeded to the Cape Verde Islands in the hope of recruiting his health, and finding some government vessel at that place.

The navy department, on application by the society, ordered the U. S. schooner Porpoise, Lieutenant Commandant Skinner, with the Rev. R. R. Gurley, to proceed to the coast of Africa. These gentlemen were appointed by the government and society to examine into the affairs of the colony, and into the reports in circulation prejudicial to the agent. The Porpoise reached the Cape Verde Islands soon after Mr. Ashmun's arrival there; and he returned with the commissioners to the colony. As the result of communications received by the board from the commissioners, Messrs. Skinner and Gurley, a resolution was passed, completely exonerating Mr. Ashmun from the calumnious charges which had been made against him, and expressing their cordial approbation of his conduct.

The commissioners, on the conclusion of their investigation, deeply impressed with the zeal and ability of Mr. Ashmun, left him in charge of the colony as formerly. But previously to the reception of the report of the commissioners, and of the resolution above noticed, that body had appointed Dr. John W. Peaco, already selected as the agent of the government, to be their agent also. On the 25th of April, after their acquittal of Mr. Ashmun, they modified this resolution by reappointing him colonial agent, requesting and authorizing Dr. Peaco to give assistance and support to Mr. Ashmun in the fulfilment of his duties, and to assume the charge of those duties, in case of "the absence, inability, or death of Mr. Ashmun."

At the suggestion of the commissioners, a greater share in the government of the colony was conferred on the people. The general consequence of these proceedings was, that comparative tranquillity and energy prevailed.

Mr. Ashmun had made the important acquisition of the rich tract of land, afterwards the location of the settlement on the St. Paul's River, extending twenty miles into the interior, and of unequalled fertility. The colony now seemed to be emerging from the difficulties which often had threatened its very existence. Four day-schools, in addition to the Sunday-schools, were in operation; two churches had been erected; a religious influence more generally pervaded the community; the acclimating fever was becoming less fatal; many of the colonists preferred the climate to that of the United States; they were living in comparative comfort. In addition to the rich tract of country lying on St. Paul's River, the right of occupancy was obtained at Young Cesters and Grand Bassa. The adjoining tribes regarded the colonists so favorably as to desire to come partially under their jurisdiction; and sixty of their children were adopted as children of the colony. A Spanish slave-factory, near Monrovia, was destroyed, and the slaves recaptured and freed by the colonists.

At Tradetown, there were three slave-factories, guarded by two armed vessels, with crews of thirty men each, besides twenty men, mostly Spaniards, well armed, on shore. On the 9th of April, the Columbian man-of-war schooner "San Jacinto," Captain Chase, arrived at Monrovia, and offered to co-operate with Mr. Ashmun and Dr. Peaco for the purpose of breaking up this slave establishment. The offer was accepted; and Mr. Ashmun, accompanied by Captain Cochran, of the "Indian Chief," who gallantly volunteered his services, with two companies of the colonial militia, embarked in the San Jacinto for Tradetown. There they fortunately found the Columbian man-of-war-brig "El Vincendor," Captain Cottrell, mounting twelve guns; which vessel had, the same afternoon, captured one of the slave-vessels, the brigantine Teresa. Captain Cottrell united his forces with the others.

On the following morning, while the vessels covered the landing, they pulled for the shore, through a passage of not more than five or six fathoms wide, lined on both sides with rocks, and across which, at times, the surf broke furiously, endangering the boats and the lives of the assailants. The boat in which were Mr. Ashmun and Captain Cottrell was capsized in the surf, and a number of men were thrown upon the rocks. Nothing daunted, although Mr. Ashmun was badly injured, they made a dash upon the enemy, which was met by a galling fire from the Spanish slavers. The colonists and their allies rapidly advanced upon the town, demolished their slight palisades, and before the enemy had time to rally behind their defences, forced them to retreat, in great confusion, into the jungle.

As soon as the colonists found themselves in quiet possession of the town, Mr. Ashmun demanded from King West the delivery of all the slaves belonging to the factories. The king was told that if this was not complied with, not a vestige of Tradetown should be left. On the same day the Kroomen of King West brought in thirty or forty slaves, evidently the refuse of those which they held.

The natives, notwithstanding, collected, and, in conjunction with the Spaniards, continued to rush out occasionally from the jungle and direct their fire upon the invaders. The surgeon of the San Jacinto was badly wounded, and several of the colonists slightly. A peaceable settlement was now impossible. On the 12th, after the recaptured slaves had been sent on board, the town was fired, and at three o'clock all were embarked. The explosion of two hundred kegs of powder consummated the destruction of Tradetown.

The annihilation of Tradetown and of the slave-factories was a severe blow to the traffic, which was felt as far south as the Bight of Benin. It convinced the slave-traders that their commerce was insecure, inasmuch as a powerful enemy to their crimes had gained a permanent establishment on the coast.

Here is developed an influence for the suppression of the most atrocious commerce which has ever existed. The writer, however, by no means concurs in opinion with the zealous friends of colonization, that the slave-trade can be suppressed on the entire coast of Africa by Liberia alone. Yet it is an established fact that within her jurisdiction of six hundred miles of sea-coast and thirty miles inland, it has been effectually extirpated.

At this period many piratical vessels, well armed, were hovering about the coast. A brig from Portland, and a schooner from Baltimore, were robbed of a large amount of specie, by a vessel mounting twelve guns, manned principally by Spaniards. Scarcely an American merchant vessel had, for a year or more, been on the coast as low down as 6° North, without suffering either insult or plunder from these vessels. Mr. Ashmun then erected a battery for the protection of vessels at anchor, while he represented to the Secretary of the Navy the necessity of the constant presence of a man-of-war on the African coast for the protection of legal commerce.

Five of the most important stations from Cape Mount to Tradetown, one hundred and fifty miles, now belonged to the colony by purchase or perpetual lease, and all Europeans were excluded, or attempted to be, from possessions within their limits. On the 18th of August, Dr. Peaco was compelled from ill health to return to the United States.

The native chiefs not unfrequently proposed to the colonists to aid them in their wars, promising as an inducement the whole of the enemy's country. This was of course declined, on the ground that the colony was established for the benefit, and not for the destruction of their neighbors; and that their military means were sacred to the purpose of self-defence. The kings were now favorable to the colony, and began to appreciate the benefits of legal trade.

The U. S. schooner *Shark*, and the U. S. sloop-of-war *Ontario*, arrived on the coast during the year 1827, and besides affording aid to the colony, rendered good service towards the suppression of the slave-trade.

A reinforcement of emigrants was received; the school system reorganized and put in comparatively efficient condition, under the superintendence of the Rev. G. M'Gill, a colored teacher. The schools were all taught by colored people: the number of scholars amounted to two hundred and twenty-seven, of whom forty-five were natives. The native children belonged to the principal men in the adjoining country.

The Chief of Cape Mount, fifty-two miles N. E. from Cape Mesurado, entered into stipulations with the colo-

nial government to establish a large factory for legal
trade between it and the interior. The land north of
the St. John's River, about sixty miles southeast of Cape
Mesurado, was ceded to the colonists. In this extent of
territory there were eight eligible sites, upon which
comfortable settlements have been founded. Four
schooners were built. The colony was mainly supported by its own industry. The life of this industry was,
however, rather in trade and commerce than in agriculture, the fact being overlooked that men ought to
seek in the latter the sources of their prosperity. Liberia has suffered from the want of steady agricultural
effort. Industry like that of our Puritan fathers in
New England, would, with the Liberian soil and climate, have prevented the recurrence of difficulty, and
produced uninterrupted abundance.

On leaving Liberia, the commander of the " Ontario"
permitted eight of his crew, colored men, to remain,
furnishing them with a valuable collection of seeds, obtained in the Mediterranean and up the Archipelago.
On his arrival in the United States, the captain bore
testimony to the encouraging prospects of the colony,
and its salutary influence over the native tribes.

Mr. Ashmun's health failing from excessive labors in
the administration of the government, he was seized
in July, 1828, with a violent fever, and having been

advised by his surgeon that a return to the United States afforded the only hope of his recovery, he left Africa on the twenty-fifth of March, 1828, and reached New Haven, where he died on the twenty-fifth of August. Of Ashmun it may be said, that he united the qualities of a hero and statesman. He found the colony on the brink of extinction: he left it in peace and prosperity. He trained a people who were unorganized and disunited, to habits of discipline and self-reliance; and to crown his character, when death approached, he met it with that unshaken hope of a blissful immortality, which the true Christian alone can experience.

The remains of this honored martyr to the cause of African colonization repose in the cemetery at New Haven. At his funeral the Rev. Dr. Bacon, preaching a sermon from the text, "To what purpose is this waste," said:

"Who asks to what purpose is this waste? He is not dead to usefulness. His works still live. The light which he has kindled shall yet cheer nations unborn. His influence shall never die. What parent would exchange the memory of such a departed son, for the embrace of any living one! I would that we could stand together on the promontory of Cape Mesurado, and see what has been accomplished by those toils and exposures, which have cost this man his life. Years and ages hence, when the African mother shall be able to sit with her children under the shade of her native palm, without trembling in fear of the man-stealer and murderer, she will speak his name with thankfulness to God."

CHAPTER XIII.

LOT CAREY—DR. RANDALL—ESTABLISHMENT OF THE LIBERIA HERALD—WARS WITH THE DEYS—SLOOP-OF-WAR "JOHN ADAMS"—DIFFICULTIES OF THE GOVERNMENT—CONDITION OF THE SETTLERS.

FROM the hands of Mr. Ashmun, the government of the colony devolved upon the Rev. Lot Carey, whom necessity and the claims of humanity made a physician and a governor. Such education as he could obtain when a slave, terminated in his becoming a Baptist preacher. The colony was more indebted to him than to any other man, except Ashmun, for its memorable defence in 1822. During the few months of Dr. Carey's administration, the affairs of the colony were prosperous. His death was caused, with that of eight others, by an explosion, while filling cartridges in the old agency-house. Mr. Waring was elected to supply the vacancy occasioned by Carey's decease.

The society appointed Dr. Richard Randall as successor to Ashmun, who, accompanied by Dr. Mechlin, the colored surgeon, arrived in December, 1828, and assumed the supervision of the colony. Dr. Randall possessed great firmness of purpose, and benevolence of disposition, superadded to extensive scientific knowledge. He had been a surgeon in the army, and afterwards filled the chair of chemistry in Columbia College. But his death, in four months after his arrival on the coast, deprived the colonists of his invaluable services. The agency then devolved upon Dr. Mechlin.

In the following year, Dr. Anderson, appointed colonial physician and assistant agent, arrived with sixty emigrants. An emigrant vessel brought ninety recaptured slaves. She had sailed, the year previous, in charge of a captain who made a direct course for Monrovia, instead of keeping his northing until striking the northeast trades; and, after being at sea ninety days, was compelled to put back. Dr. Mechlin was induced, from ill health, to return to the United States, when the government devolved upon Dr. Anderson, who soon afterwards died, and A. D. Williams, the vice-agent, temporarily filled the vacancy. The schools, at this period, were sadly in want of competent teachers, which were partially supplied on the arrival of five Christian missionaries from Switzerland. The arrival of two more emigrant vessels and two missionaries from the United States, had a favorable influence on the colony.

The *Liberia Herald*, established the year previous, announced eighteen arrivals and the sailing of fourteen vessels in one month. In December, it says: "The beach is lined with Liberians of all ages, from twelve to fifty years, eager in the pursuit of traffic, and in the acquisition of camwood; and it is astonishing what little time is necessary to qualify, even the youngest, to drive as hard a bargain as any roving merchant from the land of steady habits, with his assortment of tinware, nutmegs, books, or dry-goods. Here the simile ends; for it is to be wished that our Liberians would follow their prototype in the mother country throughout, and be as careful in keeping as acquiring. The Liberian is certainly a great man; and, what is more, by the natives he is considered a white man, though many degrees from that stand; for to be thought acquainted with the white man's fashions, and to be treated as one, are considered as marks of great distinction among the Bassa and other nations." The amount of exports had reached the sum of eighty-nine thousand dollars.

Piracy still continued rife. There was no American squadron then on the coast. The schooner Mesurado was captured off Cape Mount, and all hands put to death. But while the native commerce was thus exposed and almost destroyed, the colony was extending its limits. The petty kings offered to come under its jurisdiction, on condition that settlers should be placed upon their lands, and schools established for the benefit of the native children.

The arrivals of emigrants became more frequent; six hundred being added to the colony during one year. These suffered comparatively little in the acclimating process.

In the year 1832, the colonists were again called to take the field against the Deys and a combination of other tribes. Several slaves had escaped, and sought protection in the colony; upon which the settlements at Caldwell and Mills were threatened with destruction. A brisk action, of half an hour, resulted in favor of the Liberians. This victory made an impression on the minds of the natives favorable to the future peace of the settlers. The chiefs who had been conquered appeared in Monrovia, and signed a treaty of peace, guaranteeing that traders from the interior should be allowed a free passage through their territories. The agent received a significant message from his old friend, King Boatswain, stating, that had he known of the hostility of the chiefs, it would have been unnecessary for the colonists to have marched against them.

Captain Voorhees, of the U. S. sloop-of-war *John Adams*, on his homeward-bound passage from the Mediterranean, in a letter to the Secretary of the Navy, reported favorably of the condition in which he found the colony.

In January, 1834, the Rev. J. B. Pinney, as colonial agent, and Dr. G. P. Todsen, as physician, with nine missionaries, arrived at Monrovia, and were formally received by the civil and military officers, and uniform companies. Mr. Pinney, in entering upon the duties of his office, found many abuses, which he promptly corrected. He resurveyed the lands; repaired the public buildings; satisfied the public creditors; and extinguished the jealousy between two tribes of recaptured Africans, by allowing each to elect its own officers. After a short and efficient administration, he was compelled, from ill health, to retire, when the agency devolved on Dr. Skinner.

The Liberia Herald, in 1835, was edited by Hilary Teage, a colored man, who was one of the small party first settled at Cape Mesurado. Mr. Teage filled various public offices of trust and emolument. He made an argument before the General Assembly in a divorce case, in 1851 (when the Perry was at Monrovia), for beauty of diction and sound logic seldom surpassed. The August number of the Herald states: "On the 9th instant, the brig Louisa arrived from Norfolk, Virginia, with forty-six emigrants, thirty-eight of whom are recaptured Africans, principally, we believe, from the Nunez and Pargos. They are a strolling people. A number of their countrymen, and among them some acquaintances, have found their way to this settlement: they were hailed by their redeemed brethren with the most extravagant expressions of joy."

From January to September there were nine arrivals of emigrants, which produced a great sensation among the native tribes: they gravely came to the conclusion that rice had given out in America, and suggested to the colonists to send word for the people to plant more, " or black man will have no place for set down." Dr. Skinner, suffering from ill health, returned to the United States, and the government devolved on A. D. Williams, the vice-agent.

The revenue from imports had disappeared to an extent which the vouchers of the disbursing officers did not explain. The editor of the Herald, after noticing the excitement at that period in the United States, on the passage of the "Sub-Treasury Law," quaintly remarked that " their treasury was all sub."

In the year 1837, the Mississippi Society established its new settlement, Greenville, on the Sinoe River. There were, therefore, at this period in Liberia: Monrovia, under the American Colonization Society; Bassa Cove, of the New York and Pennsylvania Societies; Greenville, of the Mississippi Society; and Cape Palmas, of the Maryland Society. These contained ten or twelve towns, and between four and five thousand emigrants.

Here was a mass of conflicting or disconnected organizations, with separate sources of authority, and separate systems of management; without common head or common spirit. Each colony was isolated amid encompassing barbarism, and far more likely, if left to itself, to fall back under the power of that which surrounded it, than to establish good policy or civilization among any portion of the savage African communities with which they were brought in contact. It was anticipated that intercourse and example, and the temptation of profit, would make them slavers; and it was said that they were so. This, although untrue, was perhaps only prevented by a change; for it now became evident, that the existing state of things was unsuitable and dangerous to the objects contemplated.

CHAPTER XIV.

THOMAS H. BUCHANAN, afterwards governor of Liberia
when it became a commonwealth, had reached Africa,
in 1836, as agent of the New York and Pennsylvania
Societies, and had acquired great experience, in establishing and superintending, during two years, the settlement at the Bassa country.

He had thus time to appreciate the condition of things
around him, before he was called to the prominent
station which he adorned as the first governor of the
commonwealth. It needed a keen eye to see light, if
any was to be got at all, through the wretched entangle-
ment of interests, vices, associations, colonies, jurisdic-
tions of natives and foreigners, which then existed. It
needed great tact, and a strong hand, to bring any thing
like order out of such confusion.

The United States had at least three associations at
work, besides that of Maryland, each with its own little

colony, established in such spots as chance seems to have directed. These occupied three districts of a tolerably definite character. There was the original settlement at Cape Mesurado, with a wing stretching to the north, so as to rest on the expanded lagoon at Cape Mount, and another wing dipping into the Junk River at the south. This was in a measure "the empire state," containing Monrovia, the capital, and several agricultural villages around it; but the Monrovians and their fellow-colonists were not, on the whole, much given to agricultural pursuits. They were shrewd at driving a trade, and liked better to compete for some gallons of palm oil, or sticks of camwood, than to be doing their duty to their fields and gardens. They had, besides, the politics and the military concerns of the nation to supervise, and were called upon to adjust claims with the neighboring settlements. The Bassa Cove villages, constituting the second district, were settling down and strengthening, after their visitation of violence and rapacity from the natives. Sinoe, the third district, with its fine river and rich lands, had received the settlement at Greenville, then flourishing. These two latter bore a very ill-defined relation to the older station at Monrovia, and to each other. There were in the territories claimed by all of them as having passed justly and by amicable means under their jurisdiction, various native tribes, with their kings and half kings; sometimes wise enough to see the advantages offered to them; sometimes pre-eminently wise in having stipulated, that in return for the territory they gave up, schools should be provided to teach them "sense," "book;" sometimes sorely perplexed by the new state of things, and always sorely tempted by strong habits, and by people at hand to take advantage of them.

It is to be remarked that between these three settlements there were two intervals of sea-coast, each about one hundred miles, which were foreign in regard to the colonies. There were also battle-fields, where slavers afloat and slavers ashore, with the occasional help of a pirate, and the countenance of Spain and Portugal, were ready to resist colonial authority, and even to withstand the opposition which they might encounter from cruisers and other sources. There were honest traders, also; that is, those who were honest as things went there, dropping their anchor everywhere as they could get purchasers for their rum and gunpowder. Nor had European powers yet made up their minds how the colonies and their claims were to be treated.

The necessity of union was a clear case to every man, and Buchanan prepared himself to accomplish it. The Bassa Cove people entertained sentiments not very conciliatory towards the Monrovians. The Mississippi people of Sinoe might come under suspicion next, and no one could imagine how far the evil would extend.

This state of things was clearly understood among the friends of the American Colonization Society and of the State societies, and the corrective was applied. A committee, comprising the names of Charles F. Mercer, Samuel L. Southard, Matthew St. Clair Clark, and Elisha Whittlesey, met at Washington, and drew up a common constitution for the colonies. Mr. Whittlesey moved, and the motion was adopted, "That no white man should become a landholder in Liberia," and that full rights of citizenship should be enjoyed by colored men alone. Political suffrage was extended to all adult males, and slavery was absolutely prohibited.

This constitution divided the territory into two provinces or counties, and having been acceded to and acted on by the different colonies, superseded and abolished the political relations of the separate establishments to the associations which had preceded it.

The American Colonization Society retained the right to disapprove, or veto, the acts of the local legislature. This last particular, as an indication of national dependence, was the characteristic distinguishing the commonwealth from the republic subsequently established.

The emancipation of the negroes under the English government was now taking effect. The United States government were beginning to realize the expediency of keeping permanently a naval force on the west coast of Africa; and notwithstanding difficulties and apprehensions resting gloomily on the future, Governor Buchanan, on landing with the new constitution, at Monrovia, on the first of April, 1839, seems to have inaugurated a new era for the African race.

He arrived with a full supply of guns and ammunition, furnished mostly from the navy department, besides a large quantity of agricultural implements, and a sugar-mill. The constitution was at once approved by the Monrovians, and in course of time it was accepted by the entire three colonies.

A firm stand was taken against the slave-trade, and the governor succeeded in getting the legislature at Monrovia and the people to back him in efforts to suppress it. His indignant appeals and strong-handed measures had their effect in turning the attention of our government to the use of the American flag in the slave-trade as a protection from British cruisers. Hear him: "The chief obstacle to the success of the very active measures pursued by the British government for the suppression of the slave-trade on the coast, is the *American flag.* Never was the proud banner of freedom so extensively used by those pirates upon liberty and humanity as at this season." He did not stop at words. An American schooner named the *Euphrates,* which had been boarded fifteen times, and three times sent to Sierra Leone, and escaped condemnation on account of her nationality, was brought into Monrovia by a British cruiser, and instantly seized by Governor Buchanan, for the purpose of sending her to the United States for trial, on suspicion of being engaged in the slave-trade.

It may here be remarked that not only this vessel, but the American sloop " *Campbell*" was also detained, and taken to Governor Buchanan, under similar circumstances. These proceedings were in direct violation of our doctrine as to the inviolability of American vessels by foreign interference; and he had no right to authorize or connive at English cruisers interfering in any degree with such vessels. These circumstances, together with the report of Governor Buchanan, that " The Euphrates is one of a number of vessels, whose names I have forwarded as engaged in the slave-trade, under American colors," will show the extent to which the American flag has been used in the traffic; and to those who have patriotism and humanity enough to vindicate the rights of that flag against foreign authority, and resist its prostitution to the slave-trade, it will conclusively prove the necessity of a well-appointed American squadron being permanently stationed on the west coast of Africa.

The Euphrates being placed in the hands of Governor

Buchanan, who had resolved on sending her to the United States for trial, was made available in a crisis when she proved of singular service as a reformed criminal against her old trade.

A Spanish slaver had established himself at Little Bassa, within fifty miles of the capital. The governor prohibited the purchase of slaves, and ordered the Spaniard off. This he disregarded. An Englishman, in the character of a legal trader, sided with the Spaniard. The governor, on Monday, the 22d of July, dispatched a force of one hundred men by land to dislodge the slavers and destroy the barracoons. The respectability, or the safety of the colony, which is the same thing, in its dealings with the mass of corrupted barbarians with which it was begirt, required summary measures. Three small schooners were sent down the coast with ammunition to assist the land force at Little Bassa. A fresh southerly wind, however, prevented these vessels from reaching their destination, leaving the land forces in a perilous predicament. Affairs looked gloomy at Monrovia as the schooners returned, after beating in vain for sixty hours.

At this juncture the schooner Euphrates, which had been seized as a slaver, was put in requisition. Being supplied with arms and ammunition, the governor himself, in three hours after the return of the vessels, was aboard, and the schooner sailed for the scene of action.

Being a *clipper*, she soon beat down the coast, and anchored before daylight off Little Bassa. On the morning of the fifth day after the colonial force had marched, a canoe was sent ashore to ascertain the state of things. The rapid daybreak showed that there was work to be done; for as the barracoon, standing in its little patch of clearance in the forest, became distinguishable, the discharge of musketry from without, replied to from within, showed plainly that beleaguering and beleaguered parties, whoever they might be, had watched through the night, to renew their interrupted strife in the morning.

It was a surprise to both parties, to find a well-known slaver at hand, and ready to take a part in the fray. The governor learned by the canoe on its return, that the colonists had seized and were holding the barracoon against the slavers and the chiefs, with the whole hue and cry of the country in arms to help them. These naturally hailed the Euphrates as an ally; and Buchanan foresaw the certainty of a fatal mistake on the part of his people, in case he should land and attempt to march up the beach, with the men he had, under the fire which, without some explanation, would be drawn upon him from the palisades of the barracoon.

In this emergency, an American sailor volunteered to convey the necessary intelligence to the besieged. In pulling off in the Kroomen's canoe, he necessarily became the object of attention and mistake to both parties. The besiegers rushed down to meet him with a friendly greeting, while Elijah Johnson sent a party to intercept him as an enemy. The sailor's bearing showed both parties, almost simultaneously, that they were wrong. The enemy, who had seized him, were charged by the colonists. A fellow, grasping a knife to stab him, was knocked down by a shot; the sailor was rescued, and taken into the barracoon.

Buchanan, aware how this would engage the attention of the combatants, had taken the men with him in the two small boats, and was pulling for the shore. The governor's boat capsized in the surf, but with no other harm than a ducking, he made his way safely to the barracoon. A brisk fight continued for some time; but, at meridian the day following, the indefatigable governor had embarked with the goods seized; and he returned to Monrovia for a fresh supply of ammunition. On his reaching again the scene of action, the refractory chiefs were persuaded to submit. With three of the slavers as prisoners, and about a dozen liberated slaves, he then returned to the capital.

At this period, the Gallinas, at the north of which the Sherboro Island shuts in the wide mouth of the river of the same name, was a den of thieves. Cesters, at the south, was not much better. Governor Buchanan was compelled to lean on the support of the British

cruisêrs. In fact, it is obvious that Liberia could not
have been founded earlier than it was, except it had
been sustained by some such authority, or directly by
that of the United States. An older and firmer condition of the slave-trade influence would have crushed it
in its birth. A few of the lawless ruffians, with their
well-armed vessels, who once frequented this coast,
could easily have done this. For want of an American
squadron, the governor assumed an authority to which
he was not entitled.

Every thing was reduced to a regular mercantile
system in carrying on the slave-trade. We have the
schooner " Hugh Boyle," from NewYork, with a crew of
nine American citizens, coming to the coast, and having
as passengers a crew of ten " citizens of the world,"
or from somewhere else. She is American, with an
American crew and papers, until she gets her slaves
on board; then her American citizens become passengers, and the " citizens of the world" take their place
as the crew, till she gets her slaves into Cuba.

Governor Buchanan, in one of his dispatches, dated
November 6th, 1839, writes: " When at Sierra Leone,
I visited a small schooner of one hundred and twenty
tons, which was just brought in, with *four hundred and
twenty-seven* slaves on board ; and of all scenes of misery I ever saw, this was most overpowering. My cheek
tingled with shame and indignation, when I was told

that the same vessel, the *Mary Cushing*, had come on the coast, and was sailed for some time under Amercan colors. When taken, the American captain was on board. He had not arrived when I left Sierra Leone, but the governor, at my instance, promised to send him down here, and deliver him up to me, to be sent to the United States. Is there any hope that our government will hang him?"

It is a question whether Buchanan had, as the agent of a private association, or the agent of the government for recaptured Africans, any right to seize the goods of British traders, or hold in custody the persons of Americans. But the governor was a man for the time and circumstances, as, taking "the responsibility," he determined to do right, and let the law of nations look out for itself.

CHAPTER XV.

WHEN a frontier rests on a savage territory, a "good look out" must be kept there, and upon every thing beyond it, as the Hollander watches his dykes and the sea. Liberia had to watch an early ally and friend of very equivocal character, already known as King Boatswain. He had founded a new Rome, like Romulus, of ragamuffins. He had made a kind of pet of Liberia, and perhaps intended to give up slaving, and take to better courses. Nothing better, however, came in his way, till all his courses ended.

The death of Boatswain, whose tribe was of his own creation, was followed by confusion among them. Gaytumba, an unscrupulous and ready man, with the assistance of Gotera, succeeded to the chief share of influence in the tribe. The Deys, from whom the colonial territory had been purchased, were near neighbors, and most convenient subjects for the slave-trade. An assault was accordingly made, and many secured.

A small remnant of the tribe took refuge in the colony ; and Gaytumba, not seeing any reason why they should not be caught and sold under colonial protection, as well as elsewhere, many were seized within the jurisdiction of the commonwealth.

The northern region was thus black with danger, and the vast woods which surrounded the settlements on the St. Paul's, became suspicious as a wild, unknown source of difficulty. There was uneasy watchfulness for months; and such preparations as circumstances would admit, were made for resistance. The storm fell on Heddington, a village at the extreme north of the settlements.

A messenger sent to negotiate had been seized and put to death, and no mercy was to be expected. All hands were on the alert. Twenty muskets, which had been provided for the settlement, were prudently kept by the missionary, Mr. Brown, ready loaded in the upper story of his house, which had around it a fence of pickets. Two carpenters were at the time inmates of the dwelling: their names deserve record, for they, Zion Harris and Demery, constituted, with the missionary, the entire force at the point of approach. Suddenly, in the morning before the men began their work, they heard the yelling and crashing of three or four hundred savages through the bushes.

This was Gaytumba's tribe: Gotera was at their head,

bringing with him a pot to cook the missionary for his next repast.   Harris and Demery placed themselves quietly at the fence, confronting the negroes as they came straggling in a mass, expecting no resistance, and exposing themselves amid the low green leaves of a cassada patch.   The two men fired into the thickest of them, and Mr. Brown commenced a destructive slaughter with his muskets overhead.   As the mass heaved backwards and forwards, a furious return of musketry, arrows, and spears was made.   Gotera, with some skill, disentangled himself with a band of resolute men, broke through the pickets at one end, and came upon Harris, standing defenceless, with his musket just discharged.   He turned to grasp a hatchet, as a last resource, but fortunately caught a musket, which a wounded colonist, in running for shelter, had placed against the pickets, and lodged its contents in Gotera's breast.   The death of their chief was the signal for a general retreat.   But ashamed and indignant at not having secured the dead body, they attempted by a rush to recover it, and were again and again driven back, till they utterly despaired, and disappeared.   This strange episode of war lasted an hour and twenty minutes.

The forest recovered its suspicious character from the prowling and threatening of the enemy spread through it; and there were reports of the gathering of more distant tribes to join Gaytumba, to make the work of destruction sure by an overwhelming rush upon the settlements.

The governor, full of warlike foresight, saw the remedy for this state of things; and, after screwing up the courage of his people, he planned an expedition against Gaytumba in his own den. For this purpose, a force of two hundred effective men, with a field-piece and a body of followers, assembled at Millsburg, on the St. Paul's River. About thirty miles from this, by the air line, in the swampy depths of the forest, was the point aimed at. Many careful arrangements were necessary to baffle spies, and keep the disaffected at bay during this desperate incursion, which the governor was about to make into the heart of the enemy's country. The fine conception had this redeeming characteristic, that it was quite beyond the enemy's understanding.

The force left Millsburg on Friday, 27th of March. Swamps and thickets soon obliged him to leave the gun behind. Through heavy rains, drenched and weary, they made their way, without any other resistance, to a bivouac in an old deserted town. Starting at daylight next morning, they forced their way through flooded streams and ponds, "in mud up to their knees, and water up to the waist." After a halt at ten o'clock, and three hours' march subsequently, they learnt that the enemy had become aware of their movements, and

was watching them.   About six miles from their destination, after floundering through the mud of a deep
ravine, followed by a weary pull up a long hill, a sharp
turn brought them in front of a rude barricade of felled
trees.   A fire of musketry from it brought to the ground
Captain Snetter, of the riflemen, who was in advance
of his men.   The men made a dash on the enemy so
suddenly that soon nobody was in front of them.   The
line moved on without stopping, and met only a straggling fire here and there, as they threaded their narrow
path through the bushes in single file.   A few men were
wounded in this disheartening march.   At length those
in advance came to a halt before the fortress, and the
rear closed up.   There the line was extended, and the
party advanced in two divisions.   The place was a kind
of square, palisaded inclosure, having outside cleared
patches here and there, intermingled with clumps of
brush.

The assailants were received with a sharp fire from
swivels and muskets, which was warmly returned.   Buchanan ordered Roberts (the present president) to lead
a reserved company round from the left, so as to take in
reverse the face attacked.   This so confounded Gaytumba's garrison that they retreated, leaving every
thing behind.   The hungry colonists became their suc-
cessors at the simmering cooking-pots.   So rapid had
the onslaught been, that the second division did not

reach in time to take a hand in it. The operation was thus completely successful, with the ultimate loss of only two men.

The place was burnt, and a lesson given, which established beyond all future challenge, the power of civilization on that coast. The banks of the St. Paul's River, with its graceful meanderings, palm-covered islands, and glorious basin spreading round into the eastward expanse of the interior, were secured for the habitations of peace and prosperity.

Great and corresponding energy was displayed by Buchanan in civil concerns. The legislature passed an act that every district should have a free school. Rules and regulations were established for the treatment of apprentices, or recaptured Africans not able to take care of themselves. Provision was made for paupers in the erection of almshouses, with schools of manual labor attached. The great point was, that the people had begun to be the government; and there, among colored men, it was shown that human nature has capacity for its highest ends on earth, and that there is no difficulty or mystery in governing society, which men of common sense and common honesty cannot overcome.

Buchanan died in harness. Drenching, travelling and over-exertion, brought on a fever when far from the means of relief. He expired on the 3d of September, 1841, in the government house at Bassa. Then and there was a remarkable man withdrawn from the work of the world. Ever through his administration he illustrated the motto of his heart: "The work is God's to which I go, and is worthy of all sacrifice." The narrative already given is his *character* and his eulogium. His deeds need no explanatory words—they have a voice to tell their own tale.

The blow given to King Boatswain's successor, Gaytumba, nearly obliterated the predatory horde which he had collected: they were scarcely heard of afterwards. A small portion of them seem to have migrated northwards, so as to hang on the skirts of more settled tribes, and carry on still, to a small extent, the practice of slaving and murder, to which they had been accustomed. The Fishmen tribe still continued to raise some disturbance. Certain points on the sea-coast gave great uneasiness; these points were the haunts of slavers. Merchant traders, at least some of them, came peddling along, establishing temporary factories for the disposal of their goods, and not unfrequently having an understanding with the slavers for their mutual benefit.

CHAPTER XVI.

ROBERTS GOVERNOR—DIFFICULTIES WITH ENGLISH TRADERS—
POSITION OF LIBERIA IN RESPECT TO ENGLAND—CASE OF THE
"JOHN SEYES"—OFFICIAL CORRESPONDENCE OF EVERETT
AND UPSHUR—TROUBLE ON THE COAST—REFLECTIONS.

TRANSACTIONS growing out of the circumstances above
mentioned, became of very grave importance. The
rights of different nations to trade on that coast had
been contested in war, and settled in peace, for centuries. The long Napoleonic wars had thrown possessions and commerce, all along the coast, into the hands
of England; and in restoring forts and factories to different nations, the intention seems to have been, to let
every thing, with the exception of the slave-trade,
revert to its old fashion. At existing factories, parties
were allowed to conduct their trade in their own way,
and to exercise whatever competing influence they
could gain with the native powers to forward their purposes. Comparatively few of the old establishments
were preserved. Everywhere else the coast had become
free to all traders; it being understood that no one was
entitled to use measures of force to the injury of
others.

If a private company of merchants in France, for instance, had taken possession of a part of the coast, driven off other traders, or seized and confiscated their goods, because they refused to pay such duties as the company chose to levy, the matter undoubtedly would have led to national complaint, and to correspondence between governments. If France disavowed all concern in these transactions, reparation would have been sought for by force. Governor Buchanan's zeal therefore sometimes outran his discretion, in the outcry he made against the English Government, for resisting his interferences with their subjects, when these men were acting on practices of very venerable antiquity, or making arrangements with the natives identical with those which he, as the Agent of the American Colonization Society, was making.

Edina, in the Bassa country, for instance, had been the resort of vessels of all nations. Private factories, for trading in ivory, palm oil, &c., were there in 1826: such places were assumed to be open ground, on which the same might occur again, or were common property. Such had been the case on almost every point occupied by the Liberian Government: hence the levying of duties and the establishment of monopolies were resisted by English traders.

England was bound to defend the property of her subjects, or to compensate them for the loss of it, if this occurred through the neglect of the government. And it no doubt appeared very strange to Great Britain, that an association of Americans should claim a right to profit by duties levied on her vessels, when there was no government responsible for their acts.

From the feeling to which these transactions had given rise, it was inferred that something in the shape of reprisals was intended by the seizure of the " John Seyes," a colonial schooner. But this ground was abandoned, by admitting the vessel to trial before the vice-admiralty court, at Sierra Leone, on suspicion of being engaged in the slave-trade. Of this there does not appear to have been evidence justifying even a shadow of suspicion. As the vessel and cargo were, by these proceedings, really lost to their proprietor, the whole case offers only the most revolting features of injustice and oppression. There was then no American squadron on the coast of Africa, to look after such interests.

This case, and many others, were in reality very hard and perplexing. The Liberian was virtually of no country. His government, in the eyes of national law, was no government. This was an evil and threatening state of things. The colonial authorities could not do right without hazard. For it was right to extend their jurisdiction, and regulate trade, and substitute fixed duties for the old irregular systems of presents or bribes to the chiefs. But they had not political law on their side.

They had the advantage, however, of a good era in the world's history.

Mr. Everett, the American Minister to England, on this subject had said, in his note to Lord Aberdeen, 30th of December, 1843 : "The undersigned greatly fears, that if the right of the settlement to act as an independent political community, and as such to enforce the laws necessary to its existence and prosperity, be denied by Her Majesty's government; and if the naval force of Great Britain be employed in protecting individual traders in violation of these laws, the effort will be to aim a fatal blow at its very existence."

The British government seemed to consider that a political community could not act as independent, which neither was in fact, nor professed to be, independent; and also supposed that it could hardly answer to its people for acknowledging a right not claimed on a foundation of fact.   But the Lords of the Admiralty gave orders to the Commodore of the squadron on the coast, for the cruisers off Liberia "to avoid involving themselves in contentions with the local authorities of the Liberian settlements upon points of uncertain legality ;" and added, "great caution is recommended to be observed in the degree of protection granted to British residents, lest, in maintaining the supposed rights of these residents, the equal or superior rights of others should be violated."

Mr. Upshur, Secretary of State, in his correspondence, announced that the American government regarded Liberia "as occupying a peculiar position, and as possessing peculiar claims to the friendly consideration of all Christian powers." There was found afterwards little difficulty in treating the matter, when put in this light.

In the mean time, circumstances looked very disheartening, when the government was committed to the hands of Joseph J. Roberts; for upon the decision of this question with England depended the stability and progress of the colonies. If they could not control their own shores, intercept evil, repulse wrong, and foster good; if they could not expel the contrabandist, secure the native chiefs from being bribed to slaving and all kinds of evil, there was an end to their progress.

Looking to the interior concerns, however, there was much that was promising. Civilization, with its peace, intelligence and high aims, was rooted in Africa. The living energy of republicanism was there. Christianity, in various influential forms, was among the people. Education was advancing, and institutions for public good coming into operation. Governor Buchanan had, among his last efforts, addressed an audience in the Lyceum at Monrovia.

Schools were supporting themselves among the colonists, although, when established for the benefit of the natives, they were maintained by missionary associations in the United States. Native hereditary enmity and faction were yielding perceptibly, in all directions, to the gentle efficacy of Christian example. All this constituted a great result.

The physical, material and political resources, or agencies, were small. A few men, in a distant land, had taken up the subject of African colonization amidst the sectional strifes, political controversies and gigantic enterprises of a mighty nation, and held fast to it. A few, of pre-eminent generosity, surrendered their slaves, or wealth, or personal endeavors, to forward it. No one could stand on Cape Mesurado, and see the intermingled churches and houses; the broad expanses of interior waters, bordered by residences, and see a people elevated far, very far, to say the least, above those of their color in other parts of the world, without the consciousness that a great work was begun. To meet everywhere the dark-browed men of Africa, solely the governors of it all, indicated a great fact in the history of the negro race.

Other movements among men were falling into a correspondence with these proceedings. A great awakening in regard to Africa was pervading Europe. The Niger expedition had entered "the valley and shadow of death," which extends its fatal circle round the white man as he penetrates among the wide lagoons, the luxuriant verdure, and sunny slopes of Africa. The world regarded it as a calamity, when the fatal consequence of this attempt came to light. Men were willing to continue the sacrifice of life and treasure, if any prospect of success should be seen. All entrances, north, south, east and west, were anxiously scrutinized to see if a safe access could be found leading into the land of mystery.

The trade with the west coast was becoming the object of keen competition. England had for years had her full share, and was grasping for more; France was straining every nerve, by purchase and otherwise, as of old, to establish herself commercially there; while the United States were sending their adventurous traders to pick up what the change in Africa would develop. Something like an earnest cordial determination was evinced to abolish the slave-trade, and substitute for it the pursuits of true and beneficial commerce.

CHAPTER XVII.

THE election of Roberts, a colored man, as governor
of the commonwealth of Liberia, totally separated and
individualized the African race as the managers of
local affairs, and made, as to internal concerns, all
things their own. He attempted to root out the inter-
lopers, with energy more patriotic than potent, and
stood up strongly for the rights of his community. He
purchased, negotiated, threatened; and in every way
did his best to accomplish the object. It was soon
seen, however, that the termination of Liberian progress as a dependent commonwealth had arrived, and
that a change was indispensable.

Liberia was, after all, as to its physical means, only
a few thousands of enlightened and determined men,
amidst an ocean of barbarism. All the emigrants
were by no means among the enlightened. Some
curious practical difficulties occurred in any political

co-operation with their American brethren. A gang
of hard-headed fellows seemed to think that it was rather
a joke, a kind of playing at government, meaning nothing
serious; therefore their respect and obedience to the
constituted authorities were very limited.

It should never be forgotten, that no change could
be greater than that to which these men were subjected,
in coming from countries where no power, authority,
or public respect, could ever rest on their race, to a country where colored men might exercise dominion, enact
laws and enforce them, and by their personal qualities
exact and attain eminence and respect. The best possible laws are only for the best state of society, and
men must grow to them; otherwise they are only like
a giant's helmet on a child's head—more a burden than
a defence.

The Liberians had no laws admitting of imprisonment for debt. There is no harm in this, where a man
has to borrow before he can become a debtor. But
the case is not so easily settled, when roguery is the
source of debt. A man who is fined when he has
nothing to pay, laughs at the judge. So it happened
in Liberia, to the embarrassment of the better class of
men.

Governor Roberts had to keep an eye on grog-selling
and grog-drinking. From the style of his reflections,
he gives fair promise of becoming a strong advocate of

the " Maine law."   There was no small number of cases
of idleness, obstinacy and heedlessness of the future;
very natural to men whose independence of station
was of very recent date, and whose independence of
character was yet to come.   The more credit is therefore due to the firm, industrious and upright, stationed
on the threshold of this vast, dark continent, with its
fury and its vice ready to burst out upon them.

The governor's resources, never very great, were
called for to regulate the intercourse between civilization and barbarism; and he found that the high moral
influence of a few hundred men around him, was a
tower of strength in dealing with the savage.   All the
kings of the northern and western districts were induced to assemble in convention in the early part of
1843, at King Bromley's town, to settle their great
disputes of long standing, and to draw up a set of rules
and regulations for their future guidance.   This was a
great step gained: a moral victory over the furious
enormities of savage life.

The kings asked the countenance and advice of the
colony, acknowledging fully its jurisdiction over them.
King Ballasada, however, sent his respectful compli-
ments, with a petition that he might be allowed to cut
the throat of King Gogomina, if opportunity offered; or
might at least have the pleasure of shooting some of
his people, because the said Gogomina had killed six

of Ballasada's "boys." Information, however, was given by Governor Roberts to King Ballasada, that the time had passed for such summary proceedings, but that the matter of shooting the six boys should be inquired into by the governor himself. Gogomina thereupon produced the six "boys" alive, and sent them home.

Much interest now began to be manifested to learn something of the interior. It was not known whither the wide valleys of the rivers might lead, or what they might contain. It was ascertained that there were the Mandingoes and other noted people somewhere beyond the deep forests, with whom communication had been held, and with whom it might be held again. The natives on a line northeast, as far as the Niger, were entirely unknown: little was really ascertained, except that the Niger was there. They knew that there were jealous tribes interposing, who stopped all commercial intercourse that did not pass through their own bloody and avaricious hands.

The governor, relying on the reputation for power and good faith which the colony had acquired, resolved to head in person an expedition of exploration along the St. Paul's River. Taking a small number of men with him, he proceeded up the river, visited the camwood country, about seventy miles inland, and found the forests greatly wasted, and the main source of supply at that time one hundred miles farther back. Kings were visited and relieved of their fears, although not of their wonder, that "the governor should be at that distance from home without engaging in war." The party had left the canoe, and after a circuit round to the eastward, they reached "Captain Sam's" town, one hundred and twenty miles east of Monrovia.

Several kings met with the president in his excursion, with whom a conversation was held, "on the subject of trade, the course and extent of the river, native wars, religion, &c." One, "who was seated in state, on a sofa of raised earth, gave us a hearty shake of the hand, and said he was glad to see us;" adding, "this country be your country, all this people be your countryman, you be first king." This king was informed by the president, "that he and his people must agree to abandon the slave-trade, to discontinue the use of sassywood, engage in no war except by permission of the colonial government." On one occasion, "Ballasada, the principal war-man of the Golah tribe, made his appearance; he entered the gate of the barricade, at the head of some twenty or thirty armed warriors, with drums beating, horns blowing, dressed in a large robe, and stepping with all the majesty of a great monarch." At Yando's town, arrangements were made for establishing a school. At Gelby, one of the missionaries preached to a large congregation—the king with most of his people being present. The audience was attentive, and, with the king, gave "a nod of the head at almost every word uttered by the interpreter."

At "Captain Sam's town," a place of great trade, they met three strangers from different tribes, anxious to have a question settled, viz.: "whether, if they carried their produce to the American settlement for sale, the colonists would beat them, take their property away, and put them in jail." Their intermediate friends had persuaded them that such would be the case, and consequently had themselves, in the mean time, become their agents, and plundered them at discretion. They had, at that time, brought a considerable quantity of produce for sale, and some of them had been kept waiting for many months. All this was fully cleared up to their satisfaction, and great extension of trade was promised. The governor says: "I have travelled considerably in the United States, but have never seen anywhere a more beautiful country than the one passed through, well timbered and watered, and the soil, I venture to assert, equal to any in the world."

President Roberts, at Monrovia, in 1850, stated to the writer, that in the interior, ore was found so pure as to be capable of being beaten into malleable iron, without the process of smelting.

Treaties were formed with all the kings, and sundry fractions of kings; introducing everywhere peace and

facilities for commerce. It may be presumed, therefore, that now the tidings are circulating through the
depths of the interior, that peace has come from the
west; and that an African people has returned to bless
their old dark continent with light and truth.

CHAPTER XVIII.

For the main evils with which Liberia was oppressed, independence was the only remedy. We have seen the nature and extent of these evils, in her equivocal position in the view of several European powers, and especially in that of the English nation. The measures necessary to carry out this great purpose were received with universal sympathy.

Individuals from all sections of our own country, bearing on them the imperial character of their nation, had transmitted it by the dark-skinned race, to vivify with liberty and self-government, the great slave-land of the world. This was perhaps an honor higher than they aimed at. The few judicious leading men of Liberia saw the necessity of making the experiment. The outlines of a constitution, as far as that already existing needed modification, were borrowed from that of the United States. A declaration of independence was drawn up and proclaimed; and on the 24th day of August, 1847, the flag of the Republic of Liberia was displayed.

Roberts, whose state of pupilage had been passed under the master mind of Buchanan, was, as might be expected, elected President of the Republic. England, France, Prussia, Belgium and Brazil have successively acknowledged the independence of Liberia. A liberal treaty of amity and commerce, based upon the equality of rights of the two nations, was entered into between England and Liberia. The ministry were probably led to the conclusion by the president's visit, that trade, regulated by the laws of a compact nation, was likely to become far more advantageous than the bribing, cheating and plundering that had occurred, with kings and half kings, and some European subjects; and had in view the increased power of the government for the suppression of the slave-trade.

The president arrived in Liberia on the 1st of February, 1849, in her majesty's steam frigate Amazon, and was saluted by her with 21 guns on landing. Other appropriate ceremonies were observed; soon after this, England presented the republic with a man-of-war schooner, with armament and stores complete.

France entered afterwards into a commercial treaty

with Liberia, and furnished a large quantity of arms. Subsequent assurances from the European powers, indicate their interest in the prosperity of the African republic.

On the 22d of February, 1849, the French flag steam frigate Penelope, accompanied by another cruiser, arrived at Monrovia. On the following day, the commander, with the officers and two hundred men, landed for the purpose of saluting the flag of the republic. They were received by three uniform companies of Monrovia, in front of Colonel Yates's residence; where three field-pieces from the French frigate had been placed. The procession was then formed and moved up Broad-street to the president's house, where the flag-staff, bearing the the Liberian colors, was standing. A salute of twenty-one guns was fired from the field-pieces, which was repeated by the French cruisers, and returned by the Liberian guns. Refreshments were provided for the men, and the officers dined with the president.

In the month of March following, several English and French cruisers placed themselves at the disposal of President Roberts, for an expedition against the Slavers who had established themselves at New Cesters. Arrangements had previously been made with some of the chiefs in that quarter, for the surrender of their lands and for the incorporation of their people, on the usual

terms, with the Liberian republic. But a portion of
the chiefs and people had been allured to the support
of the slavers, and force was required to dislodge
them.

Roberts embarked four hundred men in the cruisers,
and, accompanied by the U. S. sloop-of-war "Yorktown,"
proceeded to the scene of action. Here were foreign cruisers, transporting the troops of an African republic to
make a descent upon a European slave establishment;
such establishments as Europe had for centuries sustained on the African coast. A novel sight, certainly,
to the leader of the enemy, who was a Spaniard !

The landing was covered by the cruisers, and a well-
directed shell from the French steamer, bursting over
the heads of the natives, cleared the way for the troops
to form and march upon the barracoon, with now and
then a harmless shot from the jungle. Foreseeing the
result of a conflict, the Spaniard fired his buildings,
mounted his horse, sought safety in flight, and his rab-
ble dispersed. The establishment was strengthened by
a thick clay-wall, capable of offering a respectable
resistance. Thirty slaves were liberated. The fort was
destroyed. New Cesters was *annexed*, and the troops
returned to Monrovia.

An infectious impulse to disturbance, seems to have
come from a fruitful source in the northern interior.
For about thirty years, a war had been prevailing be-

tween revolted slaves and the chiefs, along the Gallinas River. These lingering hostilities afforded facilities for securing a good supply of slaves for exportation, which was probably the cause why the slave-trade held on so pertinaciously at the mouth of this river. Treachery, for a time, enforced quiet. The chiefs of the oppressors inveigled the leaders of the insurgents to a conference, and massacred them. Manna, who seems to have had a long familiarity with crime, directed this exploit.

President Roberts, when in England (1848), dining on one occasion with the Prussian Ambassador, the subject of purchasing the Gallinas territory was discussed. Lord Ashley and Mr. Gurney being present, pledged one thousand pounds, half the amount required to secure the territory. Benevolent individuals in the United States, also contributed for the same purpose. Possession was afterwards obtained of the Gallinas for the sum of nine thousand dollars. The price demanded was large, as the chiefs were aware that annexation to Liberia would forever cut off the lucrative slave-trade. Commissioners were appointed to settle the difficulties in the interior, open the trade in camwood, palm-oil and ivory, and furnish the people with the means of instruction in the art of agriculture. It is, however, doubtful whether the influence of the republic is sufficient to control the wars which have been so long raging in the interior. By the annexation of this territory, and in May, 1852, of the Cassa territory, Liberia practically extends its dominion, exterminating the slave-trade from Cape Lahou, eastward of Cape Palmas, to Sierra Leone, a distance of about six hundred miles of sea-coast.

The financial burdens of the government were a matter of no little anxiety. The money for the purchase of the Gallinas had been munificently contributed by Mr. Gurney and other individuals from abroad, but still there was that "national blessing—a national debt." The expedition against New Cesters was, doubtless, a great event in the history of Liberia. There was glory, which is not without its practical use; and there was gratification in the honor of having been aided, or accompanied in such an effort, by the naval forces of great nations. But glory and gratification have their disadvantages also. Very keenly did the leading men of Liberia look to the fact that there were heavy bills to be paid. The payment of a few thousand dollars was a serious affair. They wisely concluded, however, that they were following the ways of Providence in incorporating New Cesters and the Gallinas into their family. And the results have justified their proceedings.

On the 15th of February, 1850, the Secretary of State, in compliance with a resolution of the Senate of the United States, transmitted a report of the Rev. R. R. Gurley, who had a short time previously been sent out by the government to obtain information in respect to Liberia. This report contains a full account of the people, the government and the territory.

The long-standing difficulty with the British traders was brought to a crisis, by a prosecution in the Liberian courts. An appeal was made to the British commodore. Mr. Hansen, the British consul, a native African, who had been liberally educated in the United States, warmly espoused the cause of the traders. These circumstances induced the president, in May, 1852, to revisit England, where matters were satisfactorily arranged. He extended his visit to France, and was there received with attentions due to his station.

The elements of society in Liberia were not all elements of peace. Native tribes, long hostile, had submitted to union. They had promised to be very friendly, and met very lovingly together, which they no doubt considered very strange, and perhaps, for a time, found very pleasant. We should have been inclined to think this very strange, if it had continued. When old nature, old habits and old enmities recovered their strength, it required a firm hand, and one pretty well armed, too, to keep order among them. Nor did the means available always attain this end.

Dissension could not be overcome without force and punishment.

In 1850, the Veys, Deys, and Golahs had roused up their perennial quarrel about their rights and territories. A portion of them were wise enough to apply to the government to appoint a commission to settle the difficulties among them. Others took the larger liberty of attempting to settle matters in their own way. The excitement prevailed during the president's absence. In March, 1853, he proceeded, with two hundred troops, to the northward of Little Cape Mount, and, after a suitable demonstration, brought the chief offender, having the appropriate name of Boombo, to await trial at Monrovia; he was convicted, fined and sentenced to imprisonment for two years.

In November, 1850, the people of Timbo brought in a complaint against "Will Buckle," who was at the head of a gang of rogues, murdering and robbing with impunity. They asked the protection of the government, and to be received within its jurisdiction, and that Will Buckle might feel the strong arm of the law.

But an outbreak at Bassa Cove, under a chief named Grando, threatened to be the grand affair of the time. He was a shrewd, cunning subject. The president gave him a lecture. To all of it " he listened attentively, and with seeming penitence readily admitted the error of his course and the wrongs he had been guilty of, and promised never again," &c., &c. The president, however, found, as is usual in such cases, that Grando was much the same after the lecture as before. "I had scarcely left the country," says the president, "before his evil genius got the better of him." And the fact turned out to be, that his "evil genius" very nearly got the better of everybody else.

He established himself, with his people, beside a new settlement near Bassa Cove. This was exposing his penitence to too strong a temptation. He cultivated the most friendly terms with the settlers; and when he had sufficiently disarmed suspicion, he rose upon the settlement, on the 15th of November, 1851, murdered nine of the inhabitants, carried off what he could get, and took to the "bush."

Grando had taken measures to excite a considerable insurrection of confederated tribes in that region, and returned to the attack with rather a serious force, estimated at one thousand men. The assailants fought with unreflecting fierceness, as the negro does when excited, paying no attention to the artillery which opened upon them. But they made no impression on the place. Roberts proceeded to Bassa Cove in the U. S. sloop-of-war "Dale," accompanied by a reinforcement in the Liberian schooner "Lark," and prevented a third attack.

In March, 1852, Grando and his confederate, Boyer, were again arranging combinations among the tribes in the "bush." The "evil genius" complained of had contrived to bring the traders again on the stage, with their perplexing complaints about imposts and monopolies. One of these traders seems to have been instigating the disturbance.

These circumstances brought on the most extensive and most trying military campaign in which the Liberian forces have yet been engaged. It was estimated that the confederates had in the field about five thousand men. They were well supplied with ammunition, and had some artillery, and were employing their time in constructing formidable defences. To meet them, Roberts had about five hundred colonists, and the same number of natives. With these, on the 6th of January, 1852, he marched upon the enemy. A breastwork, terminating the passage through a swamp, was occupied by three times the number of its assailants. After an action of an hour and a half, this position was forced, and the enemy driven through a piece of difficult forest ground. After some resistance here, they were dislodged and chased to Grando's palisaded town. This they set on fire, and then retreated to Boyer, occupying the left bank of the New Cess river, to dispute the passage.

From this position Boyer was dislodged by the hostility of the chiefs around him, who did not join in the revolt. He retreated within the barricades of his own town. Here he had some artillery. On the 15th, Roberts came with his whole force upon this place. A fierce fight of nearly two hours took place, which resulted in the capture of the town. The loss of the enemy was considerable. The Liberians had six killed and twenty-five wounded.

Grando's allies soon discovered that they were in the wrong. Boyer fell into the same train of repentance. Grando's authority altogether expired in 1853. His own people held a council, whether they should not deliver him up to the president. This was opposed by the old men as contrary to custom. They made him prisoner, however. Boyer would, by no persuasion, be induced to put himself within the grasp of the president. He was also playing his tricks upon other people. Having in July, 1853, induced a Spanish slaver to advance him a considerable sum in doubloons, and a quantity of goods, he suddenly became strongly *anti-slavery* in his views, and sent a request to the president, and to the British steam cruiser " Pluto," to look out for the slaver, which vessel had cleared for the Gallinas, grounded in the river, and was afterwards destroyed.

Boyer himself and another worthy by the name of

Cain, who joined Grando in these disturbances, keep the Liberians on the alert, but seem gradually spreading a net for themselves, and it is to be anticipated that ere long they may be found as companions with Boombo in his captivity.

CHAPTER XIX.

NOTWITHSTANDING the heterogeneous population of
Liberia, a commendable degree of order, quiet and
comparative prosperity prevails. With such men as
President Roberts, Chief-Justice Benedict, Major-
General Lewis, Vice-President Williams, and many
other prominent persons in office and in the walks of
civil life, the government and society present an aspect
altogether more favorable than a visitor, judging them
from the race when in contact with a white population,
is prepared to find. The country is theirs—they are
lords of the soil; and in intercourse with them, it is
soon observed that they are free from that oppressive
sense of inferiority which distinguish the colored people
of this country. A visit to Monrovia is always agreeable to the African cruiser.

Monrovia, the capital, is situated immediately in the

rear of the bold promontory of Cape Mesurado, which rises to the altitude of 250 feet. The highest part of the town is eighty feet above the level of the sea. The place is laid out with as much regularity as the location will admit. Broadway is the main or principal street, running nearly at right angles with the sea. Besides this, there are twelve or fifteen more. The town contains not far from two thousand inhabitants. Many of the houses are substantially built of brick or of stone, and several of them are handsomely furnished. The humidity of the climate has greatly impaired the wooden buildings. The State-House, public stores, and the new academy are solid, substantial buildings, appropriate to their uses. There are five churches, and these are well attended. The schools will compare favorably with the former district schools in this country, which is not saying much in their favor.

The soil in the vicinity of the rocky peninsula of Mesurado is generally sandy and comparatively unproductive, except where there are alluvial deposits along the margin of the streams or creeks. The lands on the banks of the rivers—of the St. Paul's, for instance, four or five miles north of Monrovia—are very rich, of loamy clay soil, equalling in fertility the high lands of Brazil, or any other part of the world. Here more care is devoted to the culture of sugar, and increasing attention is given to agriculture. These lands readily sell at from forty to fifty dollars per acre. A fork of this river flows in a southeasterly direction, and unites with the Mesurado River at its mouth. This fork is called Stockton's Creek, in honor of Commodore Stockton. The largest rivers of Liberia are navigable only about twelve or fifteen miles before coming to the Rapids.

As the country becomes settled, and the character of its diseases better understood, the acclimating fever is less dreaded. In fact, it now rarely proves fatal. This having been passed through, the colored emigrants enjoy far better health than they did in most parts of the United States. The statistics, as President Roberts stated, show some three per cent. smaller number of deaths than in the New England States and Canada among the same class of population. The thermometer seldom rises higher than 85°, nor falls lower than 70°.

The productions of the soil are varied and abundant, —capable of sustaining an immense population. The want of agricultural industry, rather than the incapacity of the country to yield richly the fruits of the earth, has been the difficulty with the Liberians. With well-directed labor, of one-half the amount required among the farmers of the United States, a large surplus of the earth's productions, over the demands of home consumption, might be gathered. The country certainly possesses elements of great prosperity.

"A bill for the improvement of rivers and harbors" should be forthwith passed by the Liberian legislature. A country exporting articles annually amounting to the sum of eight hundred thousand dollars, and this on the increase, might make an appropriation to render landing safe from the ducking in the surf to which one is now exposed. Sharks, in great abundance, are playing about the bars of the rivers, eagerly watching the boats and canoes for their prey. Dr. Prout, a Liberian senator, and several others, have been capsized in boats and fallen victims to these sea-tigers.

A full and very interesting description of the geography, climate, productions and diseases of Africa has been published by Dr. J. W. Lugenbeel, late colonial physician, and the last white man who was United States agent in Africa.

In devising measures for the benefit of Liberia, one thing was pre-eminently to be kept in view, which was, that the people be prevented from sinking back to become mere Africans. It is believed that this danger was wholly past under the energetic administration of Buchanan, to whom too much praise cannot be awarded. He infused life and spirit into the nation, and brought out such men as Roberts and others, in whose hands we believe the republic is safe. A large majority of the emigrants having been slaves, and dependent on the will and dictation of others, many of them are thereby rendered in a measure incapable of that self-reliance which secures early success in an enterprise of this kind.

Slaves do not work like freemen.   The question, then, arises—Is this the case because they are slaves, or because they are negroes? Those who have been emancipated in the British territories have hitherto cast no favorable light on this inquiry. They do not now work as they did when compelled to work, although they are free. Neither do the Sicilians, Neapolitans, or Portuguese work as men work elsewhere. There are no men freer than the slavers, who steal children and sell them, in order that they themselves may live in vicious idleness. It is the freeman's intelligence and his higher motives of action, which produce his virtues.

The slave-trade being extirpated within the boundaries of Liberia, and the natives brought under new influences, the necessity produced for new kinds of labor has become favorable to the improvement of the African. There is now the will and ability of the native population to work in the fields. The low rate of remuneration which they require, favors the employment of capital, but keeps wages for common labor very low. It is of no use to urge upon colonists to employ their own people in preference to natives, when the former want eighty cents a day and the latter only twenty-five. These things must take their natural course. The increase of capital must be waited for ere wages can rise. But it all tells strongly in favor of settlers securing grants of land, and becomes a great inducement for colored men emigrating to Liberia who have some little capital of their own.

It is in Liberia alone that the colored man can find freedom and the incentives to higher motives of action, which are conducive to virtue. There these sources of good are found in abundance for his race. In this country he can gain the intelligence of the free population, but is excluded from the vivifying motives of the freeman. In Liberia he has both. Means are needed to sustain this condition of things. The first of these is religion, which to a great degree, pervades the community there : it is true that some of the lower forms of a vivid conception of spiritual things characterize the people; but far preferable is this, to the tendency of the age elsewhere—towards attempting to bring within the scope of human reason the higher mysteries of faith. The second is the school, which keeps both intelligence and aspiration alive, and nurtures both. Roberts is aware of this, and keeps it before the people. They will transfer, therefore, what the United States alone exemplifies, and what is vitally important to free governments, namely, a system of free public education in the common schools; such a system is that of the *graded schools* in many parts of our country, far surpassing most of the select schools, where a thorough education may be freely obtained by all the children of the community.

Liberia contains a population exceeding one hundred and fifty thousand inhabitants; not more than one-twentieth of this number are American colonists. Its growth has been gradual and healthy. The government, from its successful administration by blacks alone, for more than six years, appears to be firmly established. The country is now in a condition to receive as many emigrants as the United States can send. To the colored man who regards the highest interest of his children; to young men of activity and enterprise, Liberia affords the strongest attractions.

We would not join in any attempt to crush the aspirations of any class of men in this country. But it is an actual fact, whatever may be thought of it, that here the colored man has never risen to that position, which every one should occupy among his fellows. For suppose the wishes of the philanthropist towards him to be fully accomplished,—secure him his political rights; unfetter him in body and intellect; cultivate him in taste even; then while nominally free, he is still in bondage; for freedom must also be the prerogative of the white, as well as of the black man; and the white man must likewise be left free to form his most intimate social relations; and he is not, and never has been disposed, in this country, to unite himself with a caste, marked by so broad a distinction as exists between the two races. The testimony on these two points of those who have had abundant advantages for observation, has been uniform and conclusive. For the colored man himself then, for his children, Liberia is an open city of refuge. He there may become a freeman not only in name, but a freeman in deed and in truth.

Liberia has strong claims upon Christian aid and sympathy. Its present and prospective commercial advantages to our country, will far counterbalance the amount appropriated by private benevolence in planting and aiding the colony and the republic. Its independence ought to be acknowledged by the United States. This, according to the opinion of President Roberts, would not imply the necessity of diplomatic correspondence, while the moral and political effects, would be beneficial to both parties. England, by early acknowledging the independence of Liberia, and cultivating a good understanding with its government and people, has greatly subserved her own commercial interest, while responding to the call of British philanthropy.

CHAPTER XX.

THE Maryland Colonization Society resolved to establish a colony at Cape Palmas. Dr. James Hall, their
agent, secured the consent of the chiefs to cede the
required territory, without employing the wretched
medium of rum. These kings, to their credit, have
retained sensible names of their own, redolent of good
taste and patriotism, being Parmah, Weah Boleo, and
Baphro. As has ever been done by all wise people on
that coast, a fort was expeditiously erected, overlooking
in a peremptory way the native villages and the anchorage; since it is not, for a time at least, safe to trust in
such affairs to the conscience of the natives.

Cape Palmas is well suited for such an establishment; the climate is as good as any in tropical Africa.
The Cape itself is a small elevation or insulated hill,
sloping down towards the continent, into the general
expanse of wooded plain or forest; this, to the north

and east of the Cape, stretches out into a wide fertile flat, the waters of which drain towards the long line of sea-beach, receiving the heavy surf of the equatorial Atlantic.   The surf throws a long bulwark of sand along the mouths of the fresh-water streams, and checks them in a lagoon of ten miles in length, by about a quarter of a mile in breadth.   This water is fresh or brackish, according as either element gains the mastery, and serves the natives as a precious and fruitful fish-pond.

Of this region, a tract extending about twenty miles along the sea-shore, and as much inland, was, by purchase, brought under the jurisdiction of the Maryland Society.   Provision was made for retaining the resident natives on the lands they cultivated.   Here, in the month of February, 1834, the Maryland Colonization Society attached itself to Africa, by landing fifty-three emigrants from that State.

Their temporary dwellings were soon put up; and their fortifications erected near to populous towns crowded with natives supplied with fire-arms and ready to use them.   Vessels continued to arrive, bringing more settlers to their shores.   In 1836, an additional tract of country, east of the Cape, was procured; extending the colonial territories along the broad, rapid stream of the Cavally, to the distance of thirty miles from its mouth.   In succeeding years new settlers arrived to occupy the lands so acquired; yet all these acquisitive proceedings gave rise to scarcely any noticeable opposition. A little blustering occurred on the part of one chief, who attempted to monopolize the selling of rice to the colonists when in want; but a kind and resolute firmness removed the difficulty. Scarcely, in fact, does an instance occur in history, of an administration so uniformly successful in the operations for which it was established; and, whatever the future may offer to equal it, nothing certainly in the past has a higher claim for sympathy, than these efforts of Maryland for the benefit of her colored population.

With the same wisdom which had characterized the previous measures of the society, in 1837 Mr. Russwurm, a colored man, was appointed governor of the colony. He fulfilled the expectations formed of him. Thus one step was judiciously taken, to disengage the colored men of Africa from dependence on foreign management.

Considering, however, that Cape Palmas has been colonized from a slave state alone, and that the government has been retained in the hands of the state society, it is scarcely to be expected that the same vigor and activity should be found in its internal operations, or the same amount of influence exercised over the surrounding natives, as has been manifested in Liberia. Notwithstanding this, the beneficial influence of this colony also, on the surrounding natives, has been considerable. Six kings, of their own accord, applied to Governor Russwurm, and ceded their territories, that they might be incorporated with the colony. Every treaty contained an absolute prohibition of the slave-trade.

Cape Palmas colony, then, may be considered as now extending from the confines of her elder sister at the river Jarraway, as far to the eastward as Cape La-hou. The inland boundary may be anywhere, as the future shall settle it. The cultivated or cleared land extends parallel to the coast, over distances varying from twenty-five to fifty miles. Here comes on the dark verdure of forest, undulating over the rising lands which lead to the mountains, or whatever they may be, which feed the rivers. These streams act as lines of communication. But here also the old Portuguese influence has aimed at a monopoly of trade. Some explorations have disclosed the fact that there are powerful tribes in these lands, who, in spite of an obstacle of this kind, will soon be brought within the commercial influence of the colony.

This line of coast has at many points been a frequent haunt of slavers, and the atrocities due to native superstition have been shocking, and rendered more villanous by European trade. Commodore Perry, in 1843, as will be seen in the notice of squadrons, did

justice on some of their villages, convicted of murder
and robbery of an American vessel. The officers delivered several of the natives from torture under the
accusations of sorcery. To control such fierce materials
into quietness, or melt them to Christian brotherhood,
will require much grace from Providence, and much
kind and patient dealing from men.

In carrying out the objects of the colony, an effort
was made by the Maryland Colonization Society, which
seemed in its nature singularly promising. This consisted in establishing a joint-stock trading company, or
line of packets for carrying out emigrants and returning
with produce. It was expected that the colored people
of the state would, to some considerable extent, invest
capital in shares. With these expectations the "Liberia Packet" was launched in 1846, and made many
voyages. It was found necessary to increase the size
of vessels thus employed. But these operations were
checked by the wreck of the "Ralph Cross." It was
also found that comparatively little interest in this undertaking was awakened among the colored population,
or that they had not the means for investment in it, as
only about one-eighth of the whole amount of stock
was held by them. It is, however, an incident of
value in the history of Africa, that through facilities
thus afforded, many emigrants revisited this country
for short periods, and thus established a return line of

intercourse, inquiry, or business, which binds Africa more strongly to this land.

A movement for the elevation of the colony into an independent state, has been made by the people at Cape Palmas, and a commission has visited this country to make arrangements for the purpose. That there be full political independence granted to this people, is requisite, as an element of the great achievement now going on. This contemplates something far higher than creating merely a refuge for black men, or sticking on a patch of colored America on the coast of Africa like an ill-assorted graft, for which the old stock is none the better. Liberia is the restoration of the African in his highest intellectual condition to that country in which his condition had become the most degraded. The question is to be settled whether that condition can be retained, or so improved that he may keep pace with the rest of the world.

It is a necessary element in this proceeding that he be self-governing. It is to the establishment of this point that all men look to decide the dispute, whether negro races are to remain forever degraded or not. Time and patience, however, and much kind watchfulness, may be required before this experiment be deemed conclusive. Let many failures be anticipated ere a certain result is secured. Let no higher claims be made on the negro than on other races. Would a colony of Frenchmen, Spaniards, Portuguese, Sicilians, if left to themselves, offer a fairer prospect of success than Liberia now offers? Few persons would have confidence in the stability of republican institutions among these races, if so placed.

Let then the black man be judged fairly, and not presumed to have become all at once and by miracle, of a higher order than old historic nations, through many generations of whom the political organization of the world has been slowly developing itself. There will be among them men who are covetous, or men who are tyrannical, or men who would sacrifice the public interests or any others to their own: men who would now go into the slave-trade if they could, or rob hen-roosts, or intrigue for office, or pick pockets, rather than trouble their heads or their hands with more honorable occupations. It should be remembered by visitors that such things will be found in Liberia; not because men are black, but because men are men.

It should not be forgotten that the experiment in respect to this race is essentially a new one. The nonsense about Hannibal, and Terence, and Cyprian, and Augustine, being negro Africans, should have been out of the heads of people long ago. A woolly-headed, flat-nosed African, in ancient times, would have created as great a sensation at the head of an army, or in the chair of a professor, as it would now in the United

States or in England. These men were Asiatics or Europeans, rather than Africans: the Great Desert being properly the northern boundary of the African 'race. The African has never reached in fact, until the settlement of Liberia, a higher rank than a king of Dahomey, or the inventor of the last fashionable grisgris to prevent the devil from stealing sugar-plums. No philosopher among them has caught sight of the mysteries of nature; no poet has illustrated heaven, or earth, or the life of man; no statesman has done any thing to lighten or brighten the links of human policy. In fact, if all that negroes of all generations have ever done, were to be obliterated from recollection forever, the world would lose no great truth, no profitable art, no exemplary form of life. The loss of all that is African would offer no memorable deduction from any thing but the earth's black catalogue of crimes. Africa is guilty of the slavery under which she suffered; for her people made it, as well as suffered it.

The great experiment, therefore, is as to the effect of instruction given to such a race from a higher one. It has had its success, and promises more. But many patient endeavors must still be used. The heroism of the missionary is still needed. Such men as Mills, Ashmun, Wilson, and Bishop Payne, will be required to give energy to this work in various forms. But there will be henceforth, it is to be hoped, less demand for the exposure of American life. There should be found in the colored people of the United States, with whom the climate agrees, the source of supply for African missions, till, in a few years, Liberia itself send them forth, with words of life to their brethren throughout the length and breadth of the continent.

Like all sinful men, the African needs faith. But you must dig deeper in him, before you find any thing to plant it on. The grain of mustard-seed meets a very hard soil there, and the thorns are deep. It is a conquest to get him to believe that there is any virtue in man. They have never had a Socrates, to talk wisdom to them; nor a Cyrus, who was not a slave-merchant; nor a Pythagoras, to teach that kindness was a virtue. Hence the difficulty which the Christian missionary has had with them, has been to satisfy their minds as to the miraculous phenomenon of there being a good man. It has been always found that there was many a consultation among their sages as to the peculiar trade or purpose the missionary might have in view, in coming as he came; and very generally the more good they saw, the more evil they suspected. The first thing which, in most instances, opened their eyes, has been in his inculcating peace; for they saw no fees coming to him for it, and of course no looking out for plunder.

The civilized world, as well as the savage, need the

example of the missionary. The true courage of faith is a blessing to mankind. Besides his devotion to the highest interests of men, the world also owes much to the educated and enlightened missionary, who has not only greatly contributed to the cause of science and literature, but has often been the means of developing the commercial resources of the countries where he has been stationed. Women, with their own peculiar heroism, which consists in fearless tenderness and patience, have also shared in this work of faith. Mrs. Judson is seen wandering through a Burman village teaching the people, with a sick child in her arms, while her husband lies in prison. And Mrs. Wilson, highly cultivated and refined, sacrificing her property, and surrendering a position in the best society of the country, is found teaching negro children in the dull and fetid atmosphere of African schools. This is true heroism, such as the gospel alone can inspire.

Christianity has, with watchful kindness, been seeking to penetrate Africa from various points of the coast. Abyssinia has long professed the Christian faith, although in a corrupt form. Its church, and that of Egypt, must soon fall under the influence of the line of communication through the Red Sea. English missionaries are at Zanzibar, and have brought to light, by their explorations in the interior, the group of mountains which raise their snowy heads south of the equator in

that neighborhood. Missionaries from the same country are also to be found at Sierra Leone and in the
Bight of Benin. From the extremity of the continent
they have, in conjunction with those of five other nations, been penetrating all the interior of the southern
angle.

The United States have also missionaries at four or
five points. There are those of the Liberian republic,
Cape Palmas, and the Mendi mission. In these places
different denominations work kindly and earnestly together. The first obvious sign of their presence is
peace. Nowhere in the world was this more needed,
or more welcome, than in the regions north and east of
Liberia, where men, for many years, had had to fight
for their own persons, that they might remain their
own, and not be sold. Every thing, as might be expected, had fallen into utter confusion. Tribes of historic character were in fragments ; towns depopulated,
cultivation suspended, and the small knots of families
which kept together, were perishing. "The women
and children," says Mr. Thompson, " were often obliged
to go out in search of berries and fruits to keep themselves from starving." To this country, which lies
along the sources of the Sierra Leone and the Gallinas
rivers on the northern confines of Liberia, the captives
on board the *Amistad* had gone in 1842. But such
was the confusion in that quarter, that it was not until

1851, that the missionary found it practicable to commence his efforts for peace. They told Mr. Thompson, " that no one but a white man could have brought it about;" and that " they had long been praying to God to send a white man to stop the war."

The Gaboon mission, since its disturbance by the French in 1844, has been re-established, and has experienced courteous treatment at the hands of the French authorities. This mission occupies the important position at which the great southern nation and language come in contact with the more energetic men of the equatorial region, and at which great light is likely to be thrown on their relations. The French also have a mission at the Gaboon.

The mission to the Zulus, in the healthy region at the southern end of the Mozambique Channel, was at one time divided between the two branches of that tribe; but in consequence of wars, was afterwards united and established in the colony of Natal. The commercial crisis in the United States in 1837, led to the proposal that this mission should be abandoned. But its influence had been so beneficial, that the Cape colonists and their government proposed to take measures to support it. Circumstances, however, enabled the American Board to decline this proposal, and they continue their operations. An effort is being made by this mission to unite all similarly engaged, in a common and uniform mode of treating the language of the south.

The Portuguese have missions, both on the east and west side of the continent.

Commander Forbes, R. N., says : " In all the countries which have given up the traffic in their fellow-men, the preaching of the Gospel and the spread of education have most materially assisted the effects of the coercive measures of our squadron."

CHAPTER XXI.

IT was the cessation of the last great European war, which assembled the matured villany of the world on the African coast to re-establish the slave-trade. This traffic had been suspended during the latter years of the contest, as England and the United States had abolished it, and the former was strong enough at sea to prevent other European powers from engaging in it. In fact, she had swept almost the whole European marine from the ocean. The treaties formed at the peace, left Europe to the strife between anarchy and despotism ; and gave up the coast of Africa to the slave-trade and piracy.

Every evil and every fear which have harassed the world since that time, seem to be the retributions of an indignant Providence. Let it not be imagined that these dealings of justice with men are at an end. What could atone for giving up the coasts of a whole continent to be ravaged by the slave-ships of France, Spain, and Portugal? What compensation for this vicious and deadly scourge has Africa yet received? The cruising, suffering, sickness, deaths and expenses of nearly half a century have not remedied the crime of signing these treaties. The ambassador, minister, or whoever he was, that signed them, bears a load of guilt, such as few mortal men have assumed.

England set about remedying this in a more commendable spirit, as soon as the years of free and unrestricted crime, which she had really granted to these nations, were run out. During about twenty years subsequently, when treaties with these powers had granted mutual right of search and capture, three hundred vessels were seized, having slaves on board. But during the latter part of this period, more than one hundred thousand half-dead negroes were annually landed from slave-vessels in Cuba and Brazil.

In 1839 the corrective was more stringently applied. Permission had then, or soon after, been wrung from different slave-trading powers, to capture vessels outward-bound for Africa, when fitted for the slave-trade, as well as after they had taken in their cargoes. The treaties provided that vessels equipped for the traffic might be captured, so as to prevent the crime. A slaver was thus to be taken, because she was a slaver; just as it is better to shoot the wolf before he has killed the sheep than afterwards. If a vessel, therefore, was found on the African coast with slave-irons, water in sufficient quantity for a slave-cargo, with a slave-deck laid for packing slaves—somewhat as the carcases of sheep and pigs in a railway train, with the exception of the fresh air—she was seized and condemned before committing the overt act. Under this arrangement, with a rigorous squadron, double the number of captures were made, during the next ten years, as compared with the previous twenty.

Seeing, then, that, as before noticed, one thousand and seventy slave-vessels were captured, and of the slaves who were not dead, a great proportion were landed at Sierra Leone, and that the whole population of that colony, although established for nearly sixty years, does not amount to more than forty-five thousand souls, young and old, it may be conceived what a fearful waste of life has arisen even from deliverance.

The efforts of this squadron were conjoined with those of France and the United States. The former had withdrawn from the treaty stipulating the right of search, and sent a squadron of her own to prevent French vessels from engaging in the slave-trade; and the United States, which never has surrendered, and never will surrender, the inviolability of her own flag to a foreign power, guaranteed, in 1842, to keep a squadron on the coast. These, together with other subsidiary means, had reduced the export of slaves in 1849 to about thirty-seven thousand, from one hundred and five thousand. And since that period the trade has lessened, until in Brazil, the greater slave-mart, it has become almost extinct; although at times it has been carried on briskly with the island of Cuba.

The subsidiary means alluded to arose out of the presence of the squadrons, and would have had no effect without them. They consist in arrangements, on the part of England, with some of the native powers, to join in checking the evil, and substitute legal trade, and in the conversion of the old slave-factories and forts into positions defensive against their former purpose.

These measures have also prepared the way for the establishment of Christian missions, as well as permitted to legitimate traffic its full development. Missions and the slave-trade have an inverse ratio between them as to their progress. When the one dwindles, the other grows. Although it was no ostensible purpose of the squadron to forward missions, yet the presence of cruisers has been essential to their establishment and success.

Trade of all kinds was originally an adjunct to the

slave-trade. Cargoes were to be sold where they could find a purchaser. Gold, ivory, dye-stuffs and pepper were the articles procured on the coast. All of these are from exhaustible sources. The great vegetable productions of the country, constituting heavy cargoes, have but lately come into the course of commerce. Hunting and roaming about supplied the former articles of commerce. The heavier articles now in demand require more industry with the hands, and a settled life. Trade thus becomes inconsistent with slavery, and hostile to it; and the more so as it becomes more dependent on the collection of oil, ground-nuts, and other products of agriculture. Covering the coast now with trading establishments, excludes the slaver. The efforts of the squadrons were necessary to carry out this proceeding, for commerce needed to be protected against the piracies of the slaver afloat and the ravages of the slaver on shore.

Exposure to capture gave origin to the barracoons. A slaver could no longer leisurely dispose of her cargo, at different points, in return for slaves who happened to be there. The crime now required concealment and rapidity. Wholesale dealers on shore had to collect victims sufficient for a cargo to be taken on board at a moment's notice. This required that the slaver should arrive at the station, with arrangements previously made with the slave-factor, ready to "take in;" or that she should bring over a cargo of goods in payment for the slaves.

In the case of falling in with British cruisers, an American slaver was inviolate, on presenting her register, or sea-letter, as a proof of nationality, and could not be searched or detained. But the risk of falling in with American cruisers, especially if co-operating with the British, led to the disguise of legal trading; with a cargo corresponding to the manifest, and all the ship's papers in form. An instance of this occurred, as will be seen, in the capture of the second slaver by the "Perry."

The American flag, in these ways, became deeply involved in the slave traffic. How far this acted injuriously to the interests of Africa, is seen in the complaints of Buchanan and Roberts, and in the reports of our ministers and consuls, and of those of the English, at Brazil. In 1849, the British consul at Rio, in his public correspondence, says: "One of the most notorious slave-dealers in this capital, when speaking of the employment of American vessels in the slave-trade, said, a few days ago: 'I am worried by the Americans, who insist upon my hiring their vessels for slave-trade.'"

Of this there is also abundant and distressing evidence from our own diplomatic officers. Besides a lengthy correspondence from a preceding minister near the court of Brazil, the President of the United States

transmitted a report from the Secretary of State, in
December, 1850, to the Senate of the United States,
with documents relating to the African slave-trade. A
resolution had previously passed the Senate, calling
upon the Executive for this information.

In these documents it is stated that " the number of
American vessels which, since the 1st of July, 1844,
until the 1st of October last (1849), sailed for the
coast of Africa from this city, is ninety-three. . . . Of
these vessels, all, except five, have been sold and delivered on the coast of Africa, and have been engaged
in bringing over slaves, and many of them have been
captured with slaves on board. . . . This pretended sale
takes place at the moment when the slaves are ready to
be shipped; the American captain and his crew going
on shore, as the slaves are coming off, while the Portuguese or Italian *passengers*, who came out from Rio
in her, all at once became the master and crew of the
vessel. Those of the American crew who do not die of
coast-fever, get back as they can, many of them being
compelled to come over in slave-vessels, in order to get
back at all. There is evidence in the records of the
consulate, of slaves having started two or three times
from the shore, and the master and crew from their
vessel in their boat, carrying with them the flag and
ship's papers; when, the parties becoming frightened,
both retroceded; the slaves were returned to the shore,

and the American master and crew again went on board the vessel. The stars and stripes were again hoisted over her, and kept flying until the cause of the alarm (an English cruiser) departed from the coast, and the embarkation was safely effected."

On the other hand, we have the following notice from Brazil : " As in former years, the slave-dealers have derived the greatest assistance and protection for their criminal purposes, from the use of the American flag, I am happy to add that these lawless and unprincipled traders are at present deprived of this valuable protection, by a late determination of the American naval commander-in-chief on this station, who has caused three vessels, illegally using the flag of the United States, and which were destined for African voyages, to be seized on their leaving this harbor. This proceeding has caused considerable alarm and embarrassment to the slave-dealers ; and, should it be continued, will be a severe blow to all slave-trading interests."

Mr. Tod, the American Minister at the court of Brazil, in a letter to the Secretary of State, says : " As my predecessors had already done, I have, from time to time, called the attention of our government to the necessity of enacting a stringent law, having in view the entire withdrawal of our vessels and citizens from this illegal commerce ; and after so much has been already written upon the subject, it may be deemed a work of supererogation to discuss it further. The interests at stake, however, are of so high a character, the integrity of our flag and the cause of humanity being at once involved in their consideration, I cannot refrain from bringing the topic afresh to the notice of my government, in the hope that the President may esteem it of such importance as to be laid before Congress, and that even at this late day, legislative action may be secured."

In this communication, a quotation is made from Mr. Proffit, one of the preceding ministers, to the Secretary of State, February, 1844, in which he says : "I regret to say this, but it is a fact not to be disguised or denied, that the slave-trade is almost entirely carried on under our flag, in American-built vessels, sold to slave-traders here, chartered for the coast of Africa, and there sold, or sold here—delivered on the coast. And, indeed, the scandalous traffic could not be carried on to any great extent, were it not for the use made of our flag, and the facilities given for the chartering of American vessels, to carry to the coast of Africa the outfit for the trade, and the material for purchasing slaves."

Mr. Wise, the American Minister, in his dispatch of February 15th, 1845, said to Mr. Calhoun:

"It is not to be denied, and I boldly assert it, that the administration of the imperial government of Brazil, is forcibly constrained by its influences, and is deeply inculpated in its guilt. With that it would, at first sight, seem the United States have nothing to do; but an intimate and full knowledge of the subject informs us, that the only mode of carrying on that trade between Africa and Brazil, at present, involves our laws and our moral responsibilities, as directly and fully as it does those of this country itself. Our flag alone gives requisite protection against the right of visit, search, and seizure; and our citizens, in all the characters of owners, consignees, of agents, and of masters and crews of our vessels, are concerned in the business, and partake of the profits of the African slave-trade, to and from the ports of Brazil, as fully as the Brazilians themselves, and others in conjunction with whom they carry it on. In fact, without the aid of our own citizens and our flag, it could not be carried on with success at all."

To exhibit the state of the slave-trade prior to the equipment treaty in 1840, we have the following instances from parliamentary papers, and other British authority:

"La Jeune Estelle, being chased by a British vessel, inclosed twelve negroes in casks, and threw them overboard."

"M. Oiseau, commander of *Le Louis*, a French vessel, in completing his cargo at Calaba, thrust the slaves into a narrow space *three feet high*, and closed the hatches. Next morning fifty were found dead. Oiseau coolly went ashore to purchase others to supply their place."

The following extract is from a report by Captain Hayes to the Admiralty, of a representation made to him respecting one of these vessels in 1832:

"The master having a large cargo of these human beings *chained together*, with more humanity than his fellows, permitted some of them to come on deck, *but still chained together*, for the benefit of the air, when they immediately commenced jumping overboard, hand in hand, and drowning in couples; and (continued the person relating the circumstance) without any cause whatever. Now these people were just brought from a situation between decks, and to which they knew they must return, where the scalding perspiration was running from one to the other..... And men dying by their side, with full in their view, living and dead bodies chained together; and the living, in addition to all their other torments, laboring under the most famishing thirst (being in very few instances allowed more than a pint of water a day); and let it not be forgotten that these unfortunate people had just been torn from their country, their families, their all! Men dragged from their wives, women from their husbands and children, girls from their mothers, and boys from their fathers; and yet in this man's eye (for heart and soul he could have none), there was no cause whatever for jumping overboard and drowning. This, in truth, is a rough picture, but it is not highly colored. The *men are chained in pairs*, and as a proof they are intended so to remain to the end of the voyage, *their fetters are not locked, but riveted by the blacksmith;* and as deaths are frequently occurring, *living men are often for a length of time confined to dead bodies:* the living man cannot be released till the blacksmith has performed the operation of cutting the clinch of the rivet with his chisel; and I have now an officer on board the Dryad, who, on examining one of these slave-vessels, found *not only living men chained to dead bodies, but the latter in a putrid state.*"*

In the notorious Spanish slaver, the *Veloz Passageira*, captured with five hundred and fifty-six slaves, after a severe action, the captain made the slaves assist to work the guns against their own deliverers. Five were killed and one desperately wounded.

"This *Veloz Passageira* had acquired so atrocious a reputation, that it became an object with our commanders to make a special search for her. Captain Arabin, of the *North Star*, having information on his homeward voyage that she would cross his course near the equator, made preparations to attack her, though the

---

* Parliamentary papers, presented 1832, B., pp. 170, 171.

North Star was of much inferior strength. Dr. Walsh, who was coming home in the British vessel, relates, that at breakfast, while the conversation was turning on the chances of meeting with the slaver, a midshipman entered the cabin, and said, in a hurried manner, that a sail was visible to the northwest. All rushed on deck, and setting their glasses, distinctly saw a large ship of three masts, apparently crossing their way. In about an hour she tacked, as if not liking their appearance, and stood away before the wind. The English captain gave chase. Escape seemed impracticable. The breeze freshened, her hull became distinctly visible, and she was now ascertained to be a slaver. She doubled, however, in all directions, and seemed to change her course each moment to avoid her pursuers. Five guns were successively fired, and the English union-flag hoisted, but without effect; and the wind now dying away, the *North Star* began to drop astern. We kept a sharp look-out, with intense interest, leaning over the netting, and silently handing the glass to one another, as if a word spoken would impede our way. Thus closed the night. When morning dawned we saw her, like a speck on the horizon, standing due north. The breeze increased, and again the British captain gained on the slaver. Again long shots were sent after her, but she only crowded more sail to escape. At twelve we were entirely within gunshot, and one of our long bow guns was again fired at her. It struck the water along side, and then for the first time she showed a disposition to stop. While we were preparing a second, she hove to, and in a short time we were alongside of her, after a most interesting chase of thirty hours; during which we ran three hundred miles."

After all she was not the ship for which Captain Arabin had been looking out, but she was full of slaves. "Behind her foremast was an enormous gun, turning on a broad circle of iron, *and enabling her to act as a pirate if her slaving speculation had failed.* She had taken in on the coast of Africa five hundred and sixty-two slaves, and had been out seventeen days, during which she had thrown overboard fifty-five.

"The slaves were all inclosed under grated hatchways between decks. The space was so low that they sat between each other's legs, and stowed so close together that there was no possibility of their lying down or at all changing their position, by night or day. As they belonged to, or were shipped on account of, different individuals, they were all branded like sheep, with the owners' marks, of different forms. These were impressed under their hearts, or on their arms, and as the mate informed me, with perfect indifference, "burnt with the red-hot iron." Over the hatchways stood a ferocious-looking fellow, with a scourge of many-twisted thongs in his hand, who was the slave-driver of the ship; and whenever he heard the slightest noise below, he shook it over them, and seemed eager to exercise it. I was quite pleased to take this hateful badge out of his hand; and I have kept it ever since as a horrid memorial of the reality, should I ever be disposed to forget the scene I witnessed.

"As soon as the poor creatures saw us looking down at them, their dark and melancholy visages brightened up. They perceived something of sympathy and kindness in our looks, which they had not been accustomed to; and feeling instinctively that we were friends, they immediately began to shout and clap their hands. One or two had picked up a few Portuguese words, and cried out, Viva! viva! The women were particularly excited. They all held up their arms, and when we bent down and shook hands with them, they could not contain their delight: they endeavored to scramble up on their knees, stretching up to kiss our hands, and we understood they knew we were coming to liberate them. Some, however, hung their heads in apparently hopeless dejection; some were greatly emaciated, and some, particularly children, seemed dying. But the circumstance which struck us most forcibly was, how it was possible for such a number of human beings to exist, packed up and wedged together as tight as they could cram, in low cells, three feet high, the greater part of which, except that immediately under the grated hatch-ways, were shut out from light and air; and this, when the thermometer, exposed to open sky, was standing in the shade on our deck at 89°. The space between decks, divided into two compartments, was three feet three inches high; the size of one was 16 feet by 18, and of the other 40 by 21; into the first were crammed the women and the girls, into the second the men and boys. Two hundred and twenty-six fellow-creatures were thus thrust into one space of 288 square feet, and three hundred and thirty into another space of 800 square feet, giving the *whole an average of* 23 *inches; and to each of the women not more than* 13 *inches.* We also found manacles and fetters of different kinds; but it appeared that they all had been taken off before we boarded. The heat of these horrid places was so great, and the odor so offensive, that it was quite impossible to enter them, even had there been room. They were measured as above when the slaves had left them. The officers insisted that the poor suffering creatures should be admitted on deck, to get air and water. . . . . On looking into the places where they had been crammed, there were found some children next the sides of the ship, in the places most remote from air and light; they were lying nearly in a torpid state, after the rest had turned out. The little creatures seemed indifferent as to life or death; and when they

were carried on deck, many of them could not stand.
After enjoying, for a short time, the unusual luxury of
air, some water was brought; it was then that the extent of their sufferings was exposed in a fearful manner.
They all rushed like maniacs towards it. No entreaties,
or threats, or blows could restrain them; they shrieked,
and struggled and fought with one another, for a drop
of this precious liquid, as if they grew rabid at the
sight of it. There is nothing which slaves, in the mid-
passage, suffer from so much as want of water. It is
sometimes usual to take out casks filled with sea-water
as ballast, and when the slaves are received on board,
to start the casks and refill them with fresh. On one
occasion, a ship from Bahia neglected to change the
contents of the casks, and on the mid-passage found, to
their horror, that they were filled with nothing but salt-
water. *All the slaves on board perished.*"

At the time of this seizure, Brazil was precluded
from the slave-trade north of the equator; but the period
had not arrived when, by treaty, the southern trade
was to be extinguished. "The captain of this slaver
was provided with papers, which exhibited an apparent
conformity to the law, and which, false as they may
have been, yet could in no way be absolutely disproved.
The accounts of the slaves themselves, who stated they
had *originally* come from parts of Africa *north* of the
line—the course which the slaver was steering—her

flight from the English cruiser—were circumstances raising suspicion the most violent; but the reader will be not a little disappointed to learn, that, with all this, the case was deemed too doubtful, in point of legal proof, to bear out a legal detention; and the slaver therefore, after nine hours of close investigation, was finally set at liberty, and suffered to proceed..... It was dark when we separated, and the last parting sounds we heard from the unhallowed ship, were the cries and shrieks of slaves, suffering under some bodily infliction."—*Walsh*, vol. ii. pp. 474–484.

The question arises, ought not humanity to have overcome all these considerations, and led to the deliverance of the victims? If one death in such circumstances had occurred, ought not a sense of justice to have led to the detention of the slaver, and the conveyance of the captain to his own government, to be tried for murder?

The traders of France were nearly in the same position with those of the United States, and there was the same necessity for guarding against the abuse of their flag. Before proceeding to the proper history of the American squadron in its efforts for the great purposes it had in view, it may be advisable briefly to notice that France, in 1845, had formed with England a treaty under which both parties engaged to keep a squadron of not less than twenty-six cruisers on the coast. The

number was afterwards, by a separate agreement, reduced on the part of France to twelve vessels.

The reasons for this, and the few captures made by
'French vessels, apply as well to the American cruisers,
and account for the nature of the stipulation in the
treaty of Washington, that the United States should
only employ on the African coast a squadron of eighty
guns. These two nations have not, as England has, the
right by treaty with other powers, to interfere with any
vessels except their own. Hence the captures made by
English cruisers necessarily outnumbered greatly the
captures made by both the other powers.

The duty of the American and French squadron was
in fact restrictive in respect to their own citizens alone;
and while indispensable for the general success of these
operations, they could not exhibit any thing like the
same amount of result in captures, whatever might be
the zeal and activity of the cruisers. Several slavers,
however, have been captured by this squadron; and its
presence has restrained the employment of the French
flag in that traffic.

CHAPTER XXII.

THERE has been noted in the history of Liberia, prior to the establishment of the commonwealth, the occasional arrival of American men-of-war on the west coast of Africa. But an organized squadron was not established until the year 1843.

The question as to the effects arising from the abuse of the American flag was brought into discussion in 1842, between American and British diplomatists. Great Britain had to acknowledge, as the slave-trade by the United States had only been declared piracy in a municipal sense, that although a vessel was fully equipped for the trade, or even had slaves on board, if American, she was in no sense amenable to British cruisers. It, however, leaves the question unsettled, How is a vessel to be ascertained to be American? The plea that any vessel, hoisting any flag, is thereby secured against all interference in all circumstances, never can be seriously offered as a principle of national law. Neither the United States nor any other power has ever acted on a dogma of this breadth. The

United States do not claim that their flag shall give immunity to those who are not American; for such a claim would render it a cover to piracy and to acts of the greatest atrocity. But any vessel which hoists the American flag, claims to be American, and therefore while she may be boarded and examined by an American cruiser, this right is not conceded to a foreign cruiser; for the flag is prima facie evidence, although not conclusive proof of nationality; and if such vessel be really American, the boarding officer will be regarded in the light of a trespasser, and the vessel will have all the protection which that flag supplies. If, on the other hand, the vessel prove not to be American, the flag illegally worn will afford her no protection. Therefore a foreign officer boarding a vessel under the flag of the United States, does it upon his own responsibility for all consequences.

These principles have been carried out in the cooperation and joint cruising with British vessels, as will hereafter be seen, with occasional exceptions of blustering and blundering, when American cruisers were absent. This state of things, however, sometimes produces a strange dilemma. The brig "Lawrence," which was really American, was captured and condemned by an English admiralty court, as a slaver, all of which was contrary to national rights. But it was made out that she was a slaver, and although the master protested, he found himself helpless. The vessel was justly condemned as a slaver, but condemned by the wrong party, which had no legal jurisdiction over her. The master was a pirate if he fell into the hands of American authorities, and thus was debarred all claim for redress.

There is no doubt that many such cases occurred, and would again on the withdrawal of the squadron. This, therefore, gave a kind of impunity to the British cruisers, in violating the rights of the American flag, and kept things in an unsound state. The only remedy for it, was in the permanent establishment of an American squadron on the coast.

Dr. Hall, the agent in the Maryland colony at Cape Palmas says, " No stronger incentive could be given to the commission of these outrageous acts on the part of the British cruisers, than the course pursued by the United States government, in declaring the slave-trade piracy, and then taking no effective steps to prevent its prosecution under their own flag!" Again: " If our force is not increased, and we continue to disregard the prostitution of our flag, annoyances to our merchantmen will more frequently occur. We shall no longer receive the protection of British cruisers, which has ever been rendered to American vessels, and without which the whole coast would be lined with robbers and pirates."

CHAPTER XXIII.

THE treaty of Washington in 1842, settled and de-
fined matters clearly and honorably, both to the United
States and Great Britain; and agreeably to the treaty,
the African squadron was established in the year following, under the command of Commodore Matthew
C. Perry, consisting of the flag-ship Macedonian, the
sloop-of-war Saratoga, the sloop-of-war Decatur, and
the brig Porpoise. The squadron selected its rendez-
vous at Porto Praya, St. Jago, one of the Cape Verde
Islands, in lat. 14° 54′ N. and long. 23° 30′ W.

One of the first acts of this squadron was the chastisement of the natives for an outrage on American
commerce.

The people of Little Berebee, eastward of Cape
Palmas, had some time previously murdered the captain and crew of the American brig "Mary Carver."
This occurrence of itself establishes one point, which is
the necessity of having cruisers on such a coast. The

safety of commerce and the general welfare of the world are promoted by inspiring wrong-doers with wholesome terror.

On two occasions, towns have been captured, and in one instance a town fired, by our squadrons on the coast of Sumatra, for similar atrocities on our merchant vessels. But the impression is soon forgotten, and the necessity for punishment occurs again. Now it may be expedient to act thus at a distance, and trust only to occasional proofs of just severity; but when wrong is ever ready to arise, it would be better that the means of correction were at hand; for in this way is the wrong-doing most readily prevented. Such, therefore, is the best arrangement for all parties.

In a country so near as Africa, and with which the United States is so closely connected, the duty of preventing evil by the presence of power, is imperative; otherwise we at once jeopardize our citizens, and lead the savage into crime.

The commodore, with the frigate Macedonian, the Saratoga, and Decatur, proceeded to Cape Palmas. Such was then the tendency to warfare, that the saluting was misinterpreted as the commencement of a fight, and brought down a hostile tribe to share in the conflict or the spoils. These natives attacked the post called Fort Tubman, eastward of Cape Palmas, and suffered some loss in being driven off.

The squadron then proceeded to Berebee. Having landed a force of about two hundred men, and called together the chiefs and head men, some palavering, and a great deal of lying on the part of the natives, took place. They had really prepared for a conflict, which on their attempting to run off, took place. In the melée, the king was unintentionally killed, eight or ten more suffered, and the palisades and houses were burnt.

Landings took place afterwards at towns along the coast, which had shared in the crime and in the spoils. A few straggling shots were fired from the shores and from the woods, but without causing any loss. The stockades and dwelling-places were committed to the flames.

Four towns were burnt, containing " from fifty to one hundred houses each, neatly built with wicker-work, and thatched with palmetto.... It was the commodore's orders to destroy property, but spare life." This was right; but we have the reflection that the penalties may not fall altogether upon the guilty, and that in every point of view the prevention of such murderous outrages as here met punishment, is, when it can be done by a show of authority, better than such retaliation.

Humanity gained in other respects by this chastisement. The capricious hostilities of the natives against the Maryland colony were checked, and their appetite for plunder brought under wholesome correction, while missionaries were secured against their violence. A native also who was being tortured, under a senseless accusation of causing sickness in a chief, was rescued. All treaties by which the colonies consent to the incorporation of the natives, stipulate that this atrocity shall cease. The thinking men among the natives feel no repugnance in giving it up. It is well that the colonial and native authorities be sustained in counteracting the furious superstition of the mob, by the power of solemn obligation.

In a letter addressed to the Secretary of the American Colonization Society, February 3d, 1844, from J. N. Lewis, acting Colonial Secretary of Liberia, it is remarked, " Some months ago the Porpoise sent home the American brigantine Uncas, under very suspicious circumstances. There can be no doubt but that her intention was to take from the coast a cargo of slaves. Still I am under the impression that your courts will acquit her. I am informed that a bill is before Congress making it criminal for vessels under the American flag to sell goods at slave-factories. If such a bill pass the Houses, the slave-traders will be much injured, as they get their principal supplies from vessels bearing the flag of your country.... Your flag is used to protect the slavers from interference by British vessels of war while they are landing their cargoes; and when the slaves are put on board they throw overboard, or otherwise destroy, the 'stars and stripes,' and depend upon the swiftness of their sailing to escape capture by a British man-of-war."

The squadron was actively employed, cruising over the entire extent of the slave-coast, rendering aid and protection to legal commerce, and checking the slave-trade carried on in American vessels. It was relieved in 1845 by the arrival of Commodore Skinner, with the sloops-of-war Jamestown, Yorktown, and Preble, and the brig Truxton.

The commander of the Decatur, on his return to the United States, in a letter addressed to the Secretary of the Massachusetts Colonization Society, alluding to the object of the Society, says that he cannot but view it "as one of the most interesting and important that can claim the attention and sympathy of the Christian and philanthropist at the present day : besides, that in a political and national point of view, it is, I think, well worthy the study of our ablest statesmen, and the fostering aid of government, in consideration of the present and future prosperity of our agricultural, manufacturing and commercial interests. For were Africa, as she is now, to be struck out of existence, all these interests would feel it a calamity; but were a requisition now made for only a single garment for each individual of the myriads of the African race, it would probably require the energies of the whole world for at least five years to come to supply it."

A letter from an officer of the Truxton, off Sierra Leone, dated March 29th, 1845, says: "Here we are in tow of Her Britannic Majesty's steamer Ardent, with an American schooner, our prize, and a Spanish brigantine, prize to the steamer, captured in the Rio Pongas, one hundred miles to the northward. We had good information when we left Monrovia, that there was a vessel in the Pongas, waiting a cargo; and on our arrival off the river, finding an English man-of-war steamer, arrangements were made to send a combined boat expedition, to make captures for both vessels." The American boats were in charge of Lieutenant Blunt.

"On coming in sight, our little schooner ran up American colors, to protect herself from any suspicion, when our boats, after running along side of her, produced the stripes and stars, much to the astonishment of those on board. She proved to be the Spitfire, of New Orleans, and ran a cargo of slaves from the same place last year. Of only about one hundred tons; but though of so small a size she stowed three hundred and forty six negroes, and landed near Matanzas, Cuba, three hundred and thirty-nine.

"Between her decks, where the slaves are packed, there is not room enough for a man to sit, unless inclining his head forward: their food, half a pint of

rice per day, with one pint of water. No one can imagine the sufferings of slaves on their passage across,
unless the conveyances in which they are taken are
examined. Our friend had none on board, but his
cargo of three hundred were ready in a barracoon,
waiting a good opportunity to start. A good hearty
negro costs but twenty dollars, or thereabouts, and is
purchased for rum, powder, tobacco, cloth, &c. They
bring from three to four hundred dollars in Cuba. The
English are doing every thing in their power to prevent
the slave-trade; and keep a force of thirty vessels on
this coast, all actively cruising. The British boats
also brought down a prize; and the steamer is at this
moment towing the Truxton, the Truxton's prize, and
her own, at the rate of six miles an hour.

"It is extremely difficult to get up these rivers to the
places where the slavers lie. The whole coast is inter-
sected by innumerable rivers, with branches pouring
into them from every quarter, and communicating with
each other by narrow, circuitous and very numerous
creeks, bordered on each side with impenetrable thickets of mangroves. In these creeks, almost concealed by
the trees, the vessels lie, and often elude the strictest
search. But when they have taken on board their living cargo, and are getting out to sea, the British are
very apt to seize them, except, alas! when they are
protected by the banner of the United States."

The Sierra Leone Watchman, of February 19th, adds, that " the slave-traders at Shebar and in the river Gallinas had been much emboldened by the prosecution of Captain Denham, in England, for his summary destruction of sundry barracoons, and openly asserted their determination to seek redress in the English courts, if they were again molested in their operations."

CHAPTER XXIV.

CAPTURE OF THE SLAVE-BARQUE "PONS"—SLAVES LANDED AT
MONROVIA—CAPTURE OF THE SLAVE-EQUIPPED VESSELS
"PANTHER," "ROBERT WILSON," "CHANCELLOR," ETC.—LET-
TER FROM THE "JAMESTOWN" IN REFERENCE TO LIBERIA—
AFFAIR WITH THE NATIVES NEAR CAPE PALMAS—SEIZURE
AND CONDEMNATION OF THE SLAVER "H. N. GAMBRILL."

ON the 30th of November, the Yorktown, Commander Bell, captured the American bark "Pons," off
Kabenda, on the south coast, with eight hundred and
ninety-six slaves on board. This vessel had been at
Kabenda about twenty days before, during which
she had been closely watched by the British cruiser
"Cygnet." The Cygnet, leaving one morning, the
master of the Pons, James Berry, immediately gave
up the ship to Gallano, the Portuguese master. During the day, so expeditious had they been, that water
and provisions were received on board, and nine hundred and three slaves were embarked; and at eight
o'clock the same evening, the Pons was under way.
Instead of standing out to sea, she kept in with the
coast during the night; and in the morning discover-

ing the British cruiser, furled sails, and drifted so close to the shore that the negroes came down to the beach in hopes of her being wrecked. She thus eluded detection. When clear of the Cygnet, she stood out to sea, and two days afterwards was captured by the Yorktown.

Commander Bell says : " The captain took us for an English man-of-war, and hoisted the American colors ; and no doubt had papers to correspond." These he threw overboard. " As soon as the slaves were recaptured, they gave a shout that could have been heard a mile."

During the night eighteen of the slaves had died, and one jumped overboard. The master accounted for the number dying from the necessity of his sending below all the slaves on deck, and closing the hatches, when he fell in with the Yorktown, in order to escape detection. Ought not every such death to be regarded as murder ?

Commander Bell says : " The vessel has no slave-deck, and upwards of eight hundred and fifty were piled, almost in bulk, on water-casks below. As the ship appeared to be less than three hundred and fifty tons, it seemed impossible that one-half could have lived to cross the Atlantic. About two hundred filled up the spar-deck alone when they were permitted to come up from below ; and yet the captain assured me that it was his intention to have taken *four hundred more* on board, if he could have spared the time.

" The stench from below was so great that it was impossible to stand more than a few minutes near the hatchways. Our men who went below from curiosity, were forced up sick in a few minutes: then all the hatches were off. What must have been the sufferings of those poor wretches, when the hatches were closed! I am informed that very often in these cases, the stronger will strangle the weaker; and this was probably the reason why so many died, or rather were found dead the morning after the capture. None but an eye-witness can form a conception of the horrors these poor creatures must endure in their transit across the ocean.

" I regret to say, that most of this misery is produced by our own countrymen. They furnish the means of conveyance in spite of existing enactments; and although there are strong circumstances against Berry, the late master of the Pons, sufficient to induce me to detain him, if I should meet him, I fear neither he nor his employers can be reached by our present laws."

In this letter to the Secretary of the Navy, Commander Bell further adds : " For twenty days did Berry wait in the roadstead of Kabenda, protected by the flag of his country, yet closely watched by a foreign man-of-war, who was certain of his intention : but the instant that cruiser is compelled to withdraw for a few hours, he springs at the opportunity of enriching himself and owners, and disgracing the flag which had protected him."

The prize "Pons" was taken to Monrovia. There the slaves were landed, and gave the people a practical exhibition of the trade by which their ancestors had been torn from their homes. In the fourteen days intervening between the capture and arrival of the vessel at Monrovia, one hundred and fifty had died.

"The slaves," says the Monrovia Herald of December 28th, "were much emaciated, and so debilitated that many of them found difficulty in getting out of the boats. Such a spectacle of misery and wretchedness, inflicted by a lawless and ferocious cupidity, so excited our people, that it became unsafe for the captain of the slaver, who had come to look on, to remain on the beach. Eight slaves died in harbor before they were landed, and the bodies were thrown overboard."

The slaves, who were from eight to thirty years of age, came starved and thirsting from on board. Caution was required in giving them food. "When it was supposed that the danger of depletion was over, water was poured into a long canoe, into which they plunged like hungry pigs into a trough—the stronger faring the best."

Still, the kindness of human nature had not altogether been obliterated by length and intensity of suffering.

Two boys, brothers, had found beside them a younger boy of the same tribe, who was ill. They contrived to nestle together on the deck, under such shelter as the cover of the long-boat offered them—a place where the pigs, if they are small enough, are generally stowed. There they made a bed of some oakum for their dying companion, and placed a piece of old canvas under his head. Night and day one was always awake to watch him. Hardship rendered their care fruitless: the night after the vessel anchored he died, and was thrown overboard.

The recaptured were apprenticed out, and kindly cared for by the Liberians. Several of them were found, when the Perry visited Monrovia, to have become members of churches, and others were attending Sunday-schools.

Several empty slavers were captured by the squadron about this period; they are thus noticed by the National Intelligencer:—"It is remarkable that within the same week, should have arrived in our ports as prizes to the American squadron, for having been engaged in the slave-trade—the Pons, above mentioned, captured by the Yorktown; the Panther, a prize of the same vessel, which arrived at Charleston on Monday; and the Robert Wilson, a prize to the sloop-of-war Jamestown, which reached Charleston on Thursday."

In 1846, the sloop-of-war Marion, brigs Dolphin and

Boxer, with the flag-ship United States, Commodore Read, constituted the squadron.

Sixty miles of additional sea-coast territory had been purchased by Governor Roberts, from the natives. The influence of traders, of the slave-trade, and even of England being thrown in the way of obtaining possession of the purchased territory, Governor Roberts made application to the commodore, that one of the vessels of the squadron might cruise for several weeks within the limited territory, for the purpose of facilitating negotiation. The Dolphin was assigned this service; her commander offered General Lewis, the agent, a passage to such points as he wished to visit, and otherwise rendered service as circumstances required.

The Dolphin was lying at Cape Mount, watching the suspicious American bark "Chancellor," which was trading with a slave-dealer named Canot. The British cruiser "Favorite" was stationed off the Cape, and suggested to the chiefs, that as they were in treaty with his government for the suppression of the slave-trade, and as Canot was on their territory making preparations for slaving, they were bound to destroy his establishment. The chiefs accordingly burnt his premises, containing a large amount of goods he had shipped at New York. Canot having been by no means secure in conscience, had left with his family and taken up his residence in Monrovia.

The Dolphin proceeded to Porto Praya for stores, and the Chancellor was watched in the mean time by the British cruisers at the Cape and at the Gallinas. Among the traverses worked by the slave-traders, the practice had been adopted, to fill canoes with slaves and send them off the coast, to be picked up by vessels in search of a cargo, which, from the blockade, could not reach the shore. In one instance, fifty of these were found in a single canoe, and taken by a British cruiser. On the return of the Dolphin, the Chancellor was seized by Commander Pope as a prize, on the ground of having a slave-deck laid, and water-casks with rice on board sufficient for a slave cargo, and sent to the United States for adjudication.

The commodore, after having cruised along the entire extent of the slave-coast, rendering such service as American interests required, was relieved, in 1847, by the sloop-of-war Jamestown, Commodore Bolton. The frigate United States then proceeded to the Mediterranean station, to complete her cruise.

The commander of the Jamestown writes, in relation to Monrovia, "It was indeed to me a novel and interesting sight, although a southern man, to look upon these emancipated slaves legislating for themselves, and discussing freely, if not ably, the principles of human rights, on the very continent, and perhaps the very spot, where some of their ancestors were sold into slavery. . . . . Liberia, I think, is now safe, and may be left after a while to stand alone. Would it not be advisable, then, for the Colonization Society to turn its attention to some other portion of the coast, and extend the area of Christian and philanthropic efforts to bettering the condition of the colored people of our country, by sowing on other parts of the coast some of the good seed which has produced so bountifully on the free soil of Liberia. . . . . In no part of the world have I met with a more orderly, sober, religious and moral community than is to be found at Monrovia. On the Sabbath, it is truly a joyful sound to hear hymns of praise offered up to Him who doth promise, ' where two or three are gathered together in His name, there He is in the midst of them;' and a pleasure to observe how very general the attendance upon divine worship is among these people. I believe every man and woman in Monrovia, of any respectability, is a member of the church. If you take a family dinner with the President (and his hospitable door is always open to strangers), a blessing is asked upon the good things before you set to. Take a dinner at Colonel Hicks's (who, by the way, keeps one of the very nicest tables), and ' mine host,' with his shiny,. black, intelligent face, will ask a blessing on the tempting viands set before you."

This may be considered a fair type of the views of

persons generally who visit Liberia, judging the people comparatively. Our estimate of them ought not
to be conformed to the standard of an American population.

The squadron confined mostly to the north coast, rendered such services as the commerce of the United
States and the interest of its citizens required, and
checked the perversion of the flag to the continuance
of the slave-trade. The year following, the commodore
was relieved by the Yorktown, bearing the broad pendant of Commodore Cooper, and with the flag-ship
proceeded to the Mediterranean.

Commodore Cooper soon after assuming the command, suffering from ill-health, returned to the United
States, and the African squadron was assigned to Commodore Gregory, who sailed in the summer of 1849,
in the U. S. sloop-of-war Portsmouth. It consisted of
the sloops-of-war John Adams, Dale, Yorktown, and
the brigs Bainbridge, Porpoise and Perry. Three or
four slavers were captured, the entire slave-coast closely
examined, and such services rendered to our commercial interests as were required.

In 1851, Commodore Lavallette, with the Germantown,
relieved Commodore Gregory. He made an active
cruise, capturing one or two suspected slavers, and
otherwise carrying out the views of the government in
the establishment of the squadron. At the expiration

of two years, the frigate Constitution arrived, bearing the broad pendant of Commodore Mayo, who now commands the squadron, consisting of the sloops-of-war Marion and Dale, with the brig Perry.

In visiting Cape Palmas in the summer of 1853, one of the unintelligible quarrels common to the coast was then raging between the Barbo people and their neighbors along the Cavally. Interfering to settle the matter was by no means acceptable. When the commodore proposed going on shore for the purpose, the proposal was met by an intimation to go away, or they would cut off his head. The launch was sent off well manned, with a howitzer. The natives assembled with a show of resistance, but a shot being thrown among them, brought the belligerents to terms. They apologized, and promised to reconcile their enmities, and took the oath of friendship.

The American schooner N. H. Gambrill, of Baltimore, attempting to re-awaken the small remains of slaving off the river Congo, was seized by the frigate Constitution on the 3d of December, arrived in New York in charge of a prize-officer, and on the 30th of January, 1854, was condemned in the U. S. Circuit Court, for having been engaged in the slave-trade.

Considering that we have had no steamers on the coast, and the number of vessels being small, the squadron has been efficient in fulfilling its duties. Its

appearance alone had great influence. It showed a
determination in our government to share in the naval
charge of these vast seas and shores. Our country
thus became present, as it were, in power to repress,
and if need be, by punishment to avenge outrages on
our citizens or their property. It checked, by important captures, the desecration of the American flag,
and has had an essential agency towards removing the
guilt of the slave-trade from the world. Had we no
squadron on the African coast, American vessels would
with impunity pursue the iniquitous traffic; our commerce would be exposed, and our citizens subject to
outrage. The nature of the proceedings of this squadron, the circumstances of its experience, and the effect
of its operations, will be more clearly apparent in the
subsequent detail of the proceedings of the U. S. brig
"Perry," during the years 1850–1851. The following
chapters will comprise a synopsis of these proceedings,
and a compilation from the correspondence in relation
to them.

CHAPTER XXV.

ON the 21st of December, 1849, the "Perry" arrived
at the Cape Verde Islands, and was reported to the
commodore of the American squadron. On the 9th
of the succeeding month a communication was received
from the commodore intimating his intention to dispatch the vessel immediately on a cruise south of the
equator : stating, that he should leave the commander
to the exercise of his own judgment in general matters ;
but as an object of the first consequence, called his
attention to the observance of every means calculated

to preserve and insure the health of his crew. He had been counselled by the experience of the fleet surgeon and others, that it was absolutely necessary for white persons to avoid exposure to the heat of the day, and to the night air on shore, and always when at anchor to lie at a sufficient distance from the shore to avoid its deleterious effects. Besides these precautions, cleanliness of ship and persons, constant ventilation, proper food and clothing, sufficiency of water, and good discipline, had hitherto produced the happiest results, and no doubt would continue to do so. A number of Kroomen sufficient to man two boats, were to be furnished at Monrovia, which would relieve the crew ordinarily from the hazards of that duty. The officers and men should not be permitted to visit the shore unnecessarily; or at all, when they could not, with certainty, return at any moment. Care was to be observed in procuring good wholesome water, and in such abundance as to insure at all times, if possible, a full allowance to the crew; and also to furnish them with fresh provisions and vegetables, whenever the opportunity offered.

A record of all vessels boarded, with a report according to the form furnished, was required.

The commander was reminded of the disposition of the government to cultivate and maintain the most friendly intercourse with all other nations or people, and was directed to govern himself accordingly.

The commodore also directed the commander of the Perry, when that vessel should be in all respects ready for sea, to proceed direct to Monrovia, where he would meet the U. S. sloop-of-war Yorktown; the commander of which had been instructed to fill up the Perry with provisions, furnish sixteen Kroomen, and to render all needful assistance required to expedite her movements. Making no unnecessary delay at Monrovia, the commander of the Perry was to proceed thence on the cruise, the limits of which would extend to the lat. of Cape St. Mary's, 13° south.

It was recommended, that from Monrovia he should proceed off from the coast, keeping well to the westward, until crossing the equator and reaching the southern limits of the cruising-ground, for the purpose of avoiding the prevailing winds and currents, which, south of the line, would be adverse to progress in-shore, but favorable to a close examination, on the return northward.

The object of the cruise was to protect the lawful commerce of the United States, and, under the laws of the United States, to prevent the flag and citizens of the United States from being engaged in the slave-trade; and to carry out, in good faith, the treaty stipulations between the United States and England.

After reaching the southern point of destination, or nearly so, the vessel was to cruise along the coast, examining the principal points, or slave-stations; such as the Salinas, Benguela, Loanda, Ambriz, River Congo, and intermediate places, back towards Monrovia : the commander acting in all cases according to the best of his judgment, upon the information he might obtain, and circumstances that might present themselves; taking care, in no case, to exceed the instructions of the Hon. Secretary of the Navy, furnished for his guidance.

Should British cruisers be met, he might act in concert with them, so far as the instructions permitted.

It was further noticed, that a number of suspected American vessels had been hovering on the coast, between Cape St. Mary's and Cape Lopez, and that some of them had left the coast with slaves. Vessels clearly liable to capture and not provided with cargoes, might be sent directly to the United States. All captives found on board were to be landed at Monrovia.

The Perry left the Cape Verde Islands on the day in which her orders were issued, and arrived at Monrovia on the 20th. She there received provisions from the Yorktown, and sixteen Kroomen from the shore. Having exchanged salutes and visits of ceremony, she sailed on her southern cruise, and arrived at St. Philip de Benguela, after a passage of forty-one days, having, during the interval, boarded three legal traders. This passage was made on the port tack by standing to the southward and westward, into the southeast trades. But the passage from the north to the south coast should, in all cases, be made in-shore on the starboard tack; as will be explained hereafter, during the third cruise of the Perry.

At Benguela, which is a Portuguese settlement, next in importance to St. Paul de Loanda, although now much dilapidated, and where the slave-trade has been carried on to a great extent, the customary exchange of a national salute and official visits was duly observed.

The commander ascertained, on his arrival, that the American merchant vessels were subject to greater restrictions than probably would have been the case had a man-of-war occasionally made her appearance in that quarter. He therefore intimated to the governor that our cruisers, in future, would visit that part of the coast more frequently than they had done for the last few years.

Information was received, that five days previous to the arrival of the Perry, an English cruiser had captured, near this place, a brig, with eight hundred slaves on board. In this case, it appeared that the vessel came from Rio de Janeiro, under American colors and papers, with an American captain and crew; and had been, when on the coast, transferred to a Brazilian captain and crew, the Americans having gone on shore with the papers. The captured slaver was sent to the Island of St. Helena for adjudication.

After remaining three days at Benguela, where neither fresh water nor provisions could be procured, the Perry weighed anchor and ran down the coast, examining all intermediate points, and boarding several vessels during the passage to Loanda. This city is the capital of Loango, and the most flourishing of the Portuguese establishments on the African coast.

In a letter announcing the arrival of the vessel, and her reception by the authorities, the Navy Department was informed that an English steamer had arrived, having recently captured a slaver, the barque Navarre, which had sailed from Rio de Janeiro to St. Catharine's, where she had fitted up for a slave cargo, and received a Brazilian captain and crew. When boarded by the English steamer, the slaver had American colors flying; and on being told by the commander that her papers were forged, and yet that he could not search the vessel, but must send her to an American cruiser, the captain then ordered the American colors to be hauled down, and the Brazilian to be hoisted, declaring that she was Brazilian property, sent the Brazilian captain and crew on deck, and gave up the vessel.

The commander of the Perry also informed the Navy Department that, soon after his arrival at Loanda, he had received from various sources information of the abuse of the American flag in connection with the slave-trade; and inclosed copies of letters and papers addressed to him by the British commissioner, and the commander of an English cruiser, which gave authentic information on the subject.

He suggested that as the legitimate commerce of the United States exceeded that of Great Britain and France, on the coast south of the equator, and the American flag had been used to cover the most extensive slave-trade, it would seem that the presence of one or two men-of-war, and the appointment of a consul, or some public functionary at that place, were desirable.

He noticed that the depôt of stores at Porto Praya was so far removed, that a vessel could barely reach the southern point of the slave-stations before she was compelled, for want of provisions, to return and replenish. A consul or storekeeper there might, as is the case with the English or French, supply that division of the squadron, and thus a force might constantly be kept on that side of the equator, where, until the arrival of the Perry, there had been no American man-of-war for a period of two years.

It had been intimated to him, as he further stated, by Americans, that if the U. S. government were aware of the atrocities committed under its flag, it might be induced to take some measures for preventing the sale of American vessels on the African coast, as in nearly every instance the vessel had been sold for the purpose of engaging in the slave-trade. But if that should be regarded as too great a check upon the commercial interests of the United States, such sale, if made on that coast, might be duly notified to the proposed consul or agent, that the vessel should be known as having changed her nationality.

All information showing the number of American vessels and American citizens engaged in the slave-trade being regarded as desirable, interviews on the subject were held not only with the Americans engaged in mercantile pursuits, but with others, from whom reliable information could be derived. A list of American vessels, which had been on the coast during the preceding year, was procured. Many of these vessels came from Rio and adjoining ports, with two sets of papers. A sea-letter had been granted by the consul in good faith, according to law, on the sale of a vessel in a foreign port; the cargo corresponded with the manifest; the consular certificate, crew list, port clearance, and all papers were in form. Several of these vessels, after discharging their cargoes, changed their flag; the American captain and crew, with flag and papers, leaving the vessel, and she instantly becoming invested with Spanish, Portuguese, or Brazilian nationality.*

By this arrangement, as the United States never has consented, and never ought to consent, even on the African coast, to grant to Great Britain, or any other power, the right of search, a slaver, when falling in with an American cruiser, would be prepared to elude search and capture by the display of a foreign ensign and papers, even had she slaves on board. And on the other hand, she might the same day fall in with a British cruiser, and by displaying her flag, and presenting the register or sea-letter, vindicate her American nationality. This illustrates the importance of men-of-war, belonging to each nation, cruising in company for the detection of slavers.

Great Britain being in treaty with Spain, Portugal, Brazil, Sardinia and other powers, the proposed mode of co-operation would lead to the detection of slavers under almost any nationality except that of France, which government has an efficient squadron of steam-

---

* The papers of the second slaver captured by the Perry were in form, excepting the crew list, which showed but one American on board, who was master of the vessel. And in a letter of instructions from the reputed owner, he was required to leave whenever the Italian supercargo directed him to do so. This shows how readily the nationality of a vessel may be changed.

ers and sailing vessels on the coast, fully prepared to vindicate her own flag.*

In reference to vessels ostensibly American, which had been engaged in the slave-trade, a British officer, on the 21st of March, 1850, in a letter inclosing a list of American vessels which had been boarded by the cruiser under his command, stated that all these vessels had afterwards taken slaves from the coast; and with the exception of the "Lucy Ann,"† captured with five hundred slaves on board by a British steamer, had escaped. The registers, or sea-letters, of these vessels appeared to be genuine; and he being unable to detect

---

* The master of the first slaver captured by the Perry, stated that had he not supposed she was an English cruiser, he would have been prepared with a foreign flag, and otherwise, to have eluded search and capture; and that on a former occasion he had been boarded by an English cruiser, when, to use his own expression, he "bluffed off John Bull with that flag;" referring to the American ensign.

† The "Lucy Ann," when captured, was boarded fifty or sixty miles to leeward, or north of Loanda. She had an American flag flying, although her papers had been deposited in the consul's office at Rio. The English boarding-officer, who was not allowed to see any papers, suspecting her character, prolonged his visit for some time. As he was about leaving the vessel, a cry or stifled groan was heard issuing from the hold. The main hatches were apparently forced up from below, although a boat was placed over them, and the heads of many people appeared. Five hundred and forty-seven slaves were found in the hold, almost in a state of suffocation. The master then hauled down the American flag, declared the vessel to be Brazilian, and gave her up.

any inaccuracies in their papers, his duty to the American flag had ceased. The vessels in his list had been boarded by himself; but the senior officer of the division was referred to, " who could give a list of many more, all of which would have been good prizes to an officer having the right of search ;" for he was well assured that they went over to that coast, fully fitted and equipped for the slave-trade.

He expressed a regret that the pleasure of making acquaintance with the commander of the Perry had only fallen to his lot at a moment when the term of his service on the western coast of Africa had expired; but was satisfied that not only on the part of the senior officer commanding the southern division, but also of his brother officers still remaining in service on the coast, the most cordial co-operation would be afforded in the suppression of the slave-trade.

The British commissioner, of the mixed commission under the treaty between Great Britain and Portugal for the suppression of the African slave-trade, also furnished a list of suspected slavers which had claimed American nationality.

On the 25th of March, the commander requested the English captain to give him a detailed account of the circumstances attending the capture of the barque Navarre, by her B. M. steamer Fire Fly.

He asked for this information, as the Navarre was

boarded when under American colors, although displaying Brazilian colors when captured.

In reply, the English captain informed him that the slave barque Navarre, seized under the Brazilian flag, on the 19th instant, had the American ensign flying at the time she was boarded. The boarding-officer having doubts of her nationality, in consequence of her papers not appearing to be regular, he himself, although ill at the time, considered it his duty to go on board, when, being convinced that her papers were false, he informed the person calling himself master of her, that it was his duty to send him to the American squadron, or in the event of not falling in with them, to New York. The master immediately went on deck and ordered the mate to haul down the American ensign—to throw it overboard—and to hoist their proper colors. The American ensign was hauled down and thrown overboard by the mate, who immediately hoisted the Brazilian ensign. A man then came on deck from below, saying that he was captain of the vessel; that she was Brazilian property, and fully fitted for the slave-trade; which the person who first appeared acknowledged, stating that he himself was a Brazilian subject. Having obtained this from them in writing, the person who first called himself captain having signed it, and having had the signing of the document witnessed by two officers, he opened her hatches, found all the Brazilian crew below, slave-deck laid, water filled, provisions for the slaves, and slave-shackles.

At this period the agent of a large and respectable commercial house in Salem, Massachusetts, established at Loanda, submitted to the commander of the Perry a copy of the treaty between the United States and Portugal, together with a letter from the Secretary of State, and a paper from an officer of the Treasury Department, exhibiting the commercial rights of the United States under said treaty.

The agent claimed that agreeably to the treaty, a portion of the duties were to be remitted when a vessel arrived direct from the United States; which claim had not been acknowledged at Loanda, on the ground that the vessels were in the habit of touching at the native ports, while the agent insisted that as these ports were not recognized as within the jurisdiction of a civilized government, the Portuguese provincial authorities had not faithfully observed the treaty stipulations.

The subject was referred to the Government.

After remaining a week in Loanda, making proper repairs on the vessel, and refreshing the crew, the Perry ran down the coast to the northward, for the purpose of cruising off Ambriz, a noted slave-station, under native authority, with several factories for legal trade. Arriving at this station the following morning, three English steam cruisers were in sight. The second lieutenant of the Perry was sent to call on the commanding officer of the southern division of the British squadron, who soon afterwards called on board the American cruiser in person.

In a letter, dated the 24th of March, the British commanding officer informed the commander of the Perry, that it afforded him great pleasure to witness the presence of a United States vessel on the southwest coast of Africa, to be employed in co-operation with British vessels in the suppression of the slave-trade. And he therefore took the liberty to transmit, by the officer of the Perry, kindly sent to wait upon him, two documents connected with Brazilian slave-vessels, which had lately come over to that coast, displaying the American ensign, and presenting to the English boarding-officer (as they had proven) fraudulent American papers.

He assured him, that in the necessary examination of these papers, every respect had been paid to the American flag, and the visit made in strict accordance with the treaty between the United States of America and Great Britain; and that it was not until the different vessels had voluntarily hauled down their ensigns and destroyed their papers, stating at the same time that they were Brazilians, that possession was taken of them. He intimated that a letter—a copy of which was inclosed—had been addressed to him by a lieutenant of the "Cyclops," who had conducted to the Island of St. Helena one of the prizes, on board of which were two American seamen, and that this letter would give some idea of the plan pursued by parties in Brazil, to equip and man Brazilian slave-vessels.

The inclosed letter, above referred to, stated that American seamen were often enticed on board of slavers, without knowing their real character until it was too late to leave them. And that the owner of a lodging-house in Rio, where two or three sailors were boarding, offered, on one occasion, to get them a ship bound to the United States, which, at the time, was loading at Vittoria—a harbor to the northward of Cape Frio. They agreed to ship; and, after receiving their advance, proceeded in a small steamer outside the harbor of Rio, when they were transferred to a schooner, in company with a number of Brazilians; and, in a few days, reached Vittoria. On joining the slaver, which was named "Pilot," they discovered her true character, but were not allowed to go on shore; and were promised, on their arrival in Africa, a good reward, with the option of returning in the vessel, or having their passage found in another. It was affirmed that these men had never seen the American consul; and the crew-list, register and other papers, were forgeries. Also that the owner of the Pilot was a Brazilian, and esteemed one of the richest men in the empire. Two slave-steamers were owned by him; and it was said that he had boasted that not a week passed that he had not had a full cargo of slaves landed on the coast. He then owned seven or eight vessels, sailing under the American flag, which he had bought in Rio, and whose papers were all forgeries. One of the vessels belonging to the rich Brazil merchant, and sailing alternately under the American and Brazilian flag, had made nine clear voyages; and on the last voyage, before she was captured, the American captain had landed at Ambriz, with part of his crew, his flag and papers; and then the vessel shipped one thousand slaves.

An American was the consignee of these vessels, bearing his country's flag. He obtained for them masters, crews, flag and papers; and received for his agency a percentage on all slaves landed from the vessels.

During the month when the Pilot was equipped at Vittoria, two other slavers were also fitting out for the slave-trade, under the American flag; viz., the "Casco" and the "Snow." The former was afterwards captured, with four hundred and fifty slaves, by the English steamer "Pluto;" the other entered the harbor of Rio under Brazilian colors, having landed her slaves outside.

The Pilot made the African coast near Benguela;

and afterwards anchored at Bahia Longa, where, there being no slaves ready for shipment—as eight hundred had been, a few days previously, shipped in a two-topsail schooner—she was ordered, by the slave-agents, to remain at sea for ten days. On making the land at the expiration of that time, the English steamers Fire Fly, Star, and Pluto, being at Ambriz, she was again ordered to sea for ten days; when, on anchoring at the latter place, she was captured by the English steamer Cyclops. She was to have shipped twelve hundred slaves, who had been for some time ready for a slave-steamer—then so strictly blockaded at Santos by the English steamer Hydra, as to prevent her leaving port.

Such was the information contained in this letter.

During this correspondence with the British officers, the Perry was cruising off Ambriz, in company with a part of the British squadron, for the purpose of boarding and searching all American vessels suspected of being engaged in the slave-trade, on that part of the coast.

After cruising for several days, the commander-in-chief of the British naval forces, bearing his pendant at the main of the steam-frigate Centaur, appeared in the offing. The Perry hauled up her courses, and saluted him with thirteen guns, which were duly returned. An official call was made on the commodore, and an arrangement settled for the joint cruising of the Perry and steamer Cyclops.

This cruising had continued for a week or more, when the arrival of the U. S. sloop-of-war John Adams constituted her commander the senior American officer south of the equator; he, accordingly, while in company, relieved the Perry of the correspondence with the British officers.

A short time after the arrival of the Adams, it became necessary for her to visit Loanda, when the Perry was again left with the Cyclops, cruising off Ambriz.

CHAPTER XXVI.

On the 13th of April, the American brigantine
Louisa Beaton, which a few days previously had been
boarded, examined, and proven to be a legal trader,
ran out of Ambriz under American colors. One or
two of the officers who had been on shore, on their return in the evening, reported that it was rumored that
the Louisa Beaton had shipped and escaped with a
cargo of slaves.

That vessel had then made a good offing, and was
out of sight. Acting under the impression of the report thus conveyed, an armed boat, in charge of the
second lieutenant and junior passed midshipman, was
dispatched on each beam, and with the Perry stood out
to sea, in the hope of overhauling the chase. At daylight, being out of sight of the land, and no sail visible,
the boats were picked up, and the vessel stood in
towards Ambriz.

During the succeeding day, on joining company with the Cyclops, the second lieutenant was sent with a message to her commander, requesting that he might remain on board, and that the Cyclops would steam out to sea, on a southwest course, with a view of overhauling the Louisa Beaton, and ascertaining if there was any foundation for this charge against her.

The proposition was readily complied with; and after running forty miles off the land, and no sail being seen, the steamer rejoined the Perry.

A letter from the commanding officer of the British division was received, dated April 15th, containing information to the following effect: that he had the pleasure of receiving the intelligence, which the commander of the Perry had kindly sent him by the lieutenant, informing him that a report had been circulated, that the American brigantine Louisa Beaton, which vessel was lying at Ambriz, in company with the British and American cruisers, on the 7th instant, had shipped a cargo of negroes. He had observed the Louisa Beaton weigh from Ambriz on the evening of the 12th instant, and pass close to the stern of the Perry, with her colors flying; and at sunset she was observed by him, close in with the land. He also sighted her next morning, and continued to see her until the evening, apparently working in-shore to the southward.

As the wind had been exceedingly light all night,

he thought it possible that the steamer might overtake her, and accordingly proposed to the lieutenant of the Perry to accompany him, and watch the proceedings of the vessel, in case they should discover her. The lieutenant having acceded to this proposal, he steamed to the westward for nearly forty miles, but saw nothing of her; and was of opinion, that the report affecting the character of the Louisa Beaton was not *then* correct, and that when intelligence next arrived from Loanda, she would be found to have reached that place.

But he believed it very probable that she had been disposed of by sale, in consequence of the slave-dealers not having been successful, as they had effected the embarkation of only two cargoes of negroes that year (1850), and therefore all the vessels that could be procured, no matter at what expense, would be eagerly sought after. But, as he had heard that there was no water at Ambriz, he had supposed it possible that arrangements were making for the Louisa Beaton's cargo to be discharged at Loanda; whence, after having procured the necessary articles and fitments required, she would probably return to Ambriz for the negroes. He remarked that this would be no new occurrence, as many American vessels had been disposed of in a similar manner, and escaped with cargoes of Africans, since he had been stationed on the coast.

Had no American man-of-war been present on the

12th instant, when the Louisa Beaton left Ambriz, he should have considered it his duty (from there having been observed, whilst in company with her on the 7th instant, a large quantity of plank, sufficient for a slave-deck, on her upper deck, together with water-casks, which would have created suspicion) to have visited her, and satisfied himself that her nationality had not been changed, by *sale*, at Ambriz; not taking it for granted, that the flag displayed by any vessel is a sufficient evidence of her nationality.

He added, that as it was probable that he might not meet the John Adams previous to the Perry's leaving the coast for Porto Praya, the commander of the Perry would oblige him, by forwarding a copy of that letter to his senior officer, for the information of the commander-in-chief of the American squadron, as it would be his duty to lay it before the British commander-in-chief, in the sincere hope that some arrangement would be made by those officers to put a stop to that nefarious system on the southwest coast of Africa.

A boat had been dispatched from the Perry to Loanda, which found the Louisa Beaton, still offering no cause of suspicion, lying in that port.

On the 17th of April, the commander of the Perry informed the British commanding officer that he had received and forwarded the above letter, agreeably to his request; intimating at the same time that he had boarded the Louisa Beaton at sea, several days before her arrival, and found her to be a legal American trader—a character which she sustained while at anchor with the several men-of-war at Ambriz; and that he had no reason, after an absence of three days, to suppose that she could, in the mean time, have fitted for a slave cargo; and therefore did not consider it to be his duty again to board her; that he was happy to inform him that the report of the Louisa Beaton's having taken slaves at Ambriz, was untrue; and that she was then at St. Paul de Loanda.

In relation to the British commander " not taking it for granted, that the flag displayed by any vessel is a sufficient evidence of her nationality," the commander of the Perry remarked that the flag which a vessel wears is *primâ facie*, although it is not conclusive proof of nationality. It is a mere emblem, which loses its true character when it is worn by those who have no right to it. On the other hand, those who lawfully display the flag of the United States, will have all the protection which it supplies. Therefore, when a foreign cruiser boards a vessel under this flag, she will do it upon her own responsibility.

On the 19th of April, the British commander acknowledged the receipt of the communication of the 17th instant, in reply to his of the 15th, in which he expressed himself glad to learn that the report of the Louisa Beaton's having shipped a cargo of slaves at Ambriz, was incorrect; but as vessels were disposed to change their nationality, and escape with slaves, " in so very short a period of time as a few hours," he would respectfully suggest the necessity of keeping a strict watch over the movements of the Louisa Beaton, should she appear again on that part of the coast.

Two armed boats were at this time frequently dispatched from the Perry a long distance in chase of vessels, when the winds were too light to enable her to overhaul them.

On one occasion, these boats had been in chase of a vessel for ten hours, and encountered, a few minutes before overhauling her, a violent squall of wind and rain. When the squall had passed over, after night-fall, the strange vessel was, for a moment, descried within long-gun shot of the Perry. A thirty-two pound shot was thrown astern of her, and, quite suddenly, the fog again enveloped her, and she became invisible.

On the return of the boats which had succeeded in boarding the chase, the commander regretted to learn that the strange vessel was a Portuguese man-of-war. In the year following, when falling in with her at Benguela, he availed himself of an early opportunity to apologize for having fired, as this had been done under the impression that the vessel was a merchantman; and for the purpose of bringing her to, in order to ascertain her character.

The John Adams, after a short stay at Loanda, again appeared off Ambriz, and resumed her cruising. The Perry's provisions had now become nearly exhausted; and she was ordered by the John Adams to proceed to the north coast with dispatches to the commodore.

The land along the southern African coast, from lat. 7° south, extending to Benguela, and even to the Cape of Good Hope, is more elevated than the coast to the northward towards the equator. Long ranges of high bluff may be seen, extending, in some cases, from twenty to thirty miles. A short distance to leeward, or north, of Ambriz, is a remarkable range of hills, with heavy blocks of granite around them, resembling, at a distance, a small village. The "granite pillar," which shoots up in the air, towering above the surrrounding blocks like a church-spire, is a good landmark to the cruisers off Ambriz. They often find themselves at daylight, after beating, during the night, to the southward, drifted down abreast of it by the northerly current.

The natives along this coast, unlike those of northern Guinea, who are bold, energetic and effective, comparatively, when muscular force is required, are marked by very opposite traits; softness, pliancy and flexibility, distinguish their moral and mental character. They are mostly below the middle stature, living in villages, in rude, rush-thatched huts; subsisting principally upon fish, and the plantain, which is the African bread-fruit tree.

These people present some of the lowest forms of humanity.

The temperature of both the air and water within southern intertropical Africa, averages, during the months of August and September, 72°, and off Benguela, on one occasion, early in July, the air temperature was as low as 60°, while in the month of February, the thermometer seldom reaches a higher point than 82°.

It is known that the southeast trade-winds prevail in the Atlantic ocean, between the African and American continents, south of the equator to the tropic of Capricon, and the northeast trade to the southward of the tropic of Cancer. It is of course generally understood, that the sun heats the equatorial regions to a higher temperature than is found anywhere else, and that the air over these regions is consequently expanded and rendered lighter than that which envelops the regions at a distance. This causes the whole mantle of air round the earth, for a short distance near the equator, to be displaced and thrown upwards (like the draft of a chimney), by the cooler and heavier air rushing in, in steadfast and continuous streams, from the north and south. The earth's revolution carries every thing on its surface somewhat against these air-currents in their progress, so that they appear to sweep aslant along the earth and sea, coming from northeast and southeast. In consequence of the greater amount of heated land being in the northern hemisphere, its peculiar wind, or the northeast trade, is narrower; while the other, the southeast trade, blowing from the greater expanse of the Southern Ocean, is broader. The latter, therefore, sometimes extends considerably beyond, or north of the equinoctial line. Thus the winds over all the Gulf of Guinea are generally from the south.

The coast of Africa, both north and south of the equator, greatly modifies the force and direction of the winds. On the southern coast the wind blows lightly, in a sea-breeze from the southwest. But at the distance of one hundred miles from the land, it begins gradually to veer round, as it connects itself with the S. E. trades. A line drawn on the chart, from the southern tropic, in 5° east to the lat. of 5° south, may be regarded as the eastern boundary of the southeast trade-winds. Hence a vessel, as in the case of the Perry, on her first passage to the southern coast, when in 10° south and 20° west, on going about and standing for the African coast by the wind, although she at first will not be able to head higher than N. E., will gradually come up to the eastward as the wind veers to the southward;

until it gradually hauls as far as S. W., and even W. S. W.—enabling her to fetch Benguela in 12° 34' south lat., although on going about she headed no higher than Prince's Island in 1° 20' north lat.

On the entire intertropical coast of Africa, it may be said that there are but two seasons, the rainy season and the dry season.

On the southern coast, the rainy season commences in November, and continues until April, although the rains are neither as frequent nor as heavy as on the northern coast, where they commence in May and continue through the month of November.

The months of March and April are the most unhealthy seasons on the southern coast, arising probably from the exhalations of the earth, which are not dispelled by the light sea-breezes prevailing at this period.

The climate of the south coast, especially from 6° south towards the Cape of Good Hope, is more healthy than on the north coast. As evidence of this, Europeans are found in comparatively great numbers in Loanda and Benguela, in the enjoyment of tolerable health.

There is a northerly current running along the southern coast of Africa, at the average rate of one mile per hour, until it is met by the Congo River, in 6° south ; where the impetuous stream of that great river breaks up this northerly current and forms one, of two miles per hour, in the direction of N. W., until it meets with the equatorial current in 2° or 3° south. The Congo will be more particularly noticed in speaking of the third southern cruise of the Perry.

The rollers on the coast are very heavy. And the breaking of the tremendous surf along the shore can often be heard at night, the distance of twenty miles from the land, reminding one of the sound of Niagara, in the vicinity of that mighty cataract.

But having in this part of the work (compilation of the correspondence) to treat more of ships, sailors and letters, than of the climate, the shore, and its inhabitants, it is time to recur to the Perry,—now squared away before the wind, with studding-sails set below and aloft, bound to Porto Praya, via Prince's Island and Monrovia, in search of the commander-in-chief of the squadron.

There are so many graphic descriptions before the public, in sea novels and naval journals, of life in a man-of-war, that it may well suffice here to remark— that a small vessel, uncomfortable quarters, salt provisions, myriads of cockroaches, an occasional tornado and deluge of rain, were ills that naval life duly encountered during the five days' passage to Prince's Island.

On the 27th of April the Perry arrived, and to the

great gratification of officers and men, the broad pendant of the commodore was descried at the main of
the U. S. sloop-of-war "Portsmouth."

The U. S. brig "Bainbridge" was also at anchor in
West Bay.

Prince's Island is ten miles in length from north to
south, and five miles in breadth. In places, it is considerably elevated, presenting, in its grotesque shafts
and projecting figures curiously formed, an exceedingly
picturesque appearance.

The natives are mostly black, and slaves; although
a few colored people are seen of a mixed race—Portuguese and African.

The island is well wooded, and the soil rich; and if
cultivated properly, would yield abundantly. Farina
is extensively manufactured.

Madame Fereira, a Portuguese lady, long resident
on the island, has no little repute for her hospitality
to African cruisers. Her taste in living here as she
does, is no more singular than that of the late clever,
eccentric and distinguished Lady Hester Stanhope,
who established herself near Sidon. Madame Fereira,
it is said, on a late visit to Europe, with abundant
means for enjoyment in a civilized state of society, was
ill at ease until the time arrived for her return to this
barbarian isle. She is ever ready, at a reasonable
price, to furnish the cruisers with wood, fresh provis-

ions and vegetables; and is never indisposed to take a hand at whist, or entertain foreigners in any other way, agreeable to their fancy.

Vessels frequently touch at Prince's Island for the purpose of obtaining fresh water, which, running down from the mountains in copious streams, is of a far better quality than can be procured on the coast.

On the arrival of the Perry, in a letter dated the 27th of April, the commander announced to the commodore the fulfilment of his instructions. The cruise had been extended to one hundred and seven days, of which eighty had been spent at sea, and the remainder at anchor, at different points of the coast.

The reply of the commodore contained his full approbation of the course pursued, stating in addition, that it was a matter of great importance to keep one of the squadron upon the southern coast; and not having provisions sufficient to enable him to proceed thither, and as the John Adams, having nearly expended her stock, would soon be compelled to return to Porto Praya, he therefore directed the commander of the Perry to make requisitions upon the flag-ship for as full a supply of provisions as could conveniently be stowed, and prepare again for immediate service on the southern coast.

CHAPTER XXVII.

ON the 6th of May, orders were given to the commander of the Perry, to proceed thence, with all practicable dispatch, to the southern coast; and to communicate with the commander of the John Adams as soon as possible. In case that vessel should have left the coast before the arrival of the Perry, her commander would proceed to cruise under former orders, and the instructions of the government.

It appeared to the commodore, in the correspondence had with some of the British officers, that in certain cases where they had boarded vessels under the flag of the United States, not having the right of search, threats had been used of detaining and sending them to the United States squadron. This he remarked was improper, and must not be admitted, or any understanding had with them authorizing such acts; adding, in substance, that if they chose to detain suspicious vessels, they must do it upon their own responsibility, without our assent or connivance. Refusing to the British government the right of search, our government has commanded us to prevent vessels and citizens of the United States from engaging in the slave-trade. These duties we must perform to the best of our ability, and we have no right to ask or receive the aid of a foreign power. "It is desirable to cultivate and preserve the good understanding which now exists between the two services; and should any differences arise, care must be taken that the discussions are temperate and respectful. You have full authority to act in concert with the British forces within the scope of our orders and duty."

On the same day, the Perry again sailed for the south coast, and after boarding several vessels, which proved to be legal traders, a *slaver* was captured, and made the subject of a communication, dated June 7th, 1850.

In this it was stated to the commodore, that the Perry, agreeably to his orders, had made the best of

U. S. BRIG PERRY, "off Ambriz, June 6ᵗʰ 1850." AMERICAN SLAVE SHIP MARTHA.

Lith. of Sarony & C.

her way for Ambriz, and arrived off that place on the
5th instant.   It was there reported that the John Adams
was probably at Loanda; and accordingly a course
was shaped for that port.   But on the 6th instant, at
three o'clock in the afternoon, a large ship with two
tiers of painted ports was made to windward, standing
in for the land towards Ambriz.   At four o'clock the
chase was overhauled, having the name " Martha,
New York," registered on her stern.   The Perry had
no colors flying.   The ship, when in range of the guns,
hoisted the American ensign, shortened sail, and backed
her main-topsail.   The first lieutenant, Mr. Rush, was
sent to board her.   As he was rounding her stern, the
people on board observed, by the uniform of the boarding-officer, that the vessel was an American cruiser.
The ship then hauled down the American, and hoisted
Brazilian colors.   The officer went on board, and asked
for papers and other proofs of nationality.   The captain denied having papers, log, or any thing else.   At
this time something was thrown overboard, when another boat was sent from the Perry, and picked up the
writing-desk of the captain, containing sundry papers
and letters, identifying the captain as an American
citizen; also indicating the owner of three-fifths of the
vessel to be an American merchant, resident in Rio de
Janeiro.   After obtaining satisfactory proof that the
ship Martha was a slaver, she was seized as a prize.

The captain at length admitted that the ship was fully equipped for the slave-trade. There were found on board the vessel, one hundred and seventy-six casks filled with water, containing from one hundred to one hundred and fifty gallons each; one hundred and fifty barrels of farina for slave-food; several sacks of beans; slave-deck laid; four iron boilers for cooking slave-provisions; iron bars, with the necessary wood-work, for securing slaves to the deck; four hundred spoons for feeding them; between thirty and forty muskets, and a written agreement between the owner and captain, with the receipt of the owner for two thousand milreis.

There being thirty-five persons on board this prize, many of whom were foreigners, it was deemed necessary to send a force of twenty-five men, with the first and second lieutenants, that the prize might be safely conducted to New York, for which place she took her departure that evening.

Soon after the Martha was discovered, she passed within hailing distance of an American brig, several miles ahead of the Perry, and asked the name of the cruiser astern; on being told, the captain, in despair, threw his trumpet on deck. But on a moment's reflection, as he afterwards stated, he concluded, notwithstanding, that she must be an English cruiser, not only from her appearance, but from the knowledge that the

Perry had left for Porto Praya, and could not in the mean time have returned to that part of the coast. Therefore finding, when within gun-shot of the vessel, that he could not escape, and must show his colors, ran up the American ensign, intending under his nationality to avoid search and capture. The boarding-officer was received at the gangway by a Brazilian captain, who strongly insisted that the vessel was Brazilian property. But the officer, agreeably to an order received on leaving the Perry, to hold the ship to the nationality first indicated by her colors, proceeded in the search. In the mean time, the American captain, notwithstanding his guise as a sailor, being identified by another officer, was sent on board the Perry. He claimed that the vessel could not lawfully be subjected to search by an American man-of-war, while under Brazilian colors. But, on being informed that he would be seized as a pirate for sailing without papers, even were he not a slaver, he admitted that she was on a slaving voyage; adding, that, had he not fallen in with the Perry, he would, during the night, have shipped eighteen hundred slaves, and before daylight in the morning, been clear of the coast.

Possession was immediately taken of the Martha, her crew put in irons, and both American and Brazilian captains, together with three or four cabin passengers (probably slave-agents), were given to understand that they would be similarly served, in case of the slightest evidence of insubordination. The accounts of the prize crew were transferred, the vessel provisioned, and in twenty-four hours after her capture, the vessels exchanged three cheers, and the Martha bore away for New York.

She was condemned in the U. S. District Court. The captain was admitted to bail for the sum of five thousand dollars, which was afterwards reduced to three thousand: he then escaped justice by its forfeiture. The American mate was sentenced to the Penitentiary for the term of two years; and the foreigners, who had been sent to the United States on account of the moral effect, being regarded as beyond our jurisdiction, were discharged.

The writing-desk thrown overboard from the Martha, soon after she was boarded, contained sundry papers, making curious revelations of the agency of some American citizens engaged in the slave-trade. These papers implicated a number of persons, who are little suspected of ever having participated in such a diabolical traffic. A citizen of New York, then on the African coast, in a letter to the captain of the Martha, says: "The French barque will be here in a few days, and, as yet, the agent has no instructions as to her taking *ebony* [negroes, slaves]. . . . From the Rio papers which I have seen, I infer that business is pretty brisk at that place. . . . . It is thought here that the brig Susan would bring a good price, as she had water on board. . . . C., an American merchant, has sold the Flood, and she was put under Brazilian colors, and gone around the Cape. The name of the brigantine in which B. came passenger was the Sotind; she was, as we are told, formerly the United States brig Boxer." Other letters found with this, stated : "The barque Ann Richardson, and brig Susan, were both sent home by a United States cruiser. The Independence cleared for Paraguay; several of the American vessels were cleared, and had sailed for Montevideo, &c., in ballast, and as I suppose bound niggerly; but where in hell they are is the big *business* of the matter. The sailors, as yet, have not been near me. I shall give myself no trouble about them. I have seen them at a distance. I am told that they are all well, but they look like death itself. V. Z. tells me they have wished a hundred times in his presence, that they had gone in the ship; for my part, I wish they were in hell, Texas, or some other nice place. B. only came down here to 'take in,' but was driven off by one of the English cruisers; he and his nigger crew were under deck, out of sight, when visited by the cruiser."*

---

* The following letter from Viscount Palmerston to Sir H. L. Bulwer, then British Minister at Washington, appears in the Parliamentary Papers of 1851. LVI. Part I.

After parting company with the Martha, the Perry proceeded to Loanda, and found English, French and Portuguese men-of-war in port. The John Adams, having exhausted her provisions, had sailed for the north coast, after having had the good fortune *to capture a slaver*. The British commissioner called aboard, and offered his congratulations on the capture of the Martha, remarking that she was the largest slaver that had been on the coast for many years; and the effect of sending all hands found in her to the United States, would prove a severe blow to the iniquitous traffic. The British cruisers, after the capture of a vessel, were in the practice of landing the slave-crews, except when they are British subjects, at some point on the coast. This is believed to be required by the governments with which Great Britain has formed treaties.

At the expiration of a few days, the Perry proceeded on a cruise down the coast, towards the Congo

---

"FOREIGN OFFICE, *November* 18, 1850.

"SIR,—I herewith transmit to you, for your information, a copy of a dispatch from the commodore in command of H. M. squadron on the west coast of Africa, respecting the circumstances under which the ship Martha was captured, on the 6th of June (1850) last, fully equipped for the slave-trade, by the U. S. brig-of-war Perry, and sent to the United States for trial.

"I have to instruct you to furnish me with a full report of the proceedings which may take place in this case before the courts of law in the United States.

"PALMERSTON."

River, encountering successively the British steamers Cyclops, Rattler, and Pluto. All vessels seen were boarded, and proved to be legal traders. Several days were spent between Ambriz and the Congo; and, learning from the Pluto—stationed off the mouth of the Congo River—that no vessels had, for a long time, appeared in that quarter, an idea, previously entertained, of proceeding up the river, was abandoned. The Perry was then worked up the coast towards Benguela.

Among the many incidents occurring:—On one occasion, at three o'clock in the morning, when the character of the vessels could not be discerned, a sail suddenly appeared, when, as usual on making a vessel at night, the battery was ordered to be cleared away, and the men sent to the guns. The stranger fired a musket, which was instantly returned. Subsequent explanations between the commanders of the cruisers were given, that the first fire was made without the knowledge of the character of the vessel; and the latter was made to repel the former, and to show the character of the vessel.

On boarding traders, the masters, in one or two instances, when sailing under a foreign flag, had requested the boarding-officer to search, and, after ascertaining her real character, to endorse the register. This elicited the following order to the boarding-officer:

" If a vessel hoists the American flag ; is of American build ; has her name and place of ownership in the United States registered on her stern ; or if she has but part of these indications of American nationality, you will, on boarding, ask for her papers, which papers you will examine and retain, if she excites suspicion of being a slaver, until you have searched sufficiently to satisfy yourself of her real character. Should the vessel be American, and doubts exist of her real character, you will bring her to this vessel ; or, if it can be done more expeditiously, you will dispatch one of your boats ; communicating such information as will enable the commander to give specific directions, or in person to visit the suspected vessel.

"If the strange vessel be a foreigner, you will, on ascertaining the fact, leave her; declining, even at the request of the captain, to search the vessel, or to endorse her character,—as it must always be borne in mind, that our government does not permit the detention and search of American vessels by foreign cruisers; and, consequently, is scrupulous in observing towards the vessels of other nations, the same line of conduct which she exacts from foreign cruisers towards her own vessels."

After cruising several days off the southern point designated in her orders, the Perry ran into Benguela. Spending a day in that place, she proceeded down the coast to the northward, occasionally falling in with British cruisers and legal traders. On meeting the Cyclops, the British commanding officer, in a letter, dated the 16th of July, stated to the commander of the Perry, that he " hastened to transmit, for his information, the following extract from a report just received from the commander of Her Britannic Majesty's steam-sloop ' Rattler,' with copies of two other documents, transmitted by the same officer ; and trusted that the same would be deemed satisfactory, as far as American interests were concerned."

The extract gave the information, that on the 2d of July, Her Majesty's steam-sloop Rattler captured the Brazilian brigantine " Volusia," of one hundred and ninety tons, a crew of seven men, and fully equipped for the slave-trade, with false papers, and sailing under the American flag ; that the crew had been landed at Kabenda, and that the vessel had been sent to St. Helena for adjudication ; and that he also inclosed certified declarations from the master, supercargo and chief mate, stating the vessel to be bona fide Brazilian property ; that they had no protest to offer, and that themselves and crew landed at Kabenda of their own free will and consent.

On the following day, the commander of the Perry, in reply to the above communication, stated that, as the brigantine in question had first displayed American colors, he wished all information which could be furnished him in relation to the character of the papers found on board; the reason for supposing them to be false, and the disposition made of them. Also, if there was a person on board, apparently an American, representing himself, in the first instance, as the captain; and if the vessel was declared to be Brazilian on first being boarded, or not until after her capture had been decided upon, and announced to the parties in charge.

In reply to this letter, on the 23d of July, the commanding officer of the British division stated that he would make known its purport to the commander who had captured the Volusia, and call upon that officer to answer the questions contained in the communication of the 17th instant, and hoped to transmit his reply prior to the Perry's departure for the north coast.

After cruising for several days in company with the English men-of-war, the vessel proceeded to Loanda, for the purpose of meeting the commodore. Arriving at that place, and leaving Ambriz without any guardianship for the morals of American traders, an order was transmitted to the acting first-lieutenant, to proceed with the launch on a cruise off Ambriz; and in boarding, searching, and in case of detaining suspected vessels, to be governed by the instructions therewith furnished him.

On the 5th of August, the British commissioner brought off intelligence that the American commodore was signalled off the harbor. The British commodore was at this date, also, to have rendezvoused at Loanda, that the subject-matter of correspondence between the officers of the two services, might be laid before their respective commanders-in-chief.

On the arrival of the American commodore, the Perry was reported, in a communication dated August the 5th, inclosing letters and papers, giving detailed information of occurrences since leaving Prince's Island, under orders of the 6th of May; also sundry documents from the commander of the British southern division, in relation to the capture of the slave-equipped brigantine Volusia; adding, that this case being similar to a number already the subjects of correspondence, he had requested further information, which the British commander of the division would probably communicate in a few days.

The letter to the commodore also stated, that our commercial intercourse with the provincial government of Portugal, and the natives of the coast, had been uninterrupted. The question arising in regard to the treaty with Portugal, whether a vessel by touching and discharging part of the cargo at a native port, is still exempt from payment of one-third of the duties on the remaining portion of the cargo, as guaranteed by treaty, when coming direct from the United States, had been submitted to our government.

On the 15th of August the Cyclops arrived at Loanda, with the commander of the British southern division on board, who, in a letter dated the 12th of August, stated, that agreeably to the promise made on the 23d ultimo, of furnishing the details from the commander who had captured the Volusia, he now furnished the particulars of that capture, which he trusted would prove satisfactory. He also gave information that the British commander-in-chief was then on the south coast, to whom all further reference must be made for additional information, in case it should be required. The reply from the officer who had captured the Volusia stated, that he had boarded her on the 2d of July off the Congo River. She had the American ensign flying, and on the production of documents, purporting to be her papers, he at once discovered the register to be false: it was written on foolscap paper, with the original signature erased; her other papers were likewise forgeries. He therefore immediately detained her. They had been presented to him by the ostensible master, apparently an American, but calling himself a Brazilian, and claiming the protection of that empire. The register and muster-roll were destroyed by the master; the remainder of the records were sent in her to St. Helena, for adjudication. The British commander further stated, that on discovering the Volusia's papers to be false, her master immediately hauled down the ensign, and called from below the remainder of the crew, twelve in number, all Brazilians.

In a letter dated the 15th of August, the above communications were acknowledged, and the British commander informed that the American commander-in-chief was also on the south coast: that all official documents must be submitted to him, and that the reply of the 12th instant, with its inclosure, had been forwarded accordingly.

The British commodore soon arrived at Loanda, and after an exchange of salutes, an interview of three hours between the two commodores took place. The captures of the Navarre, Volusia, and other vessels, with cases of interference with vessels claiming American nationality, were fully and freely discussed. The British commodore claimed that the vessels in question, were wholly, or in part Brazilian; adding, that had they been known clearly as American, no British officer would have presumed to capture, or interfere with them. The American commodore argued from documents and other testimony, that *bonâ fide* American vessels had been interfered with, and whether engaged in legal or illegal trade, they were in no sense amenable to British cruisers; the United States had made them responsible to the American government alone—subject to search and capture by American cruisers, on good grounds of suspicion and evidence of being engaged in the slave-trade; which trade the United States had declared to be piracy in a municipal sense—this offence not being piracy by the laws of nations: adding, in case of slavers, "we choose to punish our own rascals in our own way." Several discussions, at which the commander of the Perry was present, subsequently took place, without any definite results, or at least while that vessel remained at Loanda. These discussions were afterwards continued. In the commodores, both nations were represented by men of ability, capable of appreciating, expressing and enforcing the views of their respective governments.

Every person interested in upholding the rights of humanity, or concerned in the progress of Africa, will sympathize with the capture and deliverance of a wretched cargo of African slaves from the grasp of a slaver, irrespective of his nationality. But it is contrary to national honor and national interests, that the right of capture should be entrusted to the hands of any foreign authority. In a commercial point of view, if this were granted, legal traders would be molested, and American commerce suffer materially from a power which keeps afloat a force of armed vessels, more than four times the number of the commissioned men-of-war of the United States. The deck of an American vessel under its flag, is the territory of the United States, and no other authority but that of the United States must ever be allowed to exercise jurisdiction over it. Hence is apparent the importance of a well appointed United States squadron on the west coast of Africa.

On the 18th of August, the captain of an English cruiser entered the harbor with his boat, leaving the vessel outside, bringing the information that a suspected American trader was at Ambriz. The captain stated that he had boarded her, supposing she might be a Brazilian, but on ascertaining her nationality, had left her, and proceeded to Loanda, for the purpose of communicating what had transpired.

On receiving this information, the commodore ordered the Perry to proceed to Ambriz and search the vessel, and in case she was suspected of being engaged in the slave-trade, to bring her to Loanda. In the mean time a lieutenant who was about leaving the squadron as bearer of dispatches to the Government, volunteered his services to take the launch and proceed immediately to Ambriz, as the Perry had sails to bend, and make other preparations previous to leaving. The launch was dispatched, and in five hours afterwards the Perry sailed. Arriving on the following morning within twelve miles of Ambriz, the commander, accompanied by the purser and the surgeon, who volunteered their services, pulled for the suspected vessel, which proved to be the American brigantine " Chatsworth," of Baltimore.   The lieutenant, with his launch's crew, was on board.   He had secured the papers and commenced the search.   After taking the dimensions of the vessel, which corresponded to those noted in the register, examining and comparing the cargo with the manifest, scrutinizing the crew list, consular certificate, port clearance, and other papers on board, possession was taken of the Chatsworth, and the boarding-officer directed to proceed with her, in company with the Perry, to Loanda.

Both vessels having arrived, a letter to the following purport was addressed to the commodore :   " One hundred bags of farina, a large quantity of plank, sufficient to lay a slave-deck, casks and barrels of spirits, in sufficient quantity to contain water for a large slave-cargo, jerked beef, and other articles, were found on board the Chatsworth.   These articles, and others on board, corresponded generally with the manifest, which paper was drawn up in the Portuguese language.   A paper with the consular seal, authorizing the shipment of the crew, all foreigners, was also made out in the Portuguese language.   In the register, the vessel was called a brig, instead of a brigantine.   A letter of instructions from the reputed owner, a citizen of Baltimore, directed the American captain to leave the vessel whenever he should be directed to do so by the

Italian supercargo. These, together with the report
that the vessel on her last voyage had shipped a cargo
of slaves, and her now being at the most notorious
slave-station on the coast, impressed the commander of
the Perry so strongly with the belief that the Chatsworth was a slaver, that he considered it his duty to
direct the boarding-officer to take her in charge, and
proceed in company with the Perry to Loanda, that
the case might undergo a more critical examination by
the commander-in-chief."

The commodore, after visiting the Chatsworth in
person, although morally certain she was a slaver, yet
as the evidence which would be required in the United
States Courts essential to her condemnation, was wanting, conceived it to be his duty to order the commander
of the Perry to surrender the charge of that vessel, and
return all the papers to her master, and withdraw his
guard from her.

The captain of the Volusia now suddenly made his
appearance at Loanda, having in his possession the sea-
letter which the British commander who had captured
him called a register, written on a sheet of foolscap paper, which from misapprehension he erroneously
stated was destroyed by the master. This new matter
was introduced in the discussion between the two commodores. The captain of the Volusia claimed that his
vessel was *bonâ fide* American, stating that the sea-let-

ter in his possession was conclusive evidence to that effect. No other subject than that of the nationality of the vessel, while treating upon this matter with an English officer, could be introduced. The sea-letter was laid before the commanders. This document bore all the marks of a genuine paper, except in having the word " signed" occurring before the consul's signature, and partially erased. This seemed to indicate that it had been made out as a copy, and, if genuine, the consul had afterwards signed it as an original paper. The consular seal was impressed, and several other documents, duly sealed and properly certified, were attached, bearing strong evidence that the document was genuine.

The British commodore argued that the erasure of the word " signed," even if it did not invalidate the document, gave good ground for the suspicion that the document was a forgery; and she being engaged in the slave-trade, the officer who captured her regarded the claim first set forth to American nationality as groundless.

The American commodore could not permit the character of the vessel to be assigned as a reason for her capture, and confined the discussion to the papers constituting the nationality of the vessel. He regarded the consular seal as genuine, and believed that, if the paper had been a forgery, care would have been taken to have had it drawn up without any erasure, or the word "signed."

The discussion in relation to the Volusia and the Navarre, was renewed with the Chief-Justice and Judge of the Admiralty Court, soon after the arrival of the Perry at the island of St. Helena.

CHAPTER XXVIII.

ANOTHER CRUISE—CHATSWORTH AGAIN—VISIT TO THE QUEEN
NEAR AMBRIZETTE—SEIZURE OF THE AMERICAN BRIGANTINE
"LOUISA BEATON" BY A BRITISH CRUISER—CORRESPONDENCE
—PROPOSAL OF REMUNERATION FROM THE CAPTORS—SEIZURE
OF THE CHATSWORTH AS A SLAVER—ITALIAN SUPERCARGO—
MASTER OF THE LOUISA BEATON.

THE commodore, on the 24th of August, intimated
that it had been his intention to relieve the Perry from
the incessant duties which had been imposed upon her,
but regretted that he could not then accomplish it without leaving American interests in that quarter un-
protected, and that the commander would therefore
be pleased to prepare for further service on the
southern coast, with the assurance of being relieved
as soon as practicable.

Orders were issued by the commodore to resume
cruising upon the southern coast, as before, and to visit
such localities as might best insure the successful accomplishment of the purposes in view.

Authority was given to extend the cruise as far as
the island of St. Helena, and to remain there a suffi-

cient length of time to refresh the crew; and, after
cruising until the twentieth of November, then to proceed to Porto Praya, touching at Monrovia, if it was
thought proper.

The orders being largely discretionary, and the
Chatsworth still in port, and suspected of the intention
of shipping a cargo of slaves at Ambriz, the Perry
sailed, the day on which her orders were received, without giving any intimation as to her cruising-ground.
When outside of the harbor, the vessel was hauled on
a wind to the southward, as if bound up the coast, and
continued beating until out of sight of the vessels in
the harbor. She was then kept away to the northward,
making a course for Ambriz, in anticipation of the
Chatsworth's soon sailing for that place.

The cruising with the English men-of-war was resumed. A few days after leaving Loanda, when trying
the sailing qualities of the vessel with a British cruiser,
a sail was reported, standing down the land towards
Ambriz. Chase was immediately made, and, on coming within gun-shot, a gun was fired to bring the vessel
to. She hoisted American colors, but continued on her
course. Another gun, throwing a thirty-two pound
shot across her bows, brought the Chatsworth to. She
was then boarded, and again searched, without finding
any additional proof against the vessel's character.

After remaining a day or two off Ambriz, the Perry

proceeded to Ambrizette, a short distance to the northward, leaving one of the ship's boats in charge of an
officer, with orders to remain sufficiently near the
Chatsworth, and, in case she received water-casks on
board, or any article required to equip a slave-vessel,
to detain her until the return of the Perry.

When the vessel had reached her destination, the
commander conceived it to be a good opportunity to
forward the interests of American commerce, by paying
a visit of conciliation to the queen of that region.
Though warned by the British officers that the natives
were hostile to all persons engaged in suppressing the
lucrative trade in slaves, he resolved to avail himself
of the invitation of the resident American factor, and
proceed to the royal residence. Two other officers of
the vessel, the agent, and several of the gig's Kroomen,
accompanied him. On their way, a great number of
Her Majesty's loyal subjects—dressed chiefly in the
costume of their own black skins—formed the escort.
"All hands," however, were not in the native sables
exclusively, for several, of more aristocratic claims,
sported a piece of calico print, of glaring colors, over
one shoulder. The village, when first seen, resembled
a group of brown haystacks; the largest of these, as a
palace, sheltered the royal presence. The court etiquette brought the mob of gentlemen and ladies of the
escort, with and without costume, down upon their

Lith. of Sarony & C.º N.Y.

AUDIENCE TO THE PERRY'S OFFICERS, BY THE QUEEN OF AMBRIZETTE.

knees, in expectation of Her Majesty's appearance. A little withered old woman then stepped out, having, in addition to the native costume, an old red silk cloak, drawn tight around her throat, and so worn as to make her look like a loose umbrella, with two handles. She then squatted on the ground. Her prime minister aspired to be higher than African in his costume, by hanging on his long, thin person, an old full-dress French navy uniform-coat, dispensing with other material articles of clothing, except a short pair of white trowsers. The officers being seated in front, the kneeling hedge of three or four hundred black woolly heads closed behind them,—impregnating the air with their own peculiar aroma—their greasy faces upturned in humble reverence—hands joined, palm to palm, ready to applaud Her Majesty's gracious wisdom when they heard it,—the conference began. The interpreter introduced the officers, and their business, and, in the name of the commander, expressed their friendly feelings towards Her Majesty and her people; advising her to encourage trade with the American merchants in gums, copper and the products of the country, instead of selling her people as slaves, or conniving at the sale in other tribes, for the purpose of procuring goods. This speech having the honor of being directed to the royal ears, was greeted, according to etiquette, with clap, clap, clap, from all the ready hands of all the gentle-

men in waiting, who were using their knees as supports
in Her Majesty's royal presence. The prime minister,
from the inside of the French coat, then responded—
that Her Majesty had great reason to complain of the
conduct of cruisers' boats on the coast, for they were in
the habit of chasing the fishermen, and firing to bring
them to, and taking their fish, which were the principal
support of the people, without making an equivalent
return. Whereupon, clap, clap, clap, went the hands
again. Her Majesty was assured, in reply, that such
had never been, and never would be the case, in regard
to the boats of American cruisers, and that her complaints would be made known to those officers who had
the power and the disposition to remove all such cause
of grievance. The chorus of clap, clap, clap, again at
this answer concluded the ceremony. The prime minister followed the return escort at some distance, and
took occasion, at parting on the beach, to intimate that
there were certain other marks of friendly respect common at courts, and marking the usages of polished
nations. He gave no hints about gold snuff-boxes, as
might be suitable in the barbarian courts of Europe;
but intimated that his friends visiting Her Majesty, in
such instances, thought *his* humble services worthy of
two bottles of rum. Compliance with this amiable custom was declared to be wholly impracticable, as the
spirit-room casks of the Perry had been filled only with

pure (or impure) water, instead of whisky, during the cruise.

In communicating to the government, in a more official form, the object and incidents of the visit to the queen near Ambrizette, reference was made to a powerful king, residing ten miles in the interior of Ambriz, and the intention of making him a visit was announced. But the seizure of the Louisa Beaton by a British cruiser, on her return to the coast, and the impression made upon the natives by the capture of the Chatsworth as a slaver, not only occupied the intervening time before leaving for St. Helena, but rendered inland excursions by no means desirable.

On returning towards Ambriz, soon after making the land, the steamer Cyclops, with another British cruiser, was observed; and also the Chatsworth, with an American brigantine lying near her. A boat from the Cyclops, with an English officer, pulled out several miles, while the Perry was in the offing, bringing a packet of letters and papers marked as usual, " On Her Britannic Majesty's Service." These papers were accompanied by a private note from the British commander of the division, expressing great regret at the occurrence, which was officially noticed in the accompanying papers, and the earnest desire to repair the wrong.

The official papers were dated September the ninth, and contained statements relating to the *chasing, board-*

ing and *detention* of the American brigantine **Louisa Beaton**, on the seventh and eighth instant.

The particulars of the seizure of the vessel were given in a letter from the commander of the English cruiser Dolphin, directed to the British commander of the division, as follows: "I have the honor to inform you, that at daylight on the 7th instant, being about seventy miles off the land, a sail was observed on the lee bow, whilst Her Majesty's brigantine, under my command, was steering to the eastward. I made all possible sail in chase: the chase was observed making more sail and keeping away. Owing to light winds, I was unable to overtake her before 0h. 30m. A. M. When close to her and no sail shortened, I directed a signal gun to be fired abeam, and hailed the chase to shorten sail and heave to. Chase asserted he could not, and requested leave to pass to leeward; saying, if we wanted to board him, we had better make haste about it, and that 'we might fire and be damned.'

"I directed another gun to be fired across her bows, when she immediately shortened sail and hove to: it being night, no colors were observed flying on board the chase, nor was I aware of her character.

"I was proceeding myself to board her, when she bore up again, with the apparent intention of escaping. I was therefore again compelled to hoist the boat up and to close her under sail. I reached the chase on the second attempt, and found her to be the American brigantine Louisa Beaton. The master produced an American register, with a transfer of masters : this gave rise to a doubt of the authenticity of the paper, and on requesting further information, the master refused to give me any, and declined showing me his port clearance, crew list, or log-book.

"The lieutenant who accompanied me identified the mate as having been in charge of the slave-brig Lucy Ann, captured by Her Majesty's steam-sloop Rattler. Under these suspicious circumstances, I considered it my duty, as the Louisa Beaton was bound to Ambriz, to place an officer and crew on board of her, so as to confer with an American officer, or yourself, before allowing her, if a legal trader, to proceed on her voyage."

The British commander of the division, in his letter, stated, that immediately on the arrival of the vessels, he proceeded with the commander of the Dolphin and the lieutenant of the Rattler to the brigantine Louisa Beaton. Her master then presented the register, and also the transfer of masters made in Rio, in consequence of the death of the former master, but refused to show any other documents.

On examining the register, and having met the vessel before on that coast, he decided that the Louisa Beaton's nationality was perfect; but that the conduct pursued by her master, in withholding documents that should have been produced on boarding, had led to the unfortunate detention of the vessel.

The British commander further stated, that he informed the master of the Louisa Beaton that he would immediately order his vessel to be released, and that on falling in with the commander of the Perry, all due inquiry into the matter for his satisfaction should be made; but that the master positively refused to take charge again, stating that he would immediately abandon the vessel on the Dolphin's crew quitting her; and, further, requested that the vessel might be brought before the American commander.

That, as much valuable property might be sacrificed should the master carry his threat into execution, he proceeded in search of the Perry, that the case might be brought under consideration while the Dolphin was present; and on arriving at Ambriz, the cutter of the Perry was found in charge of one of her officers.

On the following morning, as he stated, accompanied by the officer in charge of the Perry's cutter, and the commander of the Dolphin, he proceeded to the Louisa Beaton, and informed her master that the detention of his vessel arose from the refusal, on his part, to show the proper documents to the boarding-officer, authorizing him to navigate the vessel in those seas; and from his mate having been identified by one of the Dolphin's officers, as having been captured in charge of a vessel having on board five hundred and forty-seven slaves, which attempted to evade search and capture by displaying the American ensign; as well as from his own suspicious maneuvering in the chase. But as he was persuaded that the Louisa Beaton was an American vessel, and her papers good, although a most important document was wanting, namely, the *sea-letter*, usually given by consular officers to legal traders after the *transfer of masters*, he should direct the commander of the Dolphin to resign the charge of the Louisa Beaton, which was accordingly done; and, that on meeting the commander of the Perry, he would lay the case before him; and was ready, if he demanded it, to give any remuneration or satisfaction, on the part of the commander of the Dolphin, for the unfortunate detention of the Louisa Beaton, whether engaged *in legal or illegal trade*, that the master might in fairness demand, and the commander of the Perry approve.

After expressing great regret at the occurrence, the British commander stated that he was requested by the captain of the Dolphin to assure the commander of the Perry, that no disrespect was intended to the flag of the United States, or even interference, on his part, with traders of America, be they legal or illegal; but the stubbornness of the master, and the identifying of one of his mates as having been captured in a

Brazilian vessel, trying to evade detection by the display of the American flag, had led to the mistake.

A postscript to the letter added, "I beg to state that the hatches of the Louisa Beaton have not been opened, nor the vessel or crew in any way examined."

On the Perry's reaching the anchorage, the Louisa Beaton was examined. The affidavit of the master, which differs not materially from the statements of the British officers, was taken. A letter by the commander of the Perry was then addressed to the British officer, stating, that he had in person visited the Louisa Beaton, conferred with her master, taken his affidavit, examined her papers, and found her to be in all respects a legal American trader. That the *sea-letter* which had been referred to, as being usually given by consular officers, was only required when the vessel changes owners, and not, as in the present case, on the appointment of a new master. The paper given by the consul authorizing the appointment of the present master, was, with the remainder of the vessel's papers, strictly in form.

The commander also stated that he respectfully declined being a party concerned in any arrangement of a pecuniary nature, as satisfaction to the master of the Louisa Beaton, for the detention and seizure of his vessel, and if such arrangement was made between the British officers and the master of the Louisa Beaton, it would be his duty to give the information to his government.

The commander added, that the government of the United States did not acknowledge a right in any other nation to visit and detain the vessels of American citizens engaged in commerce : that whenever a foreign cruiser should venture to board a vessel under the flag of the United States, she would do it upon her own responsibility for all consequences : that if the vessel so boarded should prove to be American, the injured party would be left to such redress, either in the tribunals of England, or by an appeal to his own country, as the nature of the case might require.

He also stated that he had carefully considered all the points in the several communications which the commander of the British division had sent him, in relation to the seizure of the Louisa Beaton, and he must unqualifiedly pronounce the seizure and detention of that vessel wholly unauthorized by the circumstances, and contrary both to the letter and the spirit of the eighth article of the treaty of Washington; and that it became his duty to make a full report of the case, accompanied with the communications which the British commander had forwarded, together with the affidavit of the master of the Louisa Beaton, to the government of the United States.

This letter closed the correspondence.*

The British commander-in-chief then accompanied the commander of the Perry to the Louisa Beaton, and there wholly disavowed the act of the commander of the Dolphin, stating, in the name of that officer, that he begged pardon of the master, and that he would do any thing in his power to repair the wrong; adding, "I could say no more, if I had knocked you down."

The Louisa Beaton was then delivered over to the charge of her own master, and the officer of the cutter took his station alongside of the Chatsworth.

On the 11th of September this brigantine was seized as a slaver. During the correspondence with the British officers in relation to the Louisa Beaton, an order was given to the officer of the cutter, to prevent the Chatsworth from landing the remaining part of her cargo. The master immediately called on board the Perry, with the complaint, that his vessel had been seized on a former occasion, and afterwards released by the commodore, with the endorsement of her nationality on the log-book. Since then she had been repeatedly searched, and now was prevented from disposing of her cargo; he wished, therefore, that a definite decision

---

* This correspondence, with much of that which is to be referred to hereafter, with the British officers, has been published more at length in the "Blue Book," or Parliamentary Papers, of 1851.

might be made.   A decision was made by the instant
seizure of the vessel.

Information from the master of the Louisa Beaton,
that the owner of the Chatsworth had in Rio acknowledged to him that the vessel had shipped a cargo of
slaves on her last voyage, and was then proceeding to
the coast for a similar purpose—superadded to her suspicious movements, and the importance of breaking up
this line of ostensible traders, but real slavers, running
between the coasts of Brazil and Africa—were the
reasons leading to this decision.

On announcing the decision to the master of the
Chatsworth, a prize crew was immediately sent on
board and took charge of the vessel.   The master and
supercargo then drew up a protest, challenging the act
as illegal, and claiming the sum of fifteen thousand
dollars for damages.   The supercargo, on presenting
this protest, remarked that the United States Court
would certainly release the vessel; and the *procuro*
of the owner, with other parties interested, would then
look to the captor for the amount of damages awarded.
The commander replied, that he fully appreciated the
pecuniary responsibility attached to this proceeding.

The master of the Louisa Beaton, soon after the supercargo of the Chatsworth had presented the protest,
went on shore for the purpose of having an interview
with him, and not coming off at the time specified,

apprehensions were entertained that the slave-factors had revenged themselves for his additional information—leading to the seizure of the Chatsworth. At nine o'clock in the evening, three boats were manned and armed, containing thirty officers and men,—leaving the Perry in charge of one of the lieutenants. When two of the boats had left the vessel, and the third was in readiness to follow, the master of the Louisa Beaton made his appearance, stating that his reception on shore had been any thing but pacific. Had the apprehensions entertained proved correct, it was the intention to have landed and taken possession of the town; and then to have marched out to the barracoons, liberated the slaves, and made, at least for the time being, "free soil" of that section of country.

In a letter to the commodore, dated September 14th, information was given to the following purport:

"Inclosed are affidavits, with other papers and letters, in relation to the seizure of the American brigantine Chatsworth. This has been an exceedingly complicated case, as relating to a slaver with two sets of papers, passing alternately under different nationalities, eluding detection from papers being in form, and trading with an assorted cargo.

"The Chatsworth has been twice boarded and searched by the commander, and on leaving for a short cruise off Ambrizette, a boat was dispatched with orders to watch her movements during the absence of the Perry. On returning from Ambrizette, additional evidence of her being a slaver was procured. Since then the affidavits of the master of the Chatsworth and the mate of the Louisa Beaton have been obtained, leading to further developments, until the guilt of the vessel, as will be seen by the accompanying papers, is placed beyond all question."

The Italian supercargo, having landed most of the cargo, and his business being in a state requiring his presence, was permitted to go on shore, with the assurance that he would return when a signal was made. He afterwards came within hail of the Chatsworth, and finding that such strong proofs against the vessel were obtained, he declined going on board, acknowledging to the master of the Louisa Beaton that he had brought over Brazilian papers.

The crew of the Chatsworth being foreigners, and not wishing to be sent to the United States, were landed at Ambriz, where it was reported that the barracoons contained four thousand slaves, ready for shipment; and where, it was said, the capture of the Chatsworth, as far as the American flag was concerned, would give a severe and an unexpected blow to the slave-trade.

After several unsuccessful attempts to induce the supercargo of the Chatsworth to come off to that vessel, a note in French was received from him, stating that he was "an Italian, and as such could not be owner of the American brig Chatsworth, which had been seized, it was true, but unjustly, and against the laws of all civilized nations. That the owner of the said brig would know how to defend his property, and in case the judgment should not prove favorable, the one who had been the cause of it would always bear the remorse of having ruined his countryman."

After making the necessary preliminary arrangements, the master, with a midshipman and ten men, was placed in charge of the Chatsworth; and on the 14th of September, the following order was sent to the commanding officer of the prize: "You will proceed to Baltimore, and there report yourself to the commander of the naval station, and to the Secretary of the Navy. You will be prepared, on your arrival, to deliver up the vessel to the United States marshal, the papers to the judge of the United States District Court, and be ready to act in the case of the Chatsworth as your orders and circumstances may require.

"It is advisable that you should stand as far to the westward, at least, as the longitude of St. Helena, and when in the calm latitudes make a direct north course, shaping the course for your destined port in a higher latitude, where the winds are more reliable."

On the following morning the three vessels stood out

to sea—the Perry and Louisa Beaton bound to Loanda, and the Chatsworth bearing away for the United States The crew had now become much reduced in numbers, and of the two lieutenants, master, and four passed midshipmen, originally ordered to the vessel, there remained but two passed midshipmen, acting lieutenants on board.

After a protracted trial, the Chatsworth was at length condemned as a slaver, in the U. S. District Court of Maryland.

CHAPTER XXIX.

Soon after arriving at Loanda, it was ascertained
that the masters of merchant-traders were forbidden to
visit one another on board their respective vessels, without express permission from the authorities. This regulation was even extended to men-of-war officers in
their visit to merchant vessels of their own nation. An
application was made to the authorities, remonstrating
against this regulation being applied to the United
States officers; and assurances were given which led to
the conclusion that the regulation had been rescinded.

Soon afterwards a letter to the collector, dated the
17th of September, stated that the commander of the
Perry, in company with the purser, had that evening
pulled alongside of the Louisa Beaton, and much to
his surprise, especially after the assurance of the collector that no objection would in future be raised against
the United States naval officers visiting the merchant

vessels of their own nation, the custom-house officers informed him that he could not be admitted on board: they went on board, however, but did not go below, not wishing to involve the vessel in difficulty.

The report of this circumstance was accompanied with the remark, that it was the first time that an objection had been raised to the commander's visiting a merchant vessel belonging to his own nation in a foreign port; and this had been done after the assurance had been given, that in future no obstacles should be in the way of American officers visiting American ships in Loanda.

In reply to this letter, the collector stated that he had shown, on a former occasion, that his department could give no right to officers of men-of-war to visit merchant vessels of their own nation when in port, under the protection of the Portuguese flag and nation. But in view of the friendly relations existing between Portugal and the United States, and being impressed with the belief that these visits would be made in a social, friendly character, rather than with indifference and disrespect to the authorities of that province, he would forward, and virtually had forwarded already, the orders, that in all cases, when American men-of-war are at anchor, no obstacle should be thrown in the way of their officers boarding American vessels.

He further stated, that the objections of the guards

to the commander boarding the Louisa Beaton, was the result of their ignorance of his orders, permitting visits from American vessels of war; but concluded that the opposition encountered could not have been great, as the commander himself had confessed that he had really boarded the said vessel.

On the 19th of September, the Perry sailed for the island of St. Helena. Soon after leaving port, a vessel was seen dead to windward, hull and courses down. After a somewhat exciting chase of forty-two hours, the stranger was overhauled, and proved to be a Portuguese regular trader between the Brazil and the African coast.

Several days before reaching St. Helena, the trades had so greatly freshened, together with thick, squally weather, that double-reefed topsails, with single-reefed courses, were all the sail the vessel could bear.

On the morning of the 11th of October, a glimpse of the island was caught for a few minutes. Two misty spires of rock seemed to rise up in the horizon—notched off from a ridge extended between them—the centre being Diana's peak, twenty-seven hundred feet in height. The vessel was soon again enveloped in thick squalls of rain, but the bearings of the island had been secured, and a course made for the point to be doubled. After running the estimated distance to the land, the fog again lifted, presenting the formidable island of St.

Lith. of Sarony & Co. N.Y.

SHORE AND ROADSTEAD AT JAMESTOWN, S. HELENA.

Helena close aboard, and in a moment all was obscured again.   But the point had been doubled, and soon afterwards the Perry was anchored, unseeing and unseen.

The sails were furled, the decks cleared up, when the whole scene started out of obscurity. St. Helena was in full view. A salute of twenty-one guns was fired, and promptly responded to, gun for gun, from the bristling batteries above.

Under the vast, rugged buttresses of rock—serrated with gaps between them, like the surviving parapets of a gigantic fortress, the mass of which had sunk beneath the sea—the vessel seemed shrunk to a mere speck; and close under these mural precipices, rising to the height of two thousand feet, she had, in worse than darkness, crept along within hearing of the surf.

On either bow, when anchored, were the two stupendous, square-faced bluffs, between which, liked a ruined embrasure, yawned the ravine containing Jamestown. High and distant against the sky, was frowning a battery of heavy guns, looking down upon the decks; and beyond the valley, the road zigzagged along the nine hundred feet of steep-faced, ladder hill.   Green thickets were creeping up the valleys; and plains of verdant turf here and there overlapped the precipices.

Subsequently, on an inland excursion, were seen the fantastic forms of Lot and his wife, more than fourteen hundred feet in height; and black pillars, or shafts of basaltic columns, standing high amid the snowy foam of the surf.   Patches of luxuriant vegetation were suddenly broken by astounding chasms, such as the " Devil's Punch Bowl."

This striking and majestic scenery, on an island ten miles in length and six in breadth, arises from its great height and its volcanic configuration.   The occurrence of small oceanic deposits high up on its plains, indicates fits of elevation ere it reached its present altitude. The *Yam-flowers* (the *sobriquet* of the island ladies) need not, however, fear that the joke of travellers will prove a reality, by the island again being drawn under water like a turtle's head.

Visits were received from the chief-justice, the commandant and officers of the garrison.   Invitations were sent to dine " with the mess."   The American consul, and many of the inhabitants, joined in extending unbounded hospitality to the officers, which was duly appreciated by African cruisers.   A collation to their hospitable friends, on the quarterdeck of the Perry, was also partaken of by the officers of a British cruiser, which, on leaving the island, ran across the stern of the vessel, gave three cheers, and dipped her colors.   The proprietor of Longwood, once the prison of Napoleon, received the officers and their friends at a pic-nic, when a visit was made to that secluded spot, so suggestive of interesting associations. Every means was used to leave a sense of grateful remembrance on the minds of the visitors to the island.

One watch of the crew were constantly on shore, in search of health and enjoyment.

A short time previously to leaving Loanda, information being received from the American consul at Rio, that the barque Navarre, and brigantine Volusia, already noticed, had been furnished with sea-letters as American vessels, steps were taken to ascertain from the vice-admiralty court, in St. Helena, the circumstances attending their trial and condemnation. Calls were made on several officers of the court for that purpose. Failing thus to obtain the information unofficially, a letter was drawn up and sent to the chief-justice, who was also the judge of the admiralty court. After the judge had read the letter, he held, with the commander of the Perry, a conversation of more than an hour, in reference to its contents. During this interview, the judge announced that he could not communicate, officially, the information solicited. An opportunity, however, was offered to look over the record of the proceedings. Circumstances did not seem to justify the acceptance of this proposal. It was then intimated to the commander that the letter of request would be sent to Lord Palmerston; and, in return, intimation was also given that a copy of the letter would be transmitted to the Secretary of the Navy at Washington.

The social intercourse between the parties, during this interview, was of the most agreeable character.

In the same letter to the judge of the admiralty court, that contained the above-mentioned request for documents relating to the case of the Navarre, the commander of the Perry stated that he was informed by the American consul that the Navarre was sold in Rio to a citizen of the United States; that a sea-letter was granted by the consul; that the papers were regular and true; that the owner was master, and that the American crew were shipped in the consul's office.

The commander also stated, that information from other sources had been received, that the Navarre proceeded to the coast of Africa, and when near Benguela was boarded by H. B. Majesty's brig Water-Witch, and after a close examination of her papers was permitted to pass. The captain of the Navarre, after having intimated his intention to the officer of the Water-Witch, of going into Benguela, declined doing so on learning that the Perry was there, assigning to his crew as the reason, that the Perry would take him prisoner; and at night accordingly bore up and ran down towards Ambriz. The captain also stated to a part of the crew, that *the officer of the Water-Witch* had advised him to give up the vessel to *him*, as the Perry would certainly take his vessel, and send him home, whereas *he* would only take his vessel, and let him land and go free.

On reaching Ambriz, with the American flag flying, the Navarre was boarded by the commander of H. M. steam-sloop Fire-Fly, who, on examining the papers given by the consul, and passed by the commander of the Water-Witch as being in form, *pronounced them false.* The captain of the Navarre was threatened with being taken to the American squadron, or to New York; and fearing worse consequences in case he should fall into the hands of the American cruisers, preferred giving up his vessel, *bonâ fide* American, to a British officer. Under these circumstances, he signed a paper that the vessel was Brazilian property, and he himself a Brazilian subject. The mate was ordered to haul down the American and hoist the Brazilian colors; in doing which the American crew attempted to stop him, when the English armed sailors interfered, and struck one of the American crew on the head.

The Fire-Fly arrived at Loanda a few days after the capture of the Navarre, and the representations of her commander induced the commander of the Perry to believe that the Navarre was Brazilian property, and captured with false American papers; which papers having been destroyed, no evidence of her nationality remained but the statement of the commander of the Fire-Fly. This statement, being made by a British officer, was deemed sufficient, until subsequent information led to the conclusion, that the Navarre was an American vessel, and whether engaged in *legal or illegal trade*, the course pursued towards her by the commanders of the Water-Witch and the Fire-Fly, was wholly unauthorized; and her subsequent capture by the commander of the Fire-Fly, was in direct violation of the treaty of Washington.

After this statement was drawn up, the Water-Witch being in St. Helena, it was shown to her commander.

A statement in relation to the capture and condemnation of the Volusia, was also forwarded to the chief-justice: stating, upon the authority of the American consul at Rio, that she had a sea-letter, and was strictly an American vessel, bought by an American citizen in Rio de Janeiro.

In reply to this application for a copy of the proceedings of the Admiralty Court in relation to the Navarre, the chief-justice, in a letter to the commander of the Perry, stated that he was not aware of any American vessel having been condemned in the Vice-Admiralty Court of that colony.

It was true that a barque called the Navarre had been condemned in the court, which might or might not have been American; but the circumstances under which the case was presented to the court, were such as to induce the court to conclude that the Navarre was at the time of seizure not entitled to the protection of any state or nation.

With respect to the commander's request that he should be furnished with a copy of the affidavits in the case, the judge regretted to state, that with every disposition to comply with his wishes, so far as regards the proceedings of the court, yet as the statement of the commander not only reflected upon the conduct of the officers concerned in the seizure, but involved questions not falling within the province of the court, he did not feel justified in giving any special directions in reference to the application.

Similar reasons were assigned for not furnishing a copy of the affidavits in the case of the Volusia.

In a letter to the commodore, dated October 19th, information was given substantially as follows :

"A few days previously to leaving the coast of Africa, a letter was received from the American consul at Rio, in reply to a communication from the commander of the John Adams, and directed to that office, or to the commander of any U. S. ship-of-war. This letter inclosed a paper containing minutes from the records in the consulate in relation to several American vessels, and among them the barque Navarre and brigantine Volusia were named, as having been furnished with sea-letters as American vessels. These vessels were seized on the coast of Africa, and condemned in this admiralty court, as vessels of unknown nationality.

" Availing himself of the permission to extend the cruise as far as this island, and coming into possession of papers identifying the American nationality of the Navarre and Volusia, the commander regarded it to be his duty to obtain all information in reference to the course pursued by British authorities towards these vessels for the purpose of submitting it to the Government.

" The commander called on the queen's proctor of the Vice-Admiralty Court, requesting a copy of the affidavits in the instances of the Navarre and Volusia. The proctor stated that the registrar of the court would probably furnish them. The registrar declined doing it without the sanction of the judge, and the judge declined for reasons alleged in the inclosed correspondence.

" The proctor, soon afterwards, placed a packet of papers in the hands of the commander of the Perry, containing the affidavits in question, and requested him to forward them to the British commodore. The proctor suggested to the commander that he might look over the papers. This was declined, on the ground that when the request was made for permission to examine them, unofficially, it was denied, and since having made the request officially for a copy of the papers, they could not now be received and examined at St. Helena, except in an official form. It was then intimated that the intention was to have the papers sent unofficially to the British commodore, that he might show them, if requested to do so, to the American officers."

CHAPTER XXX.

THE Perry, after ten days' acquaintance and intercourse with many exceedingly kind and hospitable
friends, reluctantly sailed for the African coast, and after a passage of ten days, beat up inside of the reef
forming the harbor, guided by the signal-lights of the
men-of-war, and anchored at Loanda. The following
morning, salutes were exchanged with the French commodore, whose broad pendant was flying at the main
of a fine steam-frigate. To the Secretary of the Navy
it was announced that no suspicious American vessel
had been on the south coast since the capture of the
Chatsworth.

After remaining two days in Loanda, cruising was
renewed, in company with the Cyclops, off Ambriz.
Soon afterwards the Cyclops was ordered to England.
The commanding officer of the southern division was

now about taking his leave of the coast. The Hon. Captain Hastings (since deceased), brother to the Earl of Huntington, was an officer of great merit, and a man of noble qualities. He was ever kind and attentive to the wants of his crew. He possessed great moral integrity of character, and sound religious principles. Notwithstanding the protracted correspondence, often involving delicate points and perplexing questions, the social friendly intercourse between the two commanders in the different services had not for a moment been interrupted. On parting the two vessels exchanged three hearty cheers.

The Perry beat up to the southward as far as Benguela, and looking into the harbor, without anchoring, proceeded to run down the coast to the northward. On approaching a Portuguese man-of-war, that vessel fired a blank cartridge from a small gun. It being daylight, and the character of both cruisers easily discernible, the object of the fire could not be conceived. A thirty-two pound shot was immediately thrown across the cruiser's bows. She then hauled down her colors, but soon afterwards hoisted them. A boat was sent for an explanation. The officer was assured that the Perry, in coming bows on, had been mistaken for a Portuguese brig, of which the cruiser was in search.

On reaching Loanda, although no vessel had arrived

to relieve the Perry, yet, as her provisions were nearly exhausted, preparations were made to leave the north coast. The day before sailing, November 29th, a letter addressed to the commander of any U. S. vessel-of-war, was left in charge of the commercial agent of the Salem House. After recapitulating the occurrences of the last cruise, the letter stated that the correspondence with the collector had secured to our merchant vessels more consideration than formerly from the custom-house; and gave information that cruisers were often met at night, and that, therefore, the Perry had always four muskets and the two bow-guns ready for service at a moment's warning. A list of signals, established between the two commodores, was inclosed. It was stated that Ambriz was considered the best cruising-ground; although the Perry had three times run up to Benguela, and once as far as Elephant Bay, having deemed it advisable to show the vessel on the entire line of coast.

It was also stated that landing the Chatsworth's crew at Ambriz having been regarded as prejudicial to the interests of the American factory, the agent had been informed that no more slave-crews would be landed at that place; and that it was believed that there were then no American vessels, with the exception of three or four legal traders, on the south coast. Although it was rumored that several vessels, fitted for the slave-trade, had gone round the Cape of Good Hope into the Mozambique Channel.

On the following day, the Perry sailed for the north coast. Off Ambriz a visit was made to the British flag steam-frigate. The cases of the Navarre and Volusia, together with other instances of interference with the American flag, were discussed with the British commodore. The copies of the affidavits, brought from St. Helena, were examined, from which, with other information in the commander's possession, it clearly appeared that, when the Navarre was first boarded off Benguela by the officer of the Water-Witch, her papers were found to be in form, and she was passed accordingly. When boarded by the Fire-Fly, a few days afterwards, the commander of that vessel declared her papers to be forgeries, and they were destroyed. The prize-officer, sent from the Fire-Fly to St. Helena in charge of the vessel, testified in the admiralty court, that he had no knowledge of the Navarre's papers. The commodore acknowledged that in the case of the Navarre there appeared, at least, some discrepancies in the different statements. Full reports, embracing these points, were made to the American commodore.

The social intercourse with the commander-in-chief had always been of the most agreeable character. Commodore Fanshawe, C. B., was Aid to the Queen,—

a man of distinguished professional abilities, and of great moral worth. He is now the admiral in command of the British naval forces in the West Indies, and on the north coast of America.

The commodore expressed his determination, while doing all in his power for the suppression of the slave-trade, not to interfere, in the least degree, with American vessels; and in cases of actual interference, attributed it, in a measure, to the want of judgment and discretion, now and then to be found among the number of twenty captains; adding, " with your extensive commerce, you ought to have more cruisers where we are so strong." He expressed his readiness to render assistance to American vessels in distress, as exemplified in having sent a vessel to the United States, which had lost her master and crew by the African fever; and in the fact that an American vessel, aground in the Congo River, had been towed off by one of his steamers. The master of this vessel refused to state his object in going up the river, which was afterwards explained by his shipping, and escaping with a cargo of slaves.

After parting with the commodore, the Perry filled away for the north coast; chased and boarded an English barque, bound to St. Helena; also boarded an American barque, which, a few days previously, had been struck by lightning. This vessel had eight hundred kegs of powder on board; her spars and rigging were much damaged.

The passage to Monrovia occupied fourteen days. The U.S. brig Porpoise had arrived on the coast, and was lying in the harbor of Monrovia. The General Assembly was in session, and the debates on the subject of resurveying the lands in one section of the country, were creditable to the speakers.

A few days after the arrival of the Perry, it being learned that the British steam-cruiser Flamer was ashore near Gray's Point, a correspondence took place with President Roberts, which will furnish some idea of the character of the president, as well as the means which Monrovia is capable of affording for assistance in such cases.

In this correspondence, the commander informed the president that he was about proceeding with the Perry to offer assistance to the Flamer; and suggested that the cases of fever among the crew should be removed to Monrovia, rather than remain subject to the discomfort of their present situation. He proposed, in case the president concurred in opinion, and accommodations could be furnished, to offer the services of the Perry in transporting the sick to Monrovia. The president, in reply, fully concurred, and recommended, by all means, that the sufferers should be immediately brought to Monrovia, where the best of accommodations would be supplied. He also sent his respects to the commander of the steamer, assuring him that he was exceedingly anxious to render all aid in his power.

On arriving at Gray's Point, the proffered assistance was declined, as one British cruiser had just arrived, and another was momentarily expected, which would transport the sick and suffering to Sierra Leone.

The Perry then proceeded to Porto Praya, and on the 8th of January, 1851, after one year's service on the south coast, reported to the commander-in-chief. Soon afterwards, the commodore was informed that a large Hamburgh ship, with a cargo exceeding in value the sum of three hundred thousand dollars, had been wrecked at night on the island of Mayo—forming one of the group of the Cape Verdes. The Perry proceeded to Mayo, for the purpose of rendering the wrecked ship all assistance in her power. The commander called on the American vice-consul, who was an intelligent, dignified black man, holding the offices of mayor and military commandant, superadded to that of vice-consul. It was found that the ship and most of her cargo had proved a total loss. The passengers and crew had escaped with their lives. Among the passengers was a clever young governess, going out to Santiago, in Chili: she proceeded to Porto Praya, where her losses were fully compensated by the contributions of the officers of the squadron. After rendering all possible assistance to the wrecked vessel and sufferers, the Perry returned to Porto Praya, and made preparations for a third southern cruise. A first lieutenant and one midshipman were ordered to the vessel, to supply, in part, the vacancies occasioned by sending home officers in charge of captured slavers.

CHAPTER XXXI.

On the 19th of February, the vessel having been
reported ready for sea, the commodore issued orders to
proceed on a cruise south of the equator, under former
orders and instructions, stopping at Monrovia and at
the island of St. Helena; and returning to Porto Praya
when provisions should be exhausted.

The vessel sailed at daylight on the following morning, and after a passage of eight days, during which
she had a long chase after an English brig, arrived at
Monrovia. Five days were spent in wooding and
watering ship. On Sunday, a colored Rev. Dr. of
Divinity in the Baptist church, preached to a large congregation, giving his own rendering of the text from
the original Greek. The effort was perhaps unusually
elaborate, in consideration of several officers forming
part of the audience.

In running down the coast, a great number of canoes, filled with natives—*sans culottes* and *sans chemises*—pulled off to the vessel. By one of these, a note addressed to the missionaries was sent into Cape Palmas, expressing regret that orders to the south coast prevented the vessel from touching either at the Cape or at the Gaboon River.

The former passage to the south coast had been made on the port tack, by standing out into the southeast trades, and forty-one days had expired on reaching Benguela. This passage was made on the starboard tack, in-shore, and occupied but twenty-two days to Ambriz—a run of four days from Benguela. The great advantages of the in-shore passage will be made manifest in a letter hereafter to be referred to. Greater alternations of weather, pleasant and squally, with now and then a strong tornado, occur in-shore; but a good look-out will enable a man-of-war to encounter all these with safety. Besides a number of legal traders, on the passage down, several British cruisers were boarded, who reported the slave-trade as being exceedingly dull.

Three days were spent in Loanda, and then cruising for the same length of time, with the new commander of the British southern division, was resumed off Ambriz. Thence the vessel proceeded down the coast towards the Congo River, where the new commander of the steamer Fire-Fly boarded the Perry, when at a distance of four miles from his own vessel. Passed the Congo, after encountering a tornado.

This river is more than two leagues broad at its mouth. At the distance of eight or ten miles seaward, in a northwesterly direction, the water preserves its freshness; and at the distance of fifty and even sixty miles, it has a black tinge. Here are often seen small islands floating seaward, formed of fibrous roots, bamboo, rushes and long grass, and covered with birds. The banks of the Congo are lined with low mangrove bushes, with clumps of a taller species interspersed, growing to the height of sixty and seventy feet. Palm-trees, and others of a smaller growth, are seen with a rich and beautiful foliage. In going up the river, the southern shore, where there is plenty of water close in with the land, should be kept aboard. The current is so strong—often running six miles an hour off Shark's Point—that an exceedingly fresh sea-breeze is necessary in order to stem the stream. The greatest strength of this current, however, is superficial, not extending more than six or eight feet in depth. The Congo, like all rivers in Africa, except the Nile, is navigable but a short distance before reaching the rapids. The great central regions being probably not less than three thousand feet in altitude above the sea, these rapids are formed by a sudden depression of the surface of the country towards the sea, or by a bed of hard rocks stretching across the basin of the river.

The slave-trade has been extensively pursued in the Congo. A British steam-cruiser, for many years, has been stationed off its mouth, making many captures. Under American nationality, however, several vessels have entered, taken in a cargo of slaves and escaped. The natives, near the mouth of the river, have been rendered treacherous and cruel by the slave-trade; but a short distance in the interior, they are represented as being civil and inoffensive, disposed to trade in elephants'-teeth and palm-oil.

After crossing the Congo, the Perry communicated with Kabenda, and the day following anchored at Loango, in company with the British cruiser stationed off that point. The British commodore arriving the next day, a letter was addressed to him, dated April 4th, asking whether any suspected vessels had been seen on the south coast, by the cruisers under his command, since the capture of the Chatsworth, on the 11th of September, 1850; also requesting that he would express his views of the present state of the slave-trade on the southern coast of Africa.

In reply, the British commodore made the following communication:

"I beg to acquaint you that the only report I have received of a suspected vessel, under American colors, having been seen on the south coast since the date you have named, was from H. M. steam-sloop Rattler, of a schooner showing American colors having approached the coast near Old Benguela Head; which vessel, when Commander Cumming landed subsequently, was reported to him, by the people on shore, to have shipped slaves near that place.

"Your inquiry applies only to the south coast; but it will not be irrelevant to the general subject and object for which we are co-operating, if I add that the schooner Bridgeton, of Philadelphia, under the American flag, was visited by Her Majesty's steam-sloop Prometheus, off Lagos, on the 22d of August, under circumstances causing much suspicion, but with papers which did not warrant her seizure by a British officer; and that I have since received information from Her Britannic Majesty's consul at Bahia, that the same vessel landed three hundred slaves there in October.

"I also take this opportunity of bringing under your notice 'another American vessel, which I observed at Sierra Leone under the American flag; and which was reported to me, by the authorities there, as being to all appearance a legal trader, with correct papers, but whose real character and ultimate object I have since had much reason to doubt.

"I inclose a copy of the formal entry of this vessel, 'The Jasper,' at the port of Sierra Leone, from which

you will observe that her cargo was shipped at the
Havana; and that in the manifest are shooks and heads
of water-casks, and that she had on board three passengers : these passengers were *Spaniards*. The Jasper
staid a short time at Sierra Leone, disposed of some
trifles of her cargo for cash, and left for Monrovia.
On proceeding a few days afterwards in the Centaur (the
flag-ship) to that place, I found that she had disposed
of more of her cargo there, also for cash, and was reported to have proceeded to the leeward coast; and I
learned from the best authority, that of the passengers,
one was recognized as being a Spanish slave-dealer
who had been expelled from Tradetown, in 1849, by
President Roberts, and that the others were a Spanish merchant, captain and supercargo; and that the
American captain had spoken of his position as being
very indefinite.

"On the second subject, my view of the present
state of the slave-trade on the south coast: It is formed on
my own observations of the line of coast from Cape St.
Paul's to this port, and from the reports which I have
received from the captains of the divisions, and the
commanders of the cruisers under my orders, as well
as from other well-informed persons on whom I can
rely, that it has never been in a more depressed state,
a state almost amounting to suppression; and that this
arises from the active exertions of Her Majesty's squad-

ron on both sides of the Atlantic, and the cordial co-
operation which has been established between the
cruisers of Great Britain and the United States on this
coast, to carry out the intention of the Washington
treaty; and latterly from the new measures of the
Brazilian government.

"Factories have been broken up at Lagos, in the
Congo, and at Ambriz; although of this I need hardly
speak, because your own observation during the past
year must satisfy you of the present state of depression
there.

"The commencement of last year was marked by an
unusual number of captures by Her Majesty's cruisers,
both in the bights and on the south coast, and also by
those by the cruisers of the United States. This year,
the capture of only one vessel equipped in the bights,
and one with slaves (a transferred Sardinian), on the
south coast, have been reported to me—a striking proof
of my view.

"The desperate measures also adopted by the slave-
dealers in the last few months to get rid of their slaves
by the employment of small vessels, formerly engaged
in the legal and coasting trade, as marked by the capture of several (named) slavers, prove the difficulty to
which they have been driven.

"The barracoons, however, along the whole line of
coast, are still reported to me to contain a great num-

ber of slaves, to ship whom, I have little doubt further attempts will be made.

" Most satisfactory, on the whole, as this state of things may be considered, still I hope it will not lead to any immediate relaxation either of our efforts or of our co-operation; but that a vigilance will be observed for a time sufficient to enable a legal trade to replace the uprooted slave-traffic, and to disperse the machinery (I may say) of the merchants connected with it, and prevent any resumption of it by them."

Leaving Loango with a fresh supply of monkeys and parrots, the Perry retraced her course to the southward, and on reaching the Congo, crossed that river in a few hours, close at its mouth, showing this to be practicable, and altogether preferable to standing off to the westward for that purpose. After crossing the river, the first lieutenant, Mr. Porter, who had seen much service in other vessels on the coast, was requested to draw up a letter addressed to the commander, containing the following information, which, after having been endorsed as fully according with experience and observation on board the Perry, was forwarded to Lieutenant Maury, in charge of the National Observatory, under the impression that it might be available in the hydrographical department. It has since been published in "Maury's Sailing Directions."

" In the season of February, March, April and May,

there is no difficulty in making the passage from Porto Praya to Ambriz in thirty days, provided the run from Porto Praya takes not more than eight days.

"The direct route, and that which approaches the great circle, leads along the coast, touching the outer soundings of St. Ann's Shoals, thence to half Cape Mount, to allow for a current when steering for Monrovia. From there, follow the coast along with land and sea breezes, assisted by the current, until you arrive at Cape Palmas. Keep on the starboard tack, notwithstanding the wind may head you in-shore (the land-breezes will carry you off), and as the wind permits, haul up for 2° west longitude. Cross the equator here if convenient, but I would not go to the westward of it. You will encounter westerly currents from thirty to fifty miles a day. In the vicinity of Prince's Island, the southwest wind is always strong. In the latitude of about 1° 30′ north there is a current: should it not be practicable to weather the island of St. Thomas, stand in, approach the coast, and you will meet with north winds to carry you directly down the coast.

"Our vessels, after arriving at Cape Palmas, have generally gone upon the port tack, because the wind carried them towards the coast or Gulf of Guinea, and seemed to favor them for the port tack the most, which, on the contrary, although slowly veering towards the southeast, was hauling more ahead, and leading them off into a current, which, under a heavy press of sail, it is impossible to work against. The consequences were, that they had to go upon the starboard tack, and retrace the ground gone over. On the starboard tack, as you proceed easterly, the action of the wind is the reverse, and it allows you to pursue the great circle course.

• " It employed one man-of-war eighty odd days to Kabenda, a port two hundred miles nearer than Ambriz, to which port (Ambriz) from Monrovia, in this vessel (the Perry), we went in twenty-three days; making thirty-one from Porto Praya. Another vessel was occupied ten to Monrovia, and forty-six to Ambriz, by the way of Prince's Island, about ten of which was lost in working to the south of Cape Palmas. In standing to the eastward, north of the equator, the current is with you—south of the equator, it is adverse.

" The practice along the coast in this vessel (the Perry), was to keep near enough to the land to have the advantage of a land and sea breeze, and to drop a kedge whenever it fell calm, or we were unable to stem the current. Upon this part of the coast, near the Congo, the lead-line does not always show the direction of the current which affects the vessel. On the bottom there is a current in an opposite direction from that on the surface; therefore, before dropping the kedge, the better way is to lower a boat and anchor her, which will show the drift of the vessel.   Between Ambriz and the Congo I have seen the under-current so strong to the southeast as to carry a twenty-four pound lead off the bottom, while the vessel was riding to a strong south-west current; but the under-current is the stronger.

"In crossing the Congo, I would always suggest crossing close at its mouth, night or day.   Going north, with the wind W. N. W., steer N. N. E. with a five or six knot breeze.   When you strike soundings on the other side, you will have made about a N. ½ E. course in the distance of nine miles, by log from 11½ fathoms off Shark's Point.   The current out of the river sets west about two knots the hour.   With the land-breeze it is equally convenient, and may be crossed in two hours. In coming from the north, with Kabenda bearing N. E. in thirteen fathoms, or from the latitude of 5° 48′, wind southwest, a S. S. E. course will carry you over in four hours, outside of Point Padron; and by keeping along shore the current will assist you in going to the north. Vessels which cross to seaward, from latitude of 5° 45′ south, and 9° west longitude, are generally six days or more to Ambriz: by the former method it occupied us (the Perry) only two days."

The vessel then proceeded to Loanda, and after remaining one day in port, beat up the coast as far as Elephants' Bay, in 13° 14′ south latitude, communicated with four British cruisers, anchored *en route* in Benguela, and there supplied a British cruiser with masts, plank and oars, for repairing a bilged launch. During a walk on shore, a Portuguese merchant was met, who spoke of the slave-trade being in a languishing state. On calling at his house, a yard in the rear was observed, capable of accommodating some three or four hundred slaves. On entering Elephants' Bay in a fresh breeze, the vessel was brought down to her double-reefed topsails.

Elephants' Bay may be termed the confines of the Great Southern Desert, and the limit of the African fever. A very few wretched inhabitants, subsisting by fishing, are found along the shores. None were seen during the Perry's visit. The soil is sandy and barren, and rains very scanty, seldom occurring more than once or twice during the year. The climate is exceedingly invigorating. The crew were permitted to haul the seine, and take a run on shore. A brackish spring was found, and around it were many tracks of wild animals. Several of the men, armed with muskets, while strolling a few miles from the shore, started up a drove of zebras, but were unsuccessful in their attempts to capture even a single prize.

The day after arriving in this bay, while one watch of the men were exercising the big guns at target-firing, and the other watch on shore familiarizing themselves with the use of small-arms, a large barque was discovered in the offing; and not conceiving any other object than that of slaving to be the business of a vessel on that desert coast, a signal-gun was fired, and the cornet hoisted for "all hands" to repair on board. The Perry was soon off under full sail in chase of the stranger. As night closed in, and the sea-breeze became light, two boats, in charge of the first and second lieutenants, were dispatched in the chase; the vessel and boats occasionally throwing up a rocket and burning a blue light to indicate their relative positions. The strange vessel was at length brought to, and boarded. She proved to be a Portuguese barque in search of ochil for dyeing purposes.

CHAPTER XXXII.

AFTER parting company with the Portuguese vessel, the Perry ran down to Loanda, from whence a letter, dated the 17th of April, was addressed to a gentleman in a prominent station at Washington, communicating in effect the following views and information:

"The slave-trade has received an effectual check within the past year. Only one suspected American vessel has been seen on the south coast, since the capture of the Chatsworth.

"In a letter from Sir George Jackson, British commissioner at Loanda, addressed to Lord Palmerston, which was shown to the commander of the Perry, it is stated that the present state of the slave-trade arises from the activity of British cruisers, the co-operation of part of the American squadron on the southern coast within the year, and its capture of two or three slavers bearing the flag of that nation, together with the measures adopted by the Brazilian government; and also that it may be said that the trade on this southern coast is now confined to a few vessels bearing the Sardinian flag.

"The British commander-in-chief has expressed himself equally sanguine as to the state of the trade; and is of the opinion that the continued presence of our vessels, in co-operation with the English, will tend to depress, if not effectually break up the traffic.

"The impression was entertained previously to joining this squadron, that the orders of our government—giving such narrow latitude to the commanders—superadded to the difficulty of getting a slaver condemned in the United States courts, that had not slaves actually on board, were almost insuperable obstacles to the American squadron's effecting any thing of consequence towards the suppression of this iniquitous traffic, or even preventing the use of our flag in the trade. But observation and experience have entirely changed these views, and led to the conclusion that if even the commodore had a small-sized steamer—which is here wanted more than on any other station—in which he might visit the cruisers at points along the line of the slave-coast, that we should no more hear of a slaver using the American flag, than we do now of his using the

British flag. Notwithstanding our legal commerce here exceeds that of Great Britain or France, yet the United States have not had, for a period of more than two years previous to the arrival of this vessel, an American man-of-war, an American consul, or a public functionary of any kind, on the southern coast of Africa. In consequence, the slave-trade has been boldly carried on under the American flag, while American legal traders have been annoyed, both by the interferences of foreign cruisers at sea, and custom-house restrictions and exactions in port.

"Checked as the slave-trade is for the time being, if vigilant cruising were to be relaxed, or the coast left without a man-of-war, this trade would soon revive; and even if with Brazil it should be suppressed, then with Cuba it would break out, with greater virulence than ever, in the Bight of Benin. Hence the importance of well-appointed cruisers for its suppression, to say nothing of their agency in the vindication of our commercial rights in the protection of legal traders.

"Eight smaller vessels, carrying the same number of guns, two of which should be steamers, would not add materially to the expense, as coal at Loanda may be purchased at ten dollars the ton, while they would prove much more efficient than the vessels composing the present squadron. These cruisers might each be assigned two hundred miles of the slave-coast, having their provisions replenished by a store-ship and flag-steamer; and once during the cruise—which should never exceed twenty months—run into the trades, or to St. Helena, for the purpose of recruiting the health of officers and men. The health of the squadron under the present sanitary regulations, is as good as that on any other station. This vessel, although in constant and active service, with her boats, after cruising for the last sixteen months, has not had a death on board. The Perry has served out no grog; and if Congress would only do the navy in general the kindness to abolish the whisky ration, which is 'evil, and only evil, and that continually,' all men-of-war, in health, comfort, morals, discipline and efficiency, would be benefited. The climate has been urged as an objection to the continuance of the squadron. This, as has been shown, is a groundless objection; and were it not, it is an unmilitary objection, as the navy is bound to perform all service, irrespective of danger to health and life, which the honor and interests of the country require. It would be a reflection on the chivalry of the service, to suppose that the African squadron could not be well officered. Withdraw the squadrons on the coast of Africa, and not only would Liberia suffer materially, but the legal trade in ivory, gum-copal, palm-oil, copper and caoutchouc, now in process of development along the line of coast, would soon be broken up, and the entire coast handed over to the tender mercies of piratical slave-traders."

Portuguese, English and French men-of-war were lying at Loanda. The Portuguese commodore had been uniformly attentive and courteous in official and social intercourse. The navy-yard was freely offered for the service of the vessel. One evening, on falling in with the commodore at sea, the Perry beat to quarters; and the first intimation given of the character of the vessel she met, was by the flag-ship running across her stern, and playing "Hail Columbia." In the last interview, the commodore alluded to our correspondence with the British officers, and expressed his gratification at the results. The French commodore was an intelligent, active officer, whose squadron had made several captures. He often expressed the wish that the Perry would visit his friends, the Rev. Mr. and Mrs. Wilson and Mr. Bushnell, at the Gaboon Mission, whom he regarded as being, in all respects, highly creditable representatives of American benevolence and culture. The character of the intercourse with the British commissioner may be inferred from a letter to be introduced hereafter. The attentions of the British consul, and in particular his politeness in furnishing news and information from England, were highly appreciated. The agent of the large and respectable house in Salem, Massachusetts, extended a liberal hospitality to the

American officers.   The governor-general of the province of Angola was a distinguished general in the Portuguese service, and supported great state.   He offered, in the complimentary style of his country, the palace and its contents to the officers of the Perry. Salutes had been exchanged with the garrison and all the commodores on the station. The attentions extended to a small cruiser, were the tribute paid to the only representative of a great and highly respected nation.

Loanda, with its seventeen thousand inhabitants, numerous fortifications, palace, churches and cathedral, its houses, many being of stone, spacious and substantial, standing as it does on an eminence, presents an impressive appearance, reminding one of a somewhat dilapidated Italian city; while the frequent passing of a palanquin, supported by two stout negroes, in which the movement is agreeably undulating, recalls the eastern luxury of locomotion.   But the wealth and prosperity of Loanda have been dependent on the slave-trade.   In the year eighteen hundred and forty-eight, the amount of goods entered for the legal trade, amounted to about ninety thousand dollars; and at the same time, there were smuggled goods for the purposes of the slave-trade, amounting to the sum of eight hundred thousand dollars.*

---

* Parliamentary reports, 1850.   H. L. evidence.

On the 17th of May, the Perry took final leave of St. Paul de Loanda, leaving a letter addressed to the commander of any U. S. cruiser on the coast, and receiving from the British commissioner, a letter expressing his views on the subject of the slave-trade, and of the agencies in operation for its suppression. After cruising a day or two off Ambriz, she bid adieu to the south African coast, and made all sail for the island of St. Helena.

The letter addressed to the commander of any U. S. cruiser, was to the following purport:

"Nothing has occurred to interrupt the cordial and harmonious co-operation with the British men-of-war, during the present cruise on the southern coast.

"The agent of the American House at Loanda asserts, that the presence of our cruisers has had a salutary effect upon his interests. Formerly there were many vexatious detentions in the clearance of vessels, prohibitions of visiting vessels, &c., which are now removed. Having no consul on the coast, he says that the interests of the House are liable to be jeopardized on frivolous pretexts, in case that a man-of-war is known to be withdrawn for any length of time."

The letter of Sir George Jackson, the commissioner, received on leaving Loanda, says:

"I have the honor to acknowledge the receipt of your letter of the 7th instant, in which, referring to my official position and long residence here, you request my opinion on the past and present state of the slave-trade, and of the measures respectively adopted for its suppression.

"From the time I left your magnificent and interesting country, I have been mostly engaged as H. M. commissioner in the mixed courts at Sierra Leone, Rio de Janeiro, and for the last five years nearly, at this place; but in all that long period, the present is the first occasion when I could have answered your inquiry with any satisfaction. When you did me the honor of calling upon me, on your first arrival here, in March, 1850, I welcomed you with those feelings of pleasure, which the recollection of kindnesses received in your country will ever excite in my breast at the sight of an American; but I was far from anticipating those benefits, in a public point of view, in a cause in which we both take so deep an interest, which, I am happy to say, have resulted from your appearance, and that of other vessels of the U. S. Navy, on this coast, which soon followed you. During the four years preceding your arrival, I did not see, and scarcely heard of one single American officer on this station. The Marion and the Boxer did, indeed, if I recollect right, anchor once or twice in this harbor, but they made no stay in these parts. What was the consequence?

"The treaty of Washington proved almost a dead

letter, as regarded one of the contracting parties. And
the abuse of the American flag became too notorious,
in promoting and abetting the slave-trade, to make it
necessary for me to refer further to it—more particularly in addressing one who, himself, witnessed that
abuse when at its height.

"The zeal and activity displayed by yourself and
brother officers, and the seizures which were the results
of them, at once changed the face of things. The
actual loss which the traffic has sustained, and still
more the dread of those further losses which they anticipated, on seeing the U. S. squadron prepared to con-
front them at those very haunts to which they had been
accustomed to repair with impunity, and determined
to vindicate the honor of their insulted flag, which they
had too long been allowed to prostitute, struck terror
into those miscreants on both sides of the Atlantic.
And from the date of those very opportune captures,
not a vessel illicitly assuming American colors has been
seen on the coast; and, as it was upon the abuse of that
flag, aided by the facility which the system of granting
sea-letters afforded, that the slave-traders have mainly
relied for the prosecution of their nefarious traffic, the
suppression of that abuse by the joint exertions of Her
Majesty's squadron with that of the United States, has
given a blow to the slave-trade which, combined with
the change of policy on that subject on the part of the

Brazilian government, will, I hope and believe, go far, if not to extinguish it altogether, at least very materially to circumscribe its operations.

"The effect of what I have above stated has, as you know, for some time past, shown itself very sensibly at this place : money is exceedingly scarce—slaves hardly find purchasers. Failures of men who have hitherto figured as among the chief merchants of this city, have already occurred, and others are anticipated, and a general want of confidence prevails.

"We must not, however, allow ourselves to be deceived either by our own too sanguine expectations, or the interested representations of others. The enemy is only defeated, not subdued; on the slightest relaxation on our part, he would rally, and the work would have to be commenced *de novo*. Nor, I should say, from my knowledge of the Brazils, must we reckon too confidently on the continuance of the measures which the Imperial Government appears now to be adopting. Giving the present administration every credit for sincerity and good intentions, we must not shut our eyes to the proofs, which have hitherto been so frequent and so overwhelming, of the power of the slave-trade interest in that country. We must act as if we still wanted the advantage of her co-operation ; and in this view it is, that I cannot too forcibly insist on the absolute necessity of the continuation of our naval exertions, which, so far from being diminished, ought as far as possible, I conceive, to be still further increased, till this hideous hydra shall be finally and forever destroyed. Then when its last head shall be cut off, colonization, which till then, like other plans, can only be regarded as auxiliary to the great work, may step in and prosper, and commerce, dipping her wings in the gall of the slain monster, shall rise triumphant.

"It would not be becoming in me, in addressing an American citizen, to do more than to testify to the mischiefs occasioned by the system I have already alluded to, of granting sea-letters; but I should hope, upon due investigation it would be found very practicable to deny such letters to vessels sailing to the coast of Africa, without at all interfering with the interest or freedom of licit trade.

"I have thus, very imperfectly, I fear, complied with your request—purposely abstaining from a detailed recapitulation of those occurrences which, if they took place in these parts, you have yourself been an eye-witness to; or with which, if they happened in a more remote quarter, you have had opportunities of being made acquainted, from better sources than I can command.

"I cannot, however, quit this subject without indulging in a feeling of gratification, if not of exultation, at the singular coincidence, or rather, I should say, contrast, between my present employment, and that which occupied me for four years in the United States.

"I was then associated with your distinguished countryman, Langdon Cheeves, engaged in appraising the value of human beings like ourselves—regarded as mere goods and chattels. I have been since that time chiefly occupied in restoring that same unhappy class to freedom and to their natural rights, and in giving effect to that increasing and disinterested perseverance in this righteous cause, on the part of my government and country, which will form one of the brightest pages in its history. Glad am I to think that the United States are disposed to join heart and hand with Great Britain in so blessed an undertaking; and oh, that I could hear my *ci-devant* and much respected colleague sympathize with me in this feeling, and know that his powerful voice and energies were exerted in the same cause!"

The run of the Perry to St. Helena occupied eight days. On approaching the island it was distinctly seen at the distance of sixty-four miles. After making a short, but an exceedingly interesting visit, the vessel sailed, making a passage of nine days to Monrovia; and from thence proceeded to Porto Praya, arriving on the 30th of June.

CHAPTER XXXIII.

MORE than eighteen months had elapsed since the
arrival of the vessel on the coast; and orders from the
Navy Department, to proceed to the United States,
were believed to be waiting at Porto Praya. No such
orders, however, were received. But instructions had
been issued by the new commodore, who had sailed a
few days previously, either to remain at Porto Praya,
or proceed to the island of Madeira. The latter alter-
native was adopted; and seven weeks were as agreeably
spent in Madeira, as was consistent with our disappoint-
ment in proceeding to this genial climate, instead of returning home, for the purpose of recruiting health and
strength, enfeebled by long service on the African
coast. A portion of the crew were daily on shore for
the sake of relaxation and enjoyment.

The princely hospitality of the American consul, Mr.
March, in opening his splendid mansion to the American officers, and at all times receiving them at his ta-

ble, is worthy of grateful acknowledgment. Several English and Portuguese families extended a generous hospitality to the officers; and the intercourse with Lord and Lady Newborough, whose steam yacht was lying in port, contributed much to the satisfaction with which the time was spent at Madeira. The noble party dipped their colors three times, on separating, which was duly acknowledged.

On returning to the Cape Verde Islands, a brisk gale from the eastward induced the Perry to run into Porto Grande, St. Vincent's Island, which is the largest and most commodious harbor in the group.

The master of an American vessel, when calling on board, in company with the consul, communicated a report that the American brigantine Louisa Beaton, a few months previously, had been denounced by the British consul to the governor-general of these islands, as a vessel engaged in the slave-trade. The American consul had heard the report, but being informed that the information was communicated *unofficially* to the governor-general, had taken no action in the case. The commander of the Perry, with the consul, then called on the collector of the port, and after learning the facts, addressed, on the 29th of September, a letter to the collector, requesting official information in reference to the agency that the British consul had had in inducing the governor-general of the Cape Verde

Islands to direct a search to be made of the Louisa Beaton, on suspicion of her being engaged in the slave-trade.

The collector, in reply, stated that the governor-general had not ordered any survey or visit on board the Louisa Beaton, but had directed him to state what was true in regard to the aforesaid vessel suspected of being employed in the slave-trade; as a representation had been made to his Excellency, by the consul for her British Majesty for these islands, in which the consul stated his belief that the said brig had on board irons, pots, and all other utensils and preparations necessary for that traffic; and also that he knew of a load of slaves being already bargained for, for the said vessel.

A letter of the same day's date was then addressed to her British Majesty's consul, stating that the commander was credibly informed that, during the month of May he had denounced the Louisa Beaton to the governor-general, on suspicion of her being engaged in the slave-trade, and requested him to state by what authority he made the denunciation; also, the grounds upon which his suspicions of the illegal character of the vessel were founded.

In reply, on the same day, the British consul stated that it was upon the very best authority that could be given; but he regretted that it was not in his power to name his authority. But that the character and former proceedings of the Louisa Beaton were quite sufficient to be referred to, to show that her proceedings were even then strongly suspected.

In a letter to the British consul, of the same day's date, the commander informed him that he regretted that the consul did not feel at liberty to disclose the authority upon which he had acted in denouncing the American brigantine Louisa Beaton, for it had been with the hope that he would in a measure be able to relieve himself of an act of interference in a matter in which he, the consul, had no concern, that chiefly induced the commander to address him. As, however, he had failed to assign any reason for that act of interference with a vessel belonging to the United States, it had become a duty to apprise him that the government of the United States would not permit an officer of any other government to interfere, officially or otherwise, with any vessel entitled to wear their flag; and that he had to suggest to the consul, that hereafter, should he have any cause to suspect any such vessel sailing in violation of a municipal law of the United States, he would content himself by giving information of the fact to some officer or agent of the United States: that such officer or agent would at all times be found near his residence.

The commander further stated that he might then,

with propriety, dismiss the subject, but that justice to the owners of the Louisa Beaton required him further to state, that the consul's information, come from what source it might, of the Louisa Beaton's being engaged in the slave-trade, was not entitled to any credit. And in reference to "the character and former proceedings of that vessel," the commander would inform him, that the British officer commanding the southern division of Her Majesty's squadron had disavowed to him, in September, eighteen hundred and fifty, the act of boarding and detaining the said brigantine Louisa Beaton by another British cruiser; and also had proposed a pecuniary remuneration for the satisfaction of the master of the said vessel; in reference to which the commander declined any agency, deeming it rather to be his duty to report the matter, which was accordingly done, to the government of the United States. And further, that in the month of June, eighteen hundred and fifty-one, he had himself examined the Louisa Beaton, at the island of St. Helena, and that at the date of his communication to the governor-general affecting her character, she was a legal trader.

On the day following, as the Perry was about leaving Porto Grande, a letter was received from the British consul, in which he remarked, that he must be permitted to say, that he could not acknowledge the right of the American commander to question his conduct in the slightest degree; that when he gave a reply to the commander's first letter, it was a mere act of courtesy upon his part; and that the language and bearing evinced in the last letter which he had received, compelled him to inform the commander that he declined any further correspondence, but to remark, that he should continue the course he had hitherto pursued, in denouncing all slave-vessels that came in his way, and should not fail to lay a copy of the correspondence before Her Majesty's government.

The Perry anchored in Porto Praya on the following day; and a letter was immediately addressed to the commodore, which furnished information of the occurrences at Porto Grande. The commander added, that in his interview, in company with the American consul, with the collector of the port, the collector had read to him a letter from the governor-general of the islands, from which it was evident that the Louisa Beaton had been denounced by the British consul. A copy of the governor-general's letter having been requested, it was refused; but when it was intimated that he ought to have informed our consul of the action of the British consul in the case, and that the relations between the United States and Portugal were of a character which should lead him to communicate, promptly, any action or information given by a foreign officer, bearing upon American vessels or American interests; the collector replied to this that he would, if officially requested, communicate the required information. This was accordingly done.

It was further stated, that, pending the correspondence, the British mail steam-packet arrived, with the Hon. David Tod, late American minister at the court of Brazil, on board, to whom the matter of the British consul's interference was referred for counsel; and that the minister approved the course pursued, remarking that it was a case of unwarrantable interference on the part of a foreign officer, which, on our part, demanded prompt notice.

While lying in Porto Praya, a suspicious-looking brigantine, under Brazilian colors, appeared off the harbor. The hull, rigging, maneuvering, and the number of men on board, indicated her to be a slaver. In a letter to the commodore, the agency of the Perry in the capture of this vessel was explained in the following terms.

"On the 13th instant, a brigantine arrived in this port, under Brazilian colors. A boat was dispatched from the Perry to ascertain (without boarding, as the custom-house boat had not visited her) where she was from, where bound, and what news she had to communicate. She reported Brazilian nationality, last from Trinidad de Cuba, with sand-ballast. As soon as the vessel had anchored the custom-house boat pulled alongside to pay the usual visit, but, without boarding her, proceeded to the Perry, when the officer stated that the said brigantine had the small-pox on board, and had been placed in quarantine. A request was then made from the authorities on shore, not to permit her to leave the port previous to the settlement of her bills for the provisions which were to be furnished. The commander deeming it rather a duty to ascertain the real character of the vessel, than to act as a police for the authorities, communicated his doubts of her having the small-pox on board, intimating that the report was probably a *ruse* for the purpose of avoiding an examination, as he strongly suspected her of being a slaver, and requested that the Perry might board the vessel. This was declined, as she was in quarantine. It was then suggested to the officer to pull under the bows of the vessel, take her papers, and submit them to a critical examination, which might give a clue to her real character. This was done; and the papers were found too informal to entitle her to the protection of any state or nation. She was then boarded by the governor and collector, who, finding no small-pox on board, requested the commander of the Perry to furnish an officer, with a gang of men, to assist in making a thorough search of the vessel. This request was complied with, in the full understanding that she was under Portuguese jurisdiction, and that the search was to be made under the direction of the collector, as a matter of accommodation, in the light of rendering assistance to a foreign service.

"After completing the search, which confirmed the suspicions of the vessel's character, the first-lieutenant of the Perry, at the request of the collector, was directed to take the slaver to the inner harbor, and to unbend her sails."

The commodore not arriving at Porto Praya, the Perry ran up to Porto Grande, and, on the twenty-second day of October, a copy of the correspondence with the British consul, in reference to the Louisa Beaton, was forwarded to the Navy Department, at Washington.

After her return to Porto Praya, to wait the arrival of the squadron, on the eleventh of November, the John Adams made her appearance, and was followed, on the succeeding day, by the flag-ship. The commodore had received triplicate orders to send the Perry to the United States. The proceedings of the vessel, during her absence from the squadron, were approved by the commodore; and on the fifteenth day of December she stood out of the harbor, homeward bound, exchanging three cheers successively with the Porpoise, the John Adams, and the Germantown.

On arriving at New York, and reporting the vessel, a letter, dated December 26th, was received from the

Secretary of the Navy, of which the following is the concluding paragraph: "The Department tenders its congratulations upon your safe return to your country and friends, after an active cruise on the coast of Africa; during which, your course has met the approbation of the Department."

CHAPTER XXXIV.

CONCLUSION—NECESSITY OF SQUADRONS FOR PROTECTION OF
  COMMERCE AND CITIZENS ABROAD—FEVER IN BRAZIL, CUBA
  AND UNITED STATES—INFLUENCE OF RECAPTURED SLAVES
  RETURNING TO THE DIFFERENT REGIONS OF THEIR OWN COUN-
  TRY—COMMERCIAL RELATIONS WITH AFRICA.

WHERE a nation has commerce, it has a dwelling-
place—a scene of action and of traffic on the sea. It
ought to find its government there also. The people
have a right to be protected, and the government is
bound to enforce that right wherever they go. If they
visit foreign countries, they have a right to just treatment. The traveller—the merchant—the missionary—
the person of whatever character, if an American
citizen, can demand justice. The sea is no foreign
territory. Where a merchant vessel bears its country's
flag, it covers its country's territory. Government is
instituted to be watchful for the interests and safety of
its citizens. A navy is the organ through which it
acts. People on shore see nothing of this kind of
governmental protection. There is there no marching
and drumming, or clearing the streets with horsemen
or footmen, or feathers and trumpets. It is the merchant who is most directly benefited by naval protec-

tion; and yet all classes share in its advantages. The planter and the manufacturer are interested in safe and free commerce; our citizens generally avow that they are also interested, by the sensitiveness with which the rights of our flag are regarded. It is more politic to prevent wrong than to punish it; therefore we have police in our streets, and locks on our doors. The shores of civilized governments are the mutual boundaries of nations. Our government is disposed to show itself there, for there are its people, and there are their interests. The shores of savage lands are our confines with savages. Just as forts are required on the frontiers of the Camanches or Utahs, so are they at Ambriz or Sumatra. Cruisers are the nation's fortresses abroad, employed for the benefit of her citizens, and the security of their commerce. It would be discreditable, as well as unsafe, to trust to a foreign power to keep down piracy in the Gulf of Guinea, or in the West Indies and in the China seas. As commerce extends, so does the necessity of its supervision and defence extend. The navy therefore requires augmentation, and for the reasons assigned in the late report of the Head of that Department, it may be inferred that it will have it, in reorganized and greatly improved efficiency.

On this subject, the following are extracts, in substance, from a lecture delivered on the evening of February 3d, 1854, before the New York Mercantile

Library Association, by the Hon. Mr. Stanton, of Tennessee, the chairman of the judiciary committee of the U. S. House of Representatives, and for a long time chairman of the naval committee of that body :

"A strong naval power is the best promoter of commerce, and hence men engaged in commercial pursuits, cannot but feel an interest in the history of the rise and progress of that navy, to which the successes of their business undertakings are principally due.   At a very early period, navies became an indispensable power in war.   The later invention of ordnance, and the still more recent application of steam as a motive power to ships of war, render it at present a question of some difficulty, to predict the extent to which naval military power may hereafter arrive.

"What we have to do in times of peace, is to maintain our naval force in the highest state of efficiency of which it is capable, and ready to enter upon action at a moment's warning.   With the lessons of the British war before us, it cannot be possible that the recent experiments of Lieutenant Dahlgren at Washington, and the discoveries which have resulted from them, will fail to prove of high practical service.   But with all our appliances or discoveries in this regard, we cannot conceal from ourselves the fact, that we are behind other nations in all that concerns the structure of our ships.

"We must have machinery and all proper appliances, as well as the raw materials, for the construction of a naval power when required. We must have independent establishments on both sides of the continent, to protect our Pacific as well as our Atlantic coasts, which should be connected by a railroad stretching across the breadth of the country. The requirements of commerce, and the advances which it has been making in increasing the facilities for navigation, will force us into improvements in our naval power, in order to uphold our commerce.

"It may be safely presumed, that at the present state of our affairs, a moderate and efficient navy would be a great civilizing power; it would hover around the path of our ships, and by the very exhibition of its power suppress all attempts to molest them in their mission of peace and brotherhood across the seas. But in addition to this, our navy is even now aiding strenuously in the march of geographical discovery, and in enlarging our stock of scientific knowledge, and our familiarity with the facts of physical philosophy. When we consider the character of our institutions—when we consider that our great interests lie in the paths of peace—we must be impressed with the fact, that the contributions to science, and the civilizing influences of our navy, are one of the most powerful means by which we can uphold our interests, and carry out our institutions to the fullest development of which they are capable.

"Under all circumstances and all disadvantages, the navy has never, at any period of our history, failed to do honor to itself, and to shed lustre on the American character. From the Revolutionary war down to the late conquest of Mexico, in every case in which its co-operation was at all possible, it has given proofs of activity and power equal to the proud and commanding position we are to occupy among the nations of the earth. We have opportunities to supply the service with the means of moral and physical progress, to free it from the shackles of old forms, and suffer it to clothe itself with the panoply of modern science, and to be identified with the spread of civilization and enlightenment over the world. It will continue to be our pride and our boast, the worthy representative upon the ocean, of the genius, the skill, and the enterprise of our people—of the boundless resources of our growing country—of the power, and grandeur, and glory, as well as the justice and humanity of our free institutions."

The legislatures of some states, the reports of some auxiliary colonization societies, the speeches of some distinguished senators and representatives in congress, the addresses of some colonization agents, have represented the great sacrifice of life and treasure in " unsuccessful efforts," by the African squadron, for the extermination of the slave-trade, and proposed to withdraw it. Whereas, it has been shown that the African squadrons, instead of being useless, have rendered *essential service.* For much as colonization has accomplished, and effectual as Liberia is in suppressing the slave-traffic within her own jurisdiction, these means and these results have been established and secured by the presence and protection of the naval squadrons of Great Britain, France and the United States. And had no such assistance been rendered, the entire coast, where we now see legal trade and advancing civilization, would have been at this day, in spite of any efforts to colonize, or to establish legal commerce, the scene of unchecked, lawless slave-trade piracy.

Strange and frightful maladies have been engendered by the cruelties perpetrated within the hold of a slaver. If any disease affecting the human constitution were brought there, we may be sure that it would be nursed into mortal vigor in these receptacles of filth, corruption and despair. Crews have been known to die by the fruit of their own crime, and leave ships almost helpless. They have carried the scourge with them. The coast fever of Africa, bad enough where it has its birth, came in these vessels, and has assumed perhaps a permanent abode in the western regions of the world. No fairer sky or healthier climate were there on earth, than in the beautiful bay, and amid the grand and picturesque scenery of Rio de Janeiro in Brazil. But it became a haunt of slavers, and the dead of Africa floated on the glittering waters, and were tumbled upon the sands of its harbor. The shipping found, in the hot summer of 1849, that death had come with the slavers. Thirty or forty vessels were lying idly at their anchors, for their crews had mostly perished. The pestilence swept along the coast of that empire with fearful malignity.

Cuba for the same crime met the same retribution. Cargoes of slaves were landed to die, and brought the source of their mortality ashore, vigorous and deadly. The fever settled there in the beginning of 1853, and came to our country, as summer approached, in merchant vessels from the West Indies. At New Orleans, Mobile, and other places it spread desolation, over which the country mourned. Let it be remembered that it is never even safe to disregard crime.

Civilized governments are now very generally united in measures for the suppression of the slave-trade. The coast of Africa itself is rapidly closing against it. The American and English colonies secure a vast extent of sea-coast against its revival. Christian missions, at many points, are inculcating the doctrines of divine truth, which, by its power upon the hearts of men, is the antagonist to such cruel unrighteousness.

The increase of commerce, and the advance of Christian civilization, will undoubtedly, at no distant date, render a naval force for the suppression of the African slave-trade unnecessary; but no power having extensive commerce ought ever to overlook the necessity of a naval force on that coast. The Secretary of the Navy, it is to be hoped, has, in his recent report, settled the question as to the continuance of the African squadron.

The increasing influence of Liberia and Cape Palmas will prove a powerful protection to their colored brethren everywhere. With them Sierra Leone will unite in feeling and purposes. Their policy will always be the same. It must necessarily happen that a close political relationship in interests and feelings will unite them all in one system of action. Their policy will be that of uncompromising hostility to the slave-trade.

There are two aspects of this question well worthy of consideration:

The Liberians are freemen, recognized as having their proper standing among the nations of the world. The people of Sierra Leone are Englishmen, having the legal rights of that kingdom. Therefore, seizing the citizens of either the one or the other community in time of peace, and carrying them captive to be sold, amounts to the greatest crime which can be committed on the ocean.

Now as this may be surmised in the case of all slavers on that coast, the guilt of the slaver in the eye of
national law becomes greater than before; and the
peril greater.   It may be presumed that if a case were
established against any slave cargo, that it contained
one of either of the above-mentioned description of
persons, the consequences to the slavers, whatever their
nation might be, would be much more serious than has
hitherto been the case.

But a principle of higher justice ought long ago to
have been kept in view, and acted upon.   Let the cai-
tiff have his " pound of flesh," but "not one drop of
blood."   If a man throttles another, or suffocates him
for want of air, or stows eight hundred people in a
ship's hold, where he knows that one or two hundred
in the "middle passage" will necessarily die, every
such death is a *murder*, and each man aboard of such
vessel who has any agency in procuring or forwarding
this cargo, is a *murderer*.   It has therefore been contrary to justice, that the perpetrators of such crimes
should have been dismissed with impunity when captured.   Such considerations ought to weigh with men
in the future.

There has been already a commencement of a coasting trade, conducted by colored men.   There is a Liberian man-of-war schooner, the " Lark," Lieutenant-
Commanding Cooper; and the English, after furnishing

the schooner, have proffered the assistance of her navy officers to instruct the young aspirants of the republic, in the art of sailing the cruiser, and in the science of naval warfare. Captain Cooper will not take exception at the remark, that it is "the day of small things" with the Liberian navy. But his flag bears the star of hope to a vigorous young naval power.

A returning of recaptured slaves, instructed and civilized, to the lands which gave them birth, has taken place. Some hundreds passed by Lagos, and were assailed and plundered. Some hundreds passed by Badagry, and were welcomed with kind treatment. The one occurrence reminded them of African darkness, obduracy and crime; the other of the softening and elevating effects which Christianity strives to introduce. They have gone to establish Christian churches, and have established them there. Such things we are sure have been reported far in the interior, and Christianity now stands contrasted with Mohammedanism, as being the deliverer, while the latter is still the enslaver. The report must also have gone over the whole broad intertropical continent, that Christian nations have joined together for African deliverance; and that for purposes so high the race of Africa has returned from the west, and by imitation of western policy and religion, is establishing a restorative influence on their own shores.

There has thus been presented a view of Africa and of its progress, as far as its condition and advancement have had any relation to our country and its flag. How far its growth in civilization has been dependent on the efforts of America has been illustrated; and how essentially the naval interference of the United States has contributed to this end, has been made evident. It cannot escape notice that this progress must in the future depend on the same means and the same efforts. Our own national interests, being those of a commercial people, require the presence of a squadron. Under its protection commerce is secure, and is daily increasing in extent and value.

It is impossible to say how lucrative this commerce may ultimately become. That the whole African coast should assume the aspect of Liberia, is perhaps not an unreasonable expectation. That Liberia will continue to grow in wealth and influence, is not improbable. There is intelligence among its people, and wisdom and energy in its councils. There is no reason to believe that this will not continue. Its position makes it an agricultural community. Other lands must afford its manufactures and its traders. There will, therefore, ever be on its shores a fair field for American enterprise.

The reduction, or annihilation of the slave-trade, is opening the whole of these vast regions to science and legal commerce. Let America take her right share in them. It is throwing wide the portals of the continent for the entrance of Christian civilization. Let our country exert its full proportion of this influence; and thus recompense to Africa the wrongs inflicted upon her people, in which hitherto all nations have participated.

THE END.